TOWNS AND TOWNSPEOPLE
IN THE FIFTEENTH CENTURY

TOWNS AND TOWNSPEOPLE IN THE FIFTEENTH CENTURY

Edited by
JOHN A.F. THOMSON

ALAN SUTTON
1988

ALAN SUTTON PUBLISHING
BRUNSWICK ROAD · GLOUCESTER · UK

ALAN SUTTON PUBLISHING INC
WOLFBORO · NEW HAMPSHIRE · USA

Copyright © D.M. Palliser, Rosemary E. Horrox,
Gervase Rosser, Stephan H. Rigby, Jennifer I. Kermode,
P.J.P. Goldberg, Norman P. Tanner, Anne E. Curry,
Michael Lynch, John A.F. Thomson 1988

First published in Great Britain in 1988 by
Alan Sutton Publishing Limited
30 Brunswick Road
Gloucester GL1 1JJ

Published in the United States of America by
Alan Sutton Publishing Inc.
Wolfboro, New Hampshire, USA

British Library Cataloguing in Publication Data

Towns and townspeople in the fifteenth century.
1. Europe. Towns. Social life, 1400–1500
I. Thomson, John A.F. (John Aidan Francis),
1934–
940'.009'732

ISBN 0-86299-469-1

Typesetting and origination by
Alan Sutton Publishing Limited, Gloucester.
Printed in Great Britain by
The Guernsey Press Company Limited
Guernsey, Channel Islands.

Acknowledgments

The publication of this work has been assisted by a grant from the Twenty-Seven Foundation.

The authors and publishers are grateful to the Museum of London for permission to reproduce the map on p.48.

Contents

Abbreviations

BIHR	Borthwick Institute of Historical Research
BIHR	*Bulletin of the Institute of Historical Research*
BL	British Library
Cal	*Calendar*
CCR	*Calendar of Close Rolls*
CChR	*Calendar of Charter Rolls*
CFR	*Calendar of Fine Rolls*
CLRO	Corporation of London Record Office
CPR	*Calendar of Patent Rolls*
EHR	*English Historical Review*
EcHR	*Economic History Review*
EETS	Early English Text Society
HMC	*Historical Manuscripts Commission*
JBS	*Journal of British Studies*
JMH	*Journal of Medieval History*
PRO	Public Record Office
RO	Record Office
SHR	*Scottish Historical Review*
TRHS	*Transactions of the Royal Historical Society*
VCH	*Victoria County History*
WAM	Westminster Abbey Muniments
WCL	Westminster City Libraries
YAJ	*Yorkshire Archaeological Journal*
YCA	York City Archives
YML	York Minster Library

Introduction

This volume comprises the papers delivered at the colloquium on fifteenth century history which met in Glasgow in September 1986. This was the sixth in a succession of such gatherings, dating back to 1970, and the third since the series of colloquia was revived at York by Professor Barrie Dobson in 1982. On this occasion the conference was more insular in its scope than had been its two immediate predecessors, at York and Nottingham, but an international character was preserved for the gathering by the welcome presence of a colleague from Germany and of an American and an Australian currently resident in Britain.

The decision to take urban life as the conference theme arose from the awareness that recent studies had shown a number of contrasting views of the late medieval town, and the discussions which took place at the colloquium, no less than the content of the papers, demonstrated clearly that many of these varied interpretations resulted from the diversity of experience between one community and another. This was equally true of economic changes, social developments, urban government and religious practices. Originally it had been hoped to include a paper on the archaeological evidence for the period, but unfortunately the illness of the invited speaker meant that this had to be dropped. The value of material remains was however stressed in a number of the papers, notably those by David Palliser, Gervase Rosser and Stephen Rigby. Of particular importance was the establishment of a precise chronology of civic building (in Palliser's case at York), because this could demonstrate the extent to which municipal resources might well change in the course of the century.[1]

During the course of the colloquium it became evident that on some questions the differences among historians of the later medieval town related less to the facts than to their interpretation. A good example of this was raised in the first paper, by David Palliser, on urban decay. Certainly in strict statistical terms one can see decline, but although wealth might have fallen in gross terms, this does not mean that there was no increase in the average wealth of individuals during the period. Still less did it preclude the possibility of particular merchants amassing large fortunes. Gross decline was also compatible with the redistribution of the nation's wealth as a whole, with the towns possessing a greater share of it by the early sixteenth century than they had in the fourteenth, and also with some towns becoming wealthier in absolute terms while others suffered from drastic decline.

The historical debate on whether the fifteenth century should be regarded as an age of decline or an age of growth is a long-standing one, but most modern discussions of the subject look back to the provocative study of A.R. Bridbury, published in 1962.[2] Indeed it is fair to say that a number of the themes considered at the colloquium look back to the questions which Bridbury raised. Not all the views expressed in the book have survived unscathed in the light of research over the intervening quarter of a century – C. Phythian-Adams's study of Coventry suggested that there at least there had been considerable decline from the mid-fifteenth century into the sixteenth, with only a temporary remission in the years immediately before 1500.[3] But as the same author also identified areas of economic growth, particularly in some of the smaller towns,[4] it is clear that his questioning of Bridbury's thesis must be regarded as only partial. Part of debate originating in Bridbury's book turns on semantic rather than purely historical questions, in whether communities should be designated as towns or as villages, but in the context of economic development the author was certainly well-advised to concentrate on the social and economic criteria for identifying towns (such as the nature of the occupations followed by the inhabitants) rather than relying on the more narrow legalistic definitions of borough status. The distinction should not, however, be overstressed – it is noteworthy that most of the towns considered in the conference papers, with the important exception of Westminster, fulfilled both the economic and the legal criteria for recognising urban status.

After the discussion of decline or growth, another characteristic of the late medieval town which received full consideration was that of the development of oligarchies in civic government. This was examined in general terms by Stephen Rigby and through a group of case studies by Jennifer Kermode. The domination of town government by small numbers of the greater merchants has long been recognised – Kingsford identified it over sixty years ago in the London mayors and aldermen of the period,[5] and the topic was also discussed in the most comprehensive study of a mercantile society in later medieval England, the classic work on the same city by S.L. Thrupp.[6] In the capital, there were occasional challenges to the ruling oligarchy, and it is evident that a similar situation existed at Southampton.[7] The colloquium papers provided further evidence of how this oligarchic control developed, through the exclusion of outsiders from a self-perpetuating group who dominated the organs of municipal government. As in London, the oligarchs never had total authority, and in many towns one finds attempts to broaden the basis of power (usually through the enlargement of the council or by the establishment of a new and larger council alongside the existing one), but in practice such increases in popular participation tended to be short-lived. Perhaps predictably, the social base from which the civic rulers was drawn was wider in the smaller towns, because of the need to spread the burdens which office involved, and a similar desire to share the expenses and responsibilities which burgess status entailed may well explain the increase in the number of freemen admitted in various towns. This strictly practical factor was probably more important in persuading the oligarchs to open the doors of privilege than any acceptance of a greater level of democracy as desirable in itself.

But although there were similarities among towns, there were also a number of divergences. Jennifer Kermode's detailed comparison of the oligarchies at York, Hull and Beverley serves as a salutary warning against the easy acceptance of any single model of urban society, and suggests that the urban history of the fifteenth century must take into consideration the local factors which affected the development of individual towns. Norman Tanner's consideration of the religious life of late medieval Norwich also stressed the unique features which existed there and suggested valuable lines of approach to the examination of regional characteristics in religion, as well as using the experience of the town as a means of testing the validity of some of the interpretations which have been advanced for the origins and establishment of the Reformation.

The growth of women's studies in recent years (which led to the conference organizer being properly reproved by one participant for its original title of 'Towns and Townsmen') made very welcome the paper by Jeremy Goldberg on the position of women in the fifteenth century town. Their role tended to be informal rather than established within the formal structures of civic life, but it seems likely that despite an increasing level of legal restrictions on them they played a considerable part in the economic life of the towns, particularly in domestic industries, and in the creation of social contacts in a neighbourhood which could create a sense of community. What was rare was for a woman to gain a position of formal authority, and it reflects the restraints on women that Marion Kent, who actually sat on the council of the York mercers' gild, was a unique example of a woman who had broken into what was customarily a male preserve.

If women were in practice part of the economic life of the town, but were not permitted to play a legal part in its activities, similar discrimination often applied to those living outside the limited area of urban jurisdiction. This relationship between the towns and the surrounding suburbs was taken up by Gervase Rosser, with particular reference to the connections of London and Westminster. Because of London's uniqueness in England compared with all other towns, which it exceeded so greatly in size,[8] this relationship may not have been altogether typical of other urban societies, but the questions raised in the paper point to further lines of investigation, such as the possible connections between London and its southern suburb of Southwark, and the conditions which existed on a smaller scale in other towns between the borough proper and the adjacent lands. Some aspects of Westminster's life were integrated with those of its larger neighbour, indeed some individuals were landowners in both the city and the suburb, but because the suburb was outside the control of the urban rulers, enterprising individuals were able to exploit the special liberties which the suburb possessed.

There were many aspects of late medieval town life which were shared with the rest of society, not least the existence of a social self consciousness which manifested itself elsewhere in such matters as sumptuary legislation or the production of courtesy books. Rosemary Horrox's paper on the urban gentry both provided a link with the theme of the previous colloquium[9] and showed convincingly that 'gentle' status was not regarded as something which was incompatible with mercantile activity. Individuals who acquired the designation of gentleman did not find it necessary to move from town to country and abandon their occupation, and lawyers who resided in a town and civic bureaucrats, although not engaged in trade, should still be regarded as townsmen. The idea of a *bourgeois gentilhomme* was not yet a theme for satire.

The two papers on towns outside England provided possible comparisons with those studied in the other contributions. Anne Curry's, on Norman towns under English rule, showed that it was not only in England that the urban historian must pay special heed to the diversity of the towns studied, as individual corporations were concerned primarily with the pursuit of their own interests. The peculiar circumstances of military occupation gave a special character to the nature of 'good lordship' in Normandy, but the patronage which a lord could extend to a town under his influence was basically similar in type to that which might exist in England. Michael Lynch's study of Scottish town life overcame the comparative paucity of the evidence to demonstrate that there too the dissimilarities between towns (themselves smaller in size than their equivalents south of the Border) were such that it is impossible to draw safe generalisations. One parallel between the two countries, however, the increasing dominance of Edinburgh and London respectively in their nation's trade, raises the question of how far the activities of government in these towns provided an incentive to and scope for economic growth during the fifteenth century.

The organizers of the colloquium would also wish to take this opportunity to thank all those who contributed to its success, the University of Glasgow for agreeing to act as host, and more especially Stephen Johnson, the Accommodation Officer, for providing administrative and secretarial back-up. Particular thanks are also due to the Manager of Wolfson Hall, Mrs Judy Rae, and her staff for the smooth running of the domestic arrangements, and to Ms Rosemary Watt, the Keeper of the Burrell Collection, for agreeing to address conference members during the afternoon excursion there. Professor Barrie Dobson and Dr Caroline Barron gave helpful advice and assistance in securing speakers, and Alan Sutton's willingness to publish the proceedings of the colloquium increases the existing debt of fifteenth century historians to him. A more unusual debt is to the Glasgow Fire Brigade, whose intervention when an anonymous pipe smoker triggered an oversensitive fire alarm on the first evening of the conference contributed to the breaking of ice among participants. The subsequent development of versions of what actually happened on this occasion has been an interesting demonstration of how variations of oral tradition can arise from the views of different parties!

J.A.F. Thomson.

Notes

1   This point has been stressed also by R.B. Dobson, 'Urban Decline in Late Medieval England', *TRHS*, 5th ser. 27 (1977), 7–8.
2   A.R. Bridbury, *Economic Growth*, (London, 1962), esp. 40–54, 56–64, 70–82.
3   C. Phythian-Adams, *Desolation of a City*, (Cambridge, 1979), 35–8.
4   Ibid., 16–19.
5   C.L. Kingsford, *Prejudice and Promise in Fifteenth Century England*, (Oxford, 1925), 107–8.
6   S.L. Thrupp, *The Merchant Class of Medieval London*, (Chicago, 1948), esp. 80ff.
7   C. Platt, *Medieval Southampton*, (London, 1973), 175–7.
8   Thrupp, op. cit., 1. W.G. Hoskins, *The Age of Plunder*, (London, 1976), 89.
9   The proceedings of this were published in, M.C.E. Jones, ed., *Gentry and Lesser Nobility in Later Medieval Europe*, (Gloucester, 1986).

1

Urban Decay Revisited[1]

D.M. Palliser
University of Hull

What were the economic fortunes of English towns as a whole in the fifteenth century? The question is hardly a new one: a century ago Thorold Rogers and Denton argued over the prosperity of both town and countryside, while in 1894 Mrs Green concluded that in the fifteenth century 'the boroughs had reached their prosperous maturity'.[2] Then came the influential pessimism of Postan, who argued that, with the exception of London, Bristol, and possibly Southampton, 'the bulk of English trading centres . . . suffered a decline'.[3] To this Bridbury was to retort 'that towns, and hence the countryside, were more prosperous then than before'.[4] And in the 1970s a fair number of monographs and articles were devoted to the theme of urban decay in the fifteenth and sixteenth centuries, a battle of the books which ended with a sharp exchange between Dyer and Phythian-Adams.[5]

The author of a recent survey notes that 'the stillness that has reigned since the appearance of the 1979 edition of the *Urban History Yearbook* does not reflect consensus but suggests that the protagonists remain entrenched in their respective positions with compromise or agreement as far away as ever'. He shrewdly remarks that one reason might be 'the lack of a firm empirical foundation', so that 'not even the most basic questions can be answered with confidence, such as when towns grew and by how much'.[6] The 'stillness' has now been broken by a renewed debate,[7] and it may be worth another attempt at a general survey of the field of conflict, even if the continuing lack of sufficient empirical data means being prepared to ask questions without being confident of knowing the answers. We need, perhaps, to remind ourselves of Reynolds' comment that too many historians of medieval England 'have considered towns almost exclusively in general surveys which, perhaps inevitably, concentrate more on what is known – or thought to be known – than on points of ignorance or controversy which might need further investigation'.[8]

The urban sector is notoriously difficult to define. Here it is taken to include all places which could be regarded as towns in an economic rather than a legal sense. That does not, however, mean excluding the small market towns as some writers have done. In a series of important studies Hilton has reminded us that, though the village markets created in the thirteenth century in vast numbers were often ephemeral and not really urban, most small market towns 'were recognizable as urban entities',[9] and formed an important part of the urban and commercial sector. Furthermore, it is not sufficient to pile up instances of towns which were, or were not, allegedly declining. Any general urban trend has to fit the evidence for the large towns as a whole (those on which the 1970s debate concentrated), the small towns as a whole, and last, but certainly not least, the capital.

The fifteenth century needs to be seen in its own right. The following discussion inevitably ranges back to the fourteenth century, and forward to the early sixteenth, if only because of the lack of intermediate tax returns, but it would be wrong to blur an already lengthy period into an even longer one. It is not relevant to cite later developments like the dissolutions of religious houses and the urban rebuilding statutes of 1535–44, or even the marvellous eye–witness evidence of John Leland which seems to be obligatory in all late medieval urban discussions. It is all too easy to let success or failure *after* 1500 cast a long shadow before: the undoubted decline of Coventry in the early sixteenth century masks the fact that it was growing and flourishing at the expense of neighbouring towns throughout the fourteenth and fifteenth centuries; the decline of Canterbury at the Reformation encourages a view of its late medieval history as one of recession even though it rose in ranking relative to other towns.

Furthermore, clarity is needed over the terms of the debate. Words like 'decline' and 'decay' have been used without rigorous definition, while there has also been a tendency 'to slide (rather than to reason) not only from population to the economy but from economic activity to prosperity'. Or, as another writer puts it, 'it is the most paradoxical feature of the present remarkable spate of intensive research into the history of English towns before the Reformation that so much of it is based on highly ambiguous evidence and yet focuses around concepts of "growth" and "decline" which can themselves be question-begging to a degree'.[10]

Towns in an economic sense were places dependent on industry and commerce rather than agriculture. They were also places where those with surplus income invested a good deal of it in urban housing rather than in rural property. If, therefore, towns were generally doing badly, we might expect the *cause* to be falling demand for the products and services of the town, whether because of an absolute decline in that demand, or because of a shift in supply from English townsmen to countryfolk or to overseas competitors. We would also expect the *results* to include lower levels of production, lower levels of wealth, lower rents, less house-building and perhaps fewer inhabitants.

Postan was emphatic 'that the total national income and wealth was declining' in the fifteenth century: and given the fact that population continued to fall or at least stagnate until about 1470 or later, that is probably correct and not surprising. Yet it need not mean that the *per capita* income of those townsmen left alive, like that of Thorold Rogers' labourers, might not have been maintained or even have risen. Postan himself conceded in the same context 'that a relative decline in the total volume of national wealth is fully compatible with the rising standard of life of the labouring classes'.[11] Furthermore, it is necessary to distinguish not only gross from *per capita* income, but also wealth from income. Total wealth might still be accumulating while incomes were declining.

II

Dobson has singled out four main types of statistical evidence relevant to the debate: freemen admissions; customs records; rent values; and taxation assessments; and all pose severe problems of interpretation and comparison. Bridbury, for instance, has put much emphasis on the levels of freemen recruitment, but Dobson has doubted whether totals of admissions 'can ever be regarded as an accurate guide to the population of the city at a particular moment', and has pointed out that the proportion of freemen to total population was not a constant, though he has since suggested that the comparatively lower rates of freemen recruitment around 1500 'may sometimes reflect a provincial town's genuine inability to attract . . . new freemen'.[12] J.C. Tingey long ago demonstrated for Norwich in Richard II's reign that freemen admissions fluctuated sharply and promptly when parliamentary statutes made burgess status more or less valuable.[13]

As for the customs records, they reveal clearly an increasing volume of wool and cloth exports, but of course they are no guide to the home market, the non-textile exports, or the relative shares of prosperity accruing to town and country. Rent values, by contrast, can be studied specifically in the towns, and here there is some conjunction of evidence for a period of buoyancy of rents in the larger towns from the 1350s to the 1420s or 1430s, followed by a downward trend for the rest of the century. Yet what this shows is a decline in demand which could be attributed to lower urban populations, and not necessarily to less prosperity for the majority of the inhabitants.

The best of an imperfect group of sources probably remains the much-cited tax assessments. Bridbury attempted to compare the lay subsidies of 1334 and 1524, and Schofield made a broader comparison, on a slightly different base, between the 1334 subsidy and those of 1514–15; both concluded that towns in general 'increased in wealth much faster than the rest of the country'.[14] Powerful attacks have been launched upon the validity of this conclusion and on the reliability and comparability of the returns,[15] though recent work on the fourteenth-century subsidies suggests that Glasscock's 1334 picture is a broadly accurate reflection of national and urban wealth, while Hadwin has suggested that the broad comparison over time between 1334 and 1515 is still acceptable.[16]

What troubles one is less the invalidity of any comparison between 1334 and 1514/24 than the margins of error involved for both dates, and also the long time-span involved. How can we disentangle fifteenth-century changes from those occurring before 1400 or even after 1500? The 1334 quotas continued to be imposed virtually unchanged throughout the fifteenth century, apart from some reliefs and abatements granted to decayed towns. With this in mind, I examined the one fifteenth-century attempt to invent a new form of taxation of lay wealth that would counterbalance the rigidity of the traditional fifteenth and tenth, the income tax of 1436.[17] Unfortunately the results are unhelpful; the returns are invaluable for the landed wealth of individuals, but being levied on a different basis from the lay subsidies, and taking no account of mercantile wealth, they cannot be used to construct an intermediate picture between 1334 and 1524.

The reliability of non-statistical evidence for the debate is even more difficult to determine. The most prominent category is the petitions of boroughs for financial relief and the king's responses to them; sporadic in the early fifteenth century, they became numerous from the 1430s, and altogether between 1433 and 1482 the Crown remitted some £73,000 in fee-farms and other tax reliefs. There are suspicious features to many of them, though Phythian-Adams has argued that 'such claims were investigated and usually confirmed by theoretically impartial commissioners'.[18] Chester's successive remissions contradict one another on the dating of decay, and Oxford and Cambridge gave mutually contradictory reasons for the impact of a university on an urban economy.[19] Some pleas may reflect, not necessarily greater poverty of the townsmen, but simply a decline of traditional revenues assigned to the payment of fee farms: thus Henry VI in 1442 accepted that Oxford's fee farm of £58–0–5d. p.a. was too high when the revenues supporting it scarcely amounted to £20 p.a. 'hiis diebus'.[20] And Reynolds has drawn attention to A.P.M. Wright's evidence 'that Exchequer procedures themselves accounted for some of the apparent difficulties in payment,' and has made the intriguing suggestion that 'the fiscal system . . . encouraged a tax-evasion culture'.[21]

At any rate, many towns which struggled to pay their farms or taxes housed merchants and craftsmen well able to find money for building churches, town halls and opulent houses. The governors of Beverley, for instance – whatever its later decline – could face with equanimity raising money for a new hall in 1434.[22] When in the following year they pleaded inability to raise a loan of 200 marks for the king because of poverty – 'three partes' of the town, they said 'was in decay' – the archbishop's provost would have none of it. They cancelled the plans to raise money for the new hall at the same time.[23] And the governors of the town found no difficulty in raising £190 for the king in 1449 and another £100 in 1450.[24]

Some remissions of taxes were more justifiable than others, but it is no accident that they were most frequent at a period when successive kings needed to buy support, between the 1440s and 1480s. Henry VI, or rather Queen Margaret, made assiduous attempts in the late 1450s to woo key towns like Coventry and York, and as soon as Edward seized the throne in 1461 he made a bid for townsmen's support with his very first parliamentary statute. All grants to boroughs and corporations made by the Lancastrian kings were to remain in force, in consideration of

> the excessive charges and costs, which the cities, boroughs, towns . . . of this realm . . . have endured and suffered, and the great poverty amongst the people of the same . . .[25]

This is apparently the earliest general statute alleging the poverty of towns as a whole, and though there was doubtless some truth in it the timing was suspicious. Edward's brother Richard similarly cultivated urban support with grants of privileges or concessions to Gloucester, Lincoln, Northampton, Oxford, Winchester, York, Scarborough and other towns, and by refusing 'divers great sums' from urban corporations on his summer progress in 1483. Henry VII likewise inaugurated his reign with a round of favourable urban charters and letters patent.

Another indicator of decline cited at the time, both by parliament and by the urban corporations, was an alleged flight from civic office. This, if established, would indeed be very serious; it was precisely the reluctance of the wealthiest citizens to take up municipal office that had signalled the decline of late Roman towns. At York, a few leading merchants began purchasing royal letters of exemption from civic offices in the 1430s and 1440s, and in 1451 the corporation decided to fine such evaders heavily.[26] Leicester imposed similar fines from 1491, and Coventry from 1495. Several writers, including myself, have called this evidence in support of urban decay, but it poses severe difficulties of interpretation. Not only do the examples and prohibitions start rather late (except at York), but there is a puzzling combination of men buying exemptions while yet serving in office shortly afterwards, while others were being barred from office on the grounds of inferior status, occupation or wealth. The explanation in York at least, argues Kermode, 'is not widescale evasion but a council keeping the lower orders out of high civic office and making a profit at the same time'. On the other hand, Rigby has argued that at Grimsby exemptions *were* a symptom, though not a cause, of urban decline.[27]

Other favourite causes of decline cited at the time were the Malthusian constraints of war and disease. The effects of civil war between 1455 and 1487 are less stressed today, since it is clear that a total of some twelve or thirteen weeks' active campaigning, spread over thirty years, had little direct impact. Charles Ross has indeed noted that to judge from the Cely papers 'one might be forgiven for believing that the Wars of the Roses never took place at all'.[28] One exception usually cited, as a result of successful Yorkist propaganda, is the Lancastrian sack of Stamford in 1461, but it has been recently been demonstrated that the damage caused was much exaggerated.[29] On the other hand, there is less reason to doubt that the indirect effects of the wars could be severe, whether in large sums extorted by both sides from towns in the front line, like Coventry, or the withdrawal of royal favour from towns which backed the wrong side. York told Henry VII that their troubles stemmed from hostility by Edward IV because of their Lancastrian sympathies, and, as Dobson has commented, 'they were in a position to know'.[30] At a more local level, of course, one should not be mesmerised by the Wars of the Roses into ignoring other military pressures. Glyndŵr's rebellions undoubtedly caused severe short-term damage to some Welsh towns, while the French wars created risks for coastal towns: the author of the *Libelle of Englyshe Polycye*, indeed, asserts that Breton ships 'raunsouned toune by toune' 'in Northfolke coostes and othere places'.[31] Bristol, by contrast, was badly hit by the peace of 1453 with the end of its Gascon links.

Then there were the epidemics, a common and very plausible cause of falling population if not necessarily of declining prosperity, especially in the unhealthy 1430s. Very many York merchants died in that decade; Wallingford complained in 1439 of many inhabitants 'consumed by pestilences and epidemics', as did Richmond (Yorks.) in 1440 and Winchester in 1440 and 1442.[32] The classic debate between Saltmarsh and Bean hinged largely on the frequency and severity of urban epidemics, further evidence on which has generally upheld Saltmarsh – they were indeed frequent and devastating in the towns. Nevertheless, it is not clear that towns did suffer more than the countryside. Most contagious mortality made no distinction, and although bubonic plague in the better recorded sixteenth and seventeenth centuries was largely an urban desease, such was less the case in the fifteenth. To cite two or three major epidemics as sufficient cause of long-term 'decay' of a town, as for Cambridge, is very dubious.[33] After all, thanks to immigration, large towns after 1538 could endure frequent epidemics with a mortality of between 15 and 30 per cent without ceasing to grow or prosper.[34] One could of course argue that in an age of stagnant or declining population, an urban cull would be less likely to be made good by immigration. More indirectly, declining wealth and population have been adduced from the quantity of buildings erected in towns. No new town walls were built after 1400 other than Alnwick's, while existing walls often decayed; few common halls were built after 1460; and the century after 1450 saw more town churches disappear 'than ever before or since' as well as few rebuilt or extended churches.[35] However, new defences and common halls were not needed for towns that had them already: and to adduce urban decay after 1450 from the lack of new town halls would be like seeing decay in twentieth-century towns because their town halls remain Victorian or Edwardian. Undoubtedly the churches are more of a problem, but many of those fabrics not demolished show much evidence of fifteenth-century enlargement and enrichment, if not total rebuilding. At York several were rebuilt in mid-century, though not after 1475, and at Norwich several others into the early sixteenth century; and once we come to the flourishing, if small, cloth towns of East Anglia, the Cotswolds and the West Country there are of course many more. And if Lavenham can be dismissed as a showy rebuilding by a short-lived boom town, the same cannot be said of Beverley, a well-known larger cloth town losing its staple industry. Falling in its ranking among the leading towns it may have been, but when the central tower of St. Mary's church collapsed in 1520, the parishioners and craft guilds found the money to rebuild the tower and much of the nave, as the datable inscriptions in wood and stone still attest.

However, Astill has commented reasonably that

> although public works such as city walls, guild halls and parish churches have been cited as illustrating an urban vitality, the same evidence could also argue for economic stagnation, much being spent on maintaining the trappings of a top-heavy civic structure.[36]

What is perhaps more relevant to the degree of urban prosperity is the amount and chronology of *domestic* building, whether deduced from documents, standing survivals or below-ground archaeology. Judging from the few quantitative estimates, there was considerable variation in this from town to town. York, for instance, enjoyed a considerable boom in house-building (as well as public building) between about 1370 and 1470, but then very little indeed from 1470 to 1570. On the other hand, the evidence of surviving buildings at Norwich suggests 'that very many houses were built between about 1470 and about 1525'.[37] Of course, the surviving houses are only a tiny, and probably untypical, minority of the total stock of late medieval housing, and for a broader picture the aid of archaeology is needed.

Archaeological evidence has great potential for the historian, yet as Astill remarks, it 'has rarely been used in the debate about the economic condition of the later medieval town'. He adds that 'the dating of most archaeological material is too inexact to contribute to many documentary debates',[38] but much has been learned over the past generation – specifically since 1961, when the major programme at Winchester began – which documentary historians ignore to their loss. Winchester itself is a good example: the Brook Street excavations revealed a picture of smaller-scale and poorer housing taking the place of substantial buildings in the fifteenth-century, and also of progressive depopulation with house sites being abandoned. On the other hand, it has been recently argued that Lincoln shows continued rebuilding of housing in the fifteenth and early sixteenth centuries with little archaeological sign of the decay suggested by the documents.[39]

It may be that one should not expect too simple a pattern from the archaeological record, but one revealing significant differences between apparently similar towns, or for that matter between different areas of the same town. Astill has drawn attention to the frequent signs of shrinkage of settlement in many small towns in the fourteenth century (and in towns like Wimborne and Langport whole suburbs abandoned) and with areas larger than individual plots 'uninhabited for most of the fifteenth century'.[40] Yet he has also pointed out the 'considerable vitality in the urban building industry' of many larger towns in the fifteenth century, and the increasing scale of industrial working, and of terraces of artisan housing, in the same towns.[41] Does this suggest that the larger towns profited economically as the smaller towns lost their trading and industrial specialisation? Does it bear out the pessimistic view that large cities like Bristol, Canterbury and York recovered in the late fourteenth and early fifteenth centuries 'at the expense of their weaker neighbours'?[42]

It may seem that there is a real danger of Rigby's recent prophecy being fulfilled: 'Students of the English town in the later middle ages may soon be in the "enviable" position of having no reliable sources at all with which to judge progress of urban life'.[43] However, Rigby himself draws some comfort from what K. Hopkins has called the 'wigwam argument': 'There are several pieces of evidence each insufficient or untrustworthy in itself , which collectively confirm a generalisation . . . Each pole would fall down by itself, but together the poles stand up, by leaning on each other . . .'[44] He has convincingly applied the method to Grimsby; and since then Britnell has published an impressive study of Colchester using a similar technique.[45]

III

If one thing is generally agreed about late medieval towns, it is that they experienced a substantial long-term fall in population (Table 1). Almost all estimates for the early sixteenth-century suggest totals at best no higher than in 1377, and by implication much lower than in 1348. Adopting Postan's doubling of the 1377 poll tax figures to give total population, rather than Russell's addition of 50 per cent which is almost certainly too low,[46] some examples from the larger towns are Coventry, down from over 9,000 in 1377 to 6,000 in the 1520s; York, down from over 14,000 to 8,000; but Bury and Colchester both stable at 5,000 or 6,000 at both dates. Even if we took Russell's lower multiplier for 1377, we should still conclude that the 1348 figures for all towns would have been well above

TABLE 1: TOWNS BY POPULATION RANKING

	1377[1]				1523–7[2]	
		No. of tax-payers x 2			Taxpayers	Est. Population
1	London			1	London	60,000
2	York	14,500		2	Norwich	1,423	10,000
3	Bristol	12,700		3	Bristol	1,101	10,000
4	Coventry	9,600		4	York	871	8,000
5	Norwich	8,000		5	Salisbury	820?	8,000
6	Lincoln	7,000		6	Exeter	807?	8,000
7	Salisbury	6,500		7	Colchester	785	5,300
8	Lynn	6,400		8?	Canterbury	784	3,000?
9	Colchester	6,000		9	Newcastle	–	?
10	Boston	5,700		10	Coventry	713	6/7,000
11	Beverley	5,300		11	Bury St Edmunds	645	5,500
12	Newcastle	5,300		?12	St Albans	640?	
13	Canterbury	5,100		?13	Lincoln	625	
14	Bury St Edmunds	4,900		14	Hereford	611	
15	Oxford	4,700		15	Oxford	542	5,000
16	Gloucester	4,500		16	Reading	523	
17	Leicester	4,200		17	Cambridge	523	2,600
18	Shrewsbury	4,200		18	Worcester	499	
19	Yarmouth	3,900		19?	Lynn	–	4,500
20	Hereford	3,800		20	Yarmouth	497	4,000
21	Cambridge	3,800		21?	Ipswich	412+?	3/4,000
22?	Plymouth	3,400		22	Northampton	477	
23	Exeter	3,100		23?	Gloucester	c466	
24	Hull	3,100		24?	Chester	–	
25	Worcester	3,100		25	Crediton	433	
26	Ipswich	3,000		26	Newbury	414	

1 W.G. Hoskins, *Local History in England* (3rd edn., 1984), p. 277; Ely omitted because figure inflated by rural dependencies.
2 Mainly drawn from Phythian-Adams, *Desolation of a City*, p. 12, and from D.M. Palliser, *The Age of Elizabeth* (1983), p. 203.

the 1520s. The major exception often cited is London, said to be growing in numbers as well as wealth; but Keene's recent work on the capital 'suggests that its population in 1300 may have been at least as great as it was in 1600', and that central Cheapside had fewer inhabitants and lower rents in the early sixteenth century than in the early fifteenth.[47]

It does not, of course, follow that urban populations declined steadily after 1348. The reduced national population led to a rise in *per capita* output of which towns were beneficiaries,[48] and some at least increased in size as well as prosperity. York and Colchester seem both to have increased in size after 1377, reaching a peak in the early fifteenth century.[49] Nevertheless, the overall pattern was one of considerable shrinkage in the long term; and there is therefore no need to be too sceptical of the apparently precise statistics of demolished and empty buildings, furnished by a few towns. Winchester is the best-known, with its claim first made in 1440, and later repeated and elaborated, that 17 parish churches, 11 streets and 987 messuages had fallen into ruin over the previous fifty years. Keene describes the 1452 list of the parish churches as 'remarkably accurate', though he adds that the number of houses given as decayed is much too high and exceeds the total of houses recorded in the city proper (without suburbs) in 1417.[50] Wallingford provides an equivalent in miniature; Henry VI's fee farm remission of 1439 rehearses that the number of parish churches had shrunk from eleven to four, and that there remained only 44 householders.[51] And at Coventry a detailed census of 1523 records 565 houses as vacant, some 26 per cent of all houses in the city.[52] Of course the hardest hit towns would have had the greatest interest in providing statistics to buttress their pleas for relief; and of course Winchester and Coventry were among the hardest hit. Nevertheless, the overall point is not disputed, that most towns had fewer inhabitants in the 1520s than in the 1340s. For Thomas Starkey 'the penury of pepul and lak of inhabytantys' was the obvious cause of urban decline: 'other chiefe groundys I fynd not many'.[53]

It would, of course, be naive to equate closure of parish churches too closely with declining population; some large medieval cities had churches out of proportion to their population needs. Nevertheless, it needs explaining why some multi-parish towns, notably London, Norwich and Worcester, kept initially their full medieval complement, while others found the burden too heavy in the fifteenth century, and either closed them then, or struggled on until empowered to close by mid-Tudor statutes. Besides Winchester, these towns included Canterbury, York, which under a statute of 1547 reduced its 40 parishes to 25, Lincoln (24 parishes to 9), and Stamford (11 to 6).[54]

However, there are two caveats to be entered before we accept an equation of shrinking population, housing and churches with 'urban decay'. One is that a smaller population need not be inconsistent with stable or even growing wealth. The other is that *national* population shrank considerably in the fourteenth century and remained at a very low level throughout the fifteenth; and one would expect a large drop in urban populations also, especially given that concentrations of humans – and also of black rats – would be especially susceptible to bubonic plague. The important question is whether they dropped more, or less, than national totals, or kept roughly in line.

The population of England on the eve of the Great Pestilence has been revised upwards by Hatcher to the range 4.5 to 6 millions;[55] and since, with a probably smaller margin of error, Wrigley and Schofield suggest 2.75 millions in 1541, that represents a population of the order of half the pre-1348 peak. How do urban figures compare? Doubling the 1377 poll-tax payers as a very rough guide (Table 1), the five provincial towns which were among the largest at both dates (Bristol, Coventry, Norwich, Salisbury, York) had a combined population of some 51,000 in 1377 and 42,000 in the 1520s. If one then inflates the former figure to allow for the national level of decline between 1348 and 1377, usually taken as about a third, one finds an urban population in the 1520s little more than half the figures for 1347. These figures are all extremely dubious, to say the least, including a whole range of assumptions about multipliers, with the margin of error widening at every stage. And one should in fairness add to this already treacherous calculation not only the huge but uncertain London total but an even bigger and more uncertain total for the smaller towns. Rodney Hilton has pointed out, on the basis of a detailed study of the West Midlands, that half of the urban population lived in small towns, and their collective population and its trend have scarcely been explored. Nevertheless, on the basis of the larger towns at least, it seems reasonable to postulate that if the whole population was halved it took place within a halving of the national total. A corporation could then assert, as did York's to Henry VII, that 'ther is not half the nombre of good men in your citie as ther hath beene in tymes past'[56] without saying more than most urban or rural areas could truthfully affirm.

To return to the small towns, if we cannot yet quantify their population we can at least estimate their numbers. Some 2–3,000 places in England received market charters before the Great Pestilence, but by the sixteenth century the number of market towns was down to something like 600.[57] The former figure is probably inflated by a good many speculative ventures which never really succeeded, but there is reason to think that at least half the functioning markets of the fourteenth century had disappeared by the sixteenth: in Staffordshire, for instance, 25 out of 45 disappeared.[58] It is further confirmation of the decline in national population, and hence of a lower demand for marketing services, compounded probably by a gradual growth of the specialisation of agriculture (which C.C. Dyer has noted as characteristic of the fourteenth and fifteenth centuries no less than the sixteenth and seventeenth) so that fewer, genuinely urban markets were needed rather than a larger number of locally-based village markets. Hilton has pointed out that 'Half of the village markets in the West Midlands disappeared, as did 60 per cent in Lincolnshire. On the other hand, in both of these areas almost all of the small urban markets survived'.[59]

Wealth is surely more relevant than population as a criterion of 'urban decay', and not absolute wealth totals either, since total productivity – if it were measurable for that period – presumably shrank both in town and countryside after the Great Pestilence. What we should look for is any quantifiable evidence either of wealth *per capita* increasing in the towns, or of a changing balance of wealth between town and country. The latter is the theme pursued by Schofield, who has argued from the comparison of the 1334 and 1515 lay subsidies that there was a threefold national increased in taxable wealth but that 'London . . . like most other towns increased in wealth much faster than the rest of the country, so that by 1515 it was almost 15 times more wealthy than it had been in 1334, accounting for 8.9 per cent of the total assessed lay wealth of the country as opposed to 2.0 per cent in 1334'.[60]

Unfortunately Schofield's published analysis is confined to counties, and does not systematically analyse the rural : urban share of taxation outside London, but Bridbury had earlier carried out, in Appendix II of his *Economic Growth*, a similar comparison of 1334 and 1524 which did just that. He found, taking the same places classified as towns in both years, that in 27 out of 28 counties the urban share of taxable wealth had increased, often dramatically: only in Staffordshire was there no rise.[61]

Now despite some understandable scepticism about the differing bases of taxation over such a long time-span, it is not clear that the broad comparisons of Schofield and Bridbury have been seriously undermined. Hadwin has suggested that Schofield's comparative base would have been better at 1290 than 1334, while Slater has found that for one county at least 1327 and 1332 would have been better, but both accept the broad validity of 1334 as a base-line.[62] The most impressive assaults on the long-term comparisons have been those of Rigby. He has pointed out that any under-valuation of urban wealth in 1334, or of over-valuation in 1524 (for both of which there is evidence), would exaggerate the apparent change between those dates. Hadwin, however, has now estimated that towns would have had to be undervalued by 60 per cent relative to villages in 1334 in order 'to negate the Bridbury thesis'. Rigby has also demonstrated that Bridbury's results in Appendix II could imply rural decline rather than urban growth: if the rural economy were in serious decline then towns might merely be declining less than the countryside. However, as Hadwin has shown, Bridbury's argument was always for a *relative* and not an *absolute* increase in urban wealth between those dates.[63]

No sufficient reason has yet, to my mind, been given to undermine the proposition that a higher *proportion* of national taxed wealth may have been located in towns in the 1520s than in the 1330s; probably, one might go on to say, in 1500 than in 1400. This certainly does not presuppose greater *absolute* wealth and does not necessarily entail universally greater prosperity; some towns did become poorer relatively as well as absolutely. It does, however, suggest that society was becoming more commercialised, a suggestion supported by Hilton in his recent study of the late medieval market towns and their relations with their hinterlands.[64] It may also have entailed more prosperity *per capita* for even humble townsmen than for their ancestors. 'Even in the 1520s, though real wages had fallen a long way from their fifteenth-century peak, skilled craftsmen could earn 25 per cent more than equivalent wage earners at the opening of the fourteenth century'.[65]

IV

Any broad view of the economic fortunes of English towns must remain, nevertheless, extremely speculative, at least until more detailed local studies have accumulated. It may be more fruitful to turn instead to the fortunes of individual towns and to the changes within the urban network and between town and countryside. If no general pattern of growth or decay can be firmly established, it may at least be possible to consider why particular towns, or groups of towns, fared relatively well or badly.

If we take the largest 26 towns in both 1377 and the 1520s, as measured, however crudely, by the numbers of taxpayers (Table 1), we find considerable changes, whether we look at the ranking order or, even more dubiously, at changes in assumed total population. Norwich, Bury, Canterbury, Worcester and probably Newcastle did apparently better than the national trend, and the most spectacular rise occurred at Exeter, which rose from 23rd place to 6th. On the other side of the balance, York, Coventry and Lincoln fared badly, and the east coast ports of Beverley, Boston and Lynn much more, as London's trade grew at their expense. What is impossible to measure in such national terms, but can be picked out by studies of regional urban networks, is the similar changes going on among smaller towns, where the fluctuations could be even more violent. Thus some towns shrank back into purely agricultural villages, or even disappeared altogether, like Chipping Dassett in Warwickshire. At the same time other small towns, especially the specialised industrial towns rather than the general-purpose market towns, were growing – Birmingham, Leeds and Manchester in particular.

Ranking by wealth, taking 1334 and c.1524, produces a similar pattern (Table 2). Among the largest towns, Coventry (this time), Salisbury and Ipswich improved their position, while York, Lincoln, Boston, Yarmouth and Oxford slipped back. Even more striking were changes in the next level of ranking: Bury, Colchester, Exeter, Lavenham, Reading and Worcester all prospered enormously relative to other towns, while Beverley and Winchester dropped heavily. A similar picture is obtained

TABLE 2: TOWNS BY TAX RANKING[1]

1334[2]		Assessed wealth	1523–7[3]		Subsidy paid
1	London	11,000	1	London	16,675
2	Bristol	2,200	2	Norwich	1,704
3	York	1,620	3	Bristol	1,072
4	Newcastle	1,333	4?	Newcastle	–
5	Boston	1,100	5	Coventry	974
6	(Yarmouth	1,000	6	Exeter	855
	(Lincoln	1,000	7	Salisbury	852
8	Norwich	946	8	Ipswich	657
9	Oxford	914	9	Lynn	576
10	Shrewsbury	800	10	Canterbury	552
11	Lynn	770	11	Reading	c470
12	(Salisbury	750	12	Colchester	426
	(Coventry	750	13	Bury St Edmunds	405
14	Ipswich	645	14	Lavenham	402
15	Hereford	605	15	York	379
16	Canterbury	599	16	Totnes	c317
17	Gloucester	541	17	Worcester	312
18	Winchester	515	18	Gloucester	c307
19	Southampton	511	19	Lincoln	298
20	Beverley	500	20	Hereford	273
21	Cambridge	466	21	Yarmouth	260
22	Newbury	412	22	Hull	256
23	Plymouth	400	23	Boston	c240
24	Newark	390	24	(Southampton	224
				(Hadleigh	c224
25	Nottingham[4]	371	26	(Wisbech	c220
26	Exeter	366		(Shrewsbury	c220

1. Chester not taxed in either list; Newcastle not taxed 1520s and position estimated.
2   R.E. Glasscock, 'England circa 1334', in H.C. Darby (ed.), A New Historical Geography of England before 1600 (1973), p. 184.
3   Hoskins, Local History in England, pp. 278–9; W.G. Hoskins, The Age of Plunder (1976), p. 13.
4   Peterborough (25th) omitted, because assessment inflated by rural dependencies.

from Bridbury's exercise of taking the ratios of individual town assessments at both dates: most towns turn out to pay up to eight times more in the latter year than the former, a few really declining towns like Boston actually paid less, while at the other extreme Lavenham's ratio was 18, Tiverton's 26 and Westminster's 43. Bridbury has, however, now regretted making these comparisons, which he describes as 'hazardous',[66] and the figures here presented in Table 2 likewise need treating with caution. Lavenham's astonishing position in 1524 was based on the assessment of one hugely wealthy family, while Coventry – despite its decline – was buoyed up by the assessments of three rich men, *all* of them much wealthier than anyone in Bristol.[67] The pitfalls of tax rankings are well illustrated by contrasting studies of Bury St Edmunds and Colchester, both of which rose considerably in ranking; while Gottfried believes that Bury was genuinely becoming wealthier, the much more convincing Britnell is not sure that even the experience of Colchester was one of growth 'through most of the period 1300–1525'.[68]

Several points seem to emerge clearly from the work done so far on the population and wealth of towns, all of them points that can usefully be pursued within the fifteenth century proper in a way that cannot be done at the national level by virtue of the sources. By doing so we can perhaps go beyond the stereotypes of the urban sector as a whole (declining or flourishing), or of the crude level of *types* of towns so doing (old-established textile towns, ports etc.).

(i)   We need not accept the orthodox opinions on individual towns simply because they have often been repeated: each case needs looking at afresh. Sometimes the result is a confirmation of the orthodoxy: thus Rigby has confirmed the commercial decline of Grimsby and Bartlett and Childs that of Hull, while Platt has confirmed the recovery of Southampton.[69] In other cases the result is less expected: Britnell has shown that Colchester was not a textile town that managed to avoid decline, while Butcher has demonstrated that Newcastle-upon-Tyne in the late fifteenth century was not the prosperous port that is often alleged.[70] And if Newcastle was not yet booming, the Cinque Ports were not yet all declining: Rye for one flourished in the fifteenth century, and in 1495 five burgesses were each assessed on £400.[71] Most surprisingly of all, the City of London itself may not have escaped recession, judging from Keene's work on Cheapside.

(ii)   Even where conventional wisdom is confirmed, it does not necessarily mean that the *reasons* for the towns' successes or misfortunes are seen in the right perspective. It is easy to argue, for instance, that the textile industry was migrating from the larger, old-established corporate towns to smaller towns or industrialising villages, which works for York but not for Worcester. It may also be deceptive to look for the causes of the *relative* decline of some towns without asking whether their previous rise had not been unexpected. It is tempting to argue this for Coventry, the only one among the largest and wealthiest half-dozen towns not to be a port or even situated on a navigable river. One reviewer of Phythian-Adams' impressive study of the city's decline has suggested that 'a longer perspective of Coventry's history might consider its prominence in the period c.1350–1470 to be a temporary inflation of its "natural" size and prosperity, otherwise occupying a similar middling level on either side of these dates – it is the boom, not the inevitable crash, which demands explanation'. Or, as the near-contemporary Camden had shrewdly observed, Coventry had prospered 'some ages since' through clothmaking and cap making, making it 'of greater resort than could be expected from its mid-land situation'.[72] As Leland put it, 'the towne rose by makynge of clothe and capps, that now decayenge, the glory of the city decayethe'; and at the time Coventry's textile industry collapsed, in the early sixteenth century, Worcester's was going from strength to strength.[73]

(iii)   Even taking the fifteenth century proper, it may be too broad to ask whether a given town was growing richer or poorer: there was much variation at a short-term level, as one would expect. Oxford and Winchester were already in decline well before 1400, whereas York and Hull seem to have remained prosperous until the 1460s and Chesterfield, taking the evidence of rents, actually grew in prosperity after 1400.[74] Many towns do seem to have become both smaller and poorer in the second half of the fifteenth century, while Bury, Exeter and Worcester went the other way. Even Colchester, which undoubtedly improved its position relative to other towns 1334–1524, had more years of decay than growth according to Britnell, while 'after 1449 it is impossible to speak of economic growth on the available evidence'.[75]

(iv)   Putting together the experience of individual towns, both large and small, with their rural hinterlands, perhaps what we should seek is neither a mere mosaic of local variations, nor a broad national trend which may not exist, but *regional* economic changes in which agrarian and urban economies moved together. Further, although it has long been argued that the sixteenth century saw the development of agriculture innovation leading ultimately to the agricultural revolution, Dyer and others have argued cogently that many of these innovations go back to the later fourteenth and fifteenth centuries. We should perhaps be looking, therefore, for a restructuring within regional economies, in which towns gained ground from one another, whether through economic change of an industrial kind – wool and cloth, leather, metal etc. – or of a purely agricultural kind affecting towns nonetheless. A booming region, for instance, could afford more prospering towns: thus in late fifteenth-century Wiltshire, Salisbury remained the largest and most prosperous textile town (it did not decline until the later sixteenth century), but there was space for the growth of Bradford-on-Avon, Trowbridge and others as well. Where the market was not expanding so much, growth in some towns led to the decline of others: the textile industry declined in York, Beverley and Ripon as it flourished in Leeds and Wakefield. The same shifts would also operate at a marketing level for agricultural produce; for instance, the small Cotswold towns (apart from the cloth towns of the Stroud valley) fell in ranking between 1334 and 1524, while those of the Avon valley and North Warwickshire rose.[76] Much has been made of the Richmond grant of 1440, rehearsing the economic decay of the town (and not fully printed in the *Calendar of Patent Rolls*), but the real point of the burgesses' complaints was not the decay of a town in isolation but the restructuring of a region in terms of the expansion of agriculture and of a marketing system to service it.[77]

(v) Finally, the country was clearly specialising agriculturally and industrially well before 1500, and some of the contrasting fortunes of towns owed less to shifts *within* regions than *between* regions. After all, Schofield's original point over twenty years ago was not so much that towns were increasing their share of the nation's taxable wealth as that there were substantial *regional* shifts in that wealth. The 1334 subsidy accounts showed the wealthiest counties to have formed a triangular swathe between Kent, Gloucestershire and the East Riding of Yorkshire, whereas in 1515 the zone of greatest wealth had shifted south and west to take in the London area, East Anglia and the West Country – a shift summarised, and over-simplified, by Platt as one from the 'wheat-producing regions' to the areas of wool and cloth.[78] The shift can still be seen in the West Country, not only in the fifteenth-century housing of the thriving Wiltshire textile towns, like Bradford and Castle Combe, but for instance at Mells in Somerset, where Abbot Selwood added a whole street for textile workers which still survives.[79] It is not at all surprising that some of the most impressive cases of relative growth in urban prosperity, like Bury, Reading and Newbury, were in this belt.

V

A final balance-sheet is very difficult – perhaps impossible. It is clear that by the period 1370–1420 the *national* population had fallen greatly and was perhaps still falling, yet the greater towns were larger and more prosperous than ever. This must have entailed a massive migration from country to town. The revealing preamble to a statute of 1405 declared that the fields were deserted, and gentry and others 'greatly impoverished', by labourers seeking apprenticeship in towns, 'and that for the pride of clothing and other evil customs that servants do use in the same'.[80] It may also be significant that many deserted villages clustered in the regions of large towns like Coventry and York. Certainly Britnell's persuasive study of Colchester argues that in the period of growth after 1350 'the town's manufacturing industry and trade stood to gain from rural crisis, which liberated manpower and capital', whereas after 1414, the town stopped growing and 'it lost its capacity to lure men away from their villages'.[81] The equation would then be – for Colchester shared its period of maximum size and prosperity with York, Norwich and other cloth towns – a *temporary* phase of growth at the expense of the countryside, followed by shrinkage as rural immigration dwindled away.

Yet it would be wrong to end on too negative a note: there was re-structuring, and not merely decay, in the fifteenth-century urban sector, a re-structuring that laid the basis for renewed urban and industrial growth in the sixteenth and seventeenth centuries. Specialisation in textiles continued to grow, and if York and Colchester declined, Norwich, Worcester and many smaller towns continued to thrive on it. And if many small market towns lost their urban and commercial character, the survivors often did very well and became more commercial as the fifteenth century advanced.

Notes

1. This paper was first written before publication of the debate between S.H. Rigby, A.R. Bridbury and J.F. Hadwin in *EcHR* 2nd ser. 39 (1986), 411–26. I am grateful to Dr Rigby and Mr Hadwin for their comments on my paper as well as their contributions in print, and in addition Mr Hadwin kindly showed me his unpublished paper on 'Long waves and sectoral shifts in the late medieval English town'. I am also grateful to Dr R.H. Britnell for his comments, and to Miss S.M. Appleton and Mrs L. Foster for making sense of my draft.
2. Mrs J.R. Green, *Town Life in the Fifteenth Century* (2 vols., 1894), I. 9.
3. M.M. Postan, 'The fifteenth century' (1939), repr. in his *Essays on Medieval Agriculture and General Problems of the Medieval Economy* (1973), p. 44.
4. A.R. Bridbury, *Economic Growth: England in the Later Middle Ages* (1962), p. 74.
5. S.H. Rigby, 'Urban decline in the later middle ages: some problems in interpreting the statistical data' (hereafter 'Statistical data'), *Urban History Yearbook 1979*, pp. 46–59; A.D. Dyer, 'Growth and decay in English towns 1500–1700', *ibid.* 60–72; C. Phythian-Adams, 'Dr Dyer's urban undulations', *ibid.* 73–6.
6. N.R. Goose, 'In search of the urban variable: towns and the English economy, 1500–1650', *EcHR* 2nd ser. 39 (1986), 165.
7. S.H. Rigby, 'Late medieval urban prosperity: the evidence of the lay subsidies', *EcHR* 2nd ser. 39 (1986), 411–16; A.R. Bridbury, 'Dr Rigby's comment: a reply', *ibid.* 417–22; J.F. Hadwin, 'From dissonance to harmony in the late medieval town', *ibid.* 423–6.
8. Susan Reynolds, *An Introduction to the History of English Medieval Towns* (1977), p. vi. Cf. J.L. Bolton, *The Medieval English Economy 1150–1500* (1980), p. 247.

9. R.H. Hilton, 'Medieval market towns and simple commodity production', *Past &
    Present* 109 (1985), 5.
10. Susan Reynolds, 'Decline and decay in late medieval towns: a look at some of the
    concepts and arguments', *Urban History Yearbook 1980*, pp. 76–8; R.B.
    Dobson, 'Model medieval vicissitudes', *Times Literary Supplement* 29 Aug. 1986.
11. Postan, *op.cit.* (n. 3), p. 42.
12. R.B. Dobson, 'Admissions to the freedom of the city of York in the later middle ages',
    EcHR 2nd ser. 26 (1973), 1–22; 'Urban decline in late medieval England', *TRHS* 5th
    ser. 27 (1977), 17.
13. J.C. Tingey, ed., *The Records of the City of Norwich*, II (1910), p. xxxix.
14. Bridbury, *Economic Growth*, pp. 77–82, 112–13; R.S. Schofield, 'The geographical
    distribution of wealth in England, 1334–1649', *EcHR* 2nd ser. 18 (1965), 483–510
    (quotation from p. 508).
15. Esp. Rigby, 'Statistical data'.
16. J.F. Hadwin, 'The medieval lay subsidies and economic history', *EcHR* 2nd ser. 36
    (1983), 200–17; T.R. Slater, 'The urban hierarchy in medieval Staffordshire', *J.
    Historical Geography* 11 (1985), 115–37.
17. Public Record Office (hereafter PRO), E 179, docs. listed in H.L. Gray, 'Incomes from
    land in England in 1436', *EHR* 49 (1934), 611 n. 1, plus E 179/217/42.
18. C. Phythian-Adams, 'Urban decay in late medieval England', in P. Abrams and E.A.
    Wrigley (eds.), *Towns in Societies: Essays in Economic History and Historical Sociology*
    (1978), p. 162.
19. R.H. Morris, *Chester in the Plantagenet and Tudor Reigns* (1894), pp. 511–24; J.
    Langton, 'Late medieval Gloucester: some data from a rental of 1455', *Trans. Inst.
    British Geographers* new ser. 2 (1977), 275; A.R. Bridbury, 'English provincial towns in
    the later middle ages', *EcHR* 2nd ser. 34 (1981), 2 (Oxford and Cambridge); S.H.
    Rigby, 'Urban decline in the later middle ages: the reliability of the non-statistical
    evidence' (hereafter 'Non-statistical evidence'), *Urban History Yearbook 1984*, pp. 45
    (Gloucester), 52–4 (Grimsby).
20. PRO, C66/453, m. 33 (*CPR 1441–6*, p. 82).
21. Reynolds, 'Decline and decay' (n. 10), p. 77.
22. Humberside County Record Office (hereafter HCRO), BC/II/3, f. 17v.
23. HCRO, BC/II/3, ff. 18r, 22, 23.
24. HCRO, BC/II/7/1, ff. 90, 92.
25. *Statutes of the Realm*, II. 381.
26. *Op.cit.* II. 359.
27. J.I. Kermode, 'Urban decline? The flight from office in late medieval York', *EcHR* 2nd
    ser. 35 (1982), 195; Rigby, 'Non-statistical evidence', p. 56.
28. C. Ross, *Richard III* (1981), p. xxxvi.
29. C.F. Richmond, 'After McFarlane', *History* 68 (1983), 51, n. 7.
30. Dobson, 'Admissions to the freedom of the city of York', p. 17, n. 3; cf. Dobson,
    'Urban decline', p. 16.
31. Sir George Warner (ed.), *The Libelle of Englyshe Polycye* (1926), p. 9.
32. PRO, C66/444, m. 11d (Wallingford); C66/446, m. 6 (Winchester 1440); C66/447,
    m. 14d (Richmond); C66/463, m. 31 (Winchester 1442).
33. E.g. H. Cam, 'The City of Cambridge', *VCH Cambridgeshire III* (1959), 12–14, arguing
    that the 15th century 'was for Cambridge, as for most English towns, a period of
    retrogression and decay', but calling in evidence only two fires (both before 1385),
    several epidemics, and the 1446 petition for tax reduction.
34. D.M. Palliser, *The Age of Elizabeth: England under the later Tudors, 1547–1603* (1983),
    pp. 51–2, 213–14.
35. Dobson, 'Urban decline', pp. 6–10.
36. G.G. Astill, 'Economic change in later medieval England: an archaeological review',

in T.H. Aston et al. (eds.), *Social Relations and Ideas: Essays in Honour of R.H. Hilton* (1983), p. 235.

37. J. Campbell, 'Norwich', in M.D. Lobel, ed., *The Atlas of Historic Towns*, II (1975), 17.
38. Astill, 'Economic change', pp. 217, 235. See also D.M. Palliser, 'The medieval period', in J. Schofield and R. Leech (eds.), *Urban Archaeology in Britain* (CBA Research Report 61, 1987), 54–68.
39. Trust for Lincolnshire Archaeology, *Archaeology in Lincolnshire 1984–1985* (1985), 53–4.
40. G.G. Astill, 'Archaeology and the smaller medieval town', *Urban History Yearbook* 1985, p. 49.
41. Astill, 'Economic change', pp. 236–9; Astill, 'Archaeology and the smaller medieval town', pp. 50–1.
42. Phythian-Adams, 'Urban decay in late medieval England', p. 167.
43. Rigby, 'Non-statistical evidence', p. 56.
44. Cited by Rigby, 'Non-statistical evidence', p. 56.
45. R.H. Britnell, *Growth and Decline in Colchester, 1300–1525* (1986), esp. pp. 3, 4.
46. M.M. Postan, 'Medieval agrarian society in its prime: England', in *The Cambridge Economic History of Europe Vol. I* (2nd edn., 1966), ed. Postan, 561–2; R.H. Hilton, 'Towns in societies – medieval England', *Urban History Yearbook 1982*, p. 8; C. Phythian-Adams, *Desolation of a City: Coventry and the Urban Crisis of the Late Middle Ages* (1979), pp. 33–4, 243–4.
47. Hilton, 'Medieval market towns', p. 3; D.J. Keene, in *Urban History Yearbook 1984*, pp. 18–20.
48. J. Hatcher, *Plague, Population and the English Economy 1348–1530* (1977), p. 34.
49. Britnell, *Growth and Decline in Colchester*, pp. 95, 159–60; D.M. Palliser, *Tudor York* (1979), pp. 201–2.
50. PRO, C66/446, m. 6; C66/453, m.31; 'A petition of the City of Winchester to Henry VI, 1450', *Archaeologia 1* (1770), 91–5; D.J. Keene, *Survey of Medieval Winchester* i, Part I (1985), pp. 96–8.
51. PRO, C66/444, m. 11d.
52. Phythian-Adams, *Desolation of a City*, p. 190.
53. J.M. Cowper, ed., *England in Henry VIII's time: a Dialogue between Cardinal Pole and Lupset by Thomas Starkey* (1871), pt. 1, p. lvii.
54. D.M. Palliser, 'The unions of parishes at York, 1547–86', *YAJ* 46 (1974), 94.
55. Hatcher, *Plague, Population and the English Economy*, p. 68.
56. A. Raine, ed., *York Civic Records* II (1941), 9.
57. A.D. Dyer, 'The market towns of southern England 1500–1700', *Southern History* 1 (1979), 125–6 (excluding Wales).
58. D.M. Palliser and A.C. Pinnock, 'The markets of medieval Staffordshire', *North Staffs. Journal of Field Studies* 11 (1971), pp. 49–63.
59. C. Dyer, *Warwickshire Farming 1349–c.1520: Preparations for Agricultural Revolution* (Dugdale Soc. Occasional Paper 27, 1981); Hilton, 'Medieval market towns', p. 10.
60. Schofield, 'Geographical distribution of wealth', p. 508.
61. Bridbury, *Economic Growth*, p. 111.
62. Hadwin, 'Medieval lay subsidies', p. 213; Slater, 'Urban hierarchy in medieval Staffordshire', pp. 120–4, 133.
63. Rigby, 'Late medieval urban prosperity', and Hadwin, 'From dissonance to harmony', *passim*.
64. Hilton, 'Medieval market towns', pp. 10, 11.
65. Britnell, *Growth and Decline in Colchester*, p. 1.
66. Bridbury, *Economic Growth*, pp. 112–13; Bridbury, 'Dr Rigby's comment', pp. 417–18.
67. W.G. Hoskins, *Provincial England* (1963), p. 73.
68. Britnell, *Growth and Decline in Colchester*, pp. 267–8.

69. Rigby, 'Non-Statistical evidence'; C. Platt, *Medieval Southampton: the Port and Trading Community, A.D. 1000–1600* (1973), pp. 141–63; J.N. Bartlett, 'The expansion and decline of York in the later middle ages', *EcHR* 2nd ser. 12 (1959–60), 17–33; W.R. Childs, ed. *The Customs Accounts of Hull 1453–1490* (1986).
70. Britnell, *Growth and Decline in Colchester*; A.F. Butcher, 'Rent, population and economic change in late-medieval Newcastle', *Northern History* 14 (1978), 67–77.
71. Green, *Town Life*, II. 17.
72. A.D. Dyer, in *Midland History* 6 (1981), p. 146; W. Camden, *Britannia*, ed. E. Gibson (1695), col. 505.
73. L. Toulmin Smith, ed., *The Itinerary of John Leland in England and Wales* (1908), II. 91, 108; A.D. Dyer, *The City of Worcester in the Sixteenth Century* (1973), pp. 93–119.
74. J. Blair, 'Religious gilds as landowners in the thirteenth and fourteenth centuries: the example of Chesterfield', in P. Riden, ed., *The Medieval Town in Britain* (1980), pp. 35–49.
75. Britnell, *Growth and Decline in Colchester*, p. 266.
76. Hilton, 'Medieval market towns', p. 11.
77. PRO, C66/447, m. 14d; *CPR 1436–1441*, p. 452.
78. Schofield, 'Geographical distribution of wealth'; C. Platt, *The English Medieval Town* (1976), pp. 90,91.
79. N. Pevsner, *The Buildings of England: North Somerset and Bristol* (1958), p. 226; M. Barley, *Houses and History* (1986), p. 79 ('Wells' for Mells).
80. Green, *Town Life*, I. 194.
81. Britnell, *Growth and Decline in Colchester*, pp. 160, 205.

2

The Urban Gentry in the Fifteenth Century

Rosemary Horrox
Cambridge

This paper is a preliminary investigation of a section of the urban community which has in the past received relatively little attention from historians. It has always been recognised that medieval merchants might aspire to gentility by buying their way into landed society beyond the town walls: a move which has sometimes been seen as the ambition of all leading townsmen, although the frequency with which that ambition was achieved has been disputed.[1] Even before this stage, while they were still active in town affairs, urban oligarchs have been seen as the equivalent of the county gentry, particularly in their peace-keeping role.[2] But none of this amounts to an explicitly urban gentry. Implicit in both definitions is the assumption that to achieve 'real' gentility a townsman must leave his employment, and preferably the town itself. Gentility is perceived as something essentially rural, and indeed the possession of a country estate has always been a seductive component in dreams of social advancement. But the reality, in the late middle ages and beyond, was more complex than this.[3] Soldiers, lawyers, administrators and household servants, as well as the archetypal country squire, could all lay some claim to being considered gentle in the fifteenth century. Given this, it is clear that the possibility of urban gentility needs to be reconsidered.

In exploring whether there was indeed an urban gentry, this paper starts from a deliberately narrow definition of the term. In what follows, urban gentry are individuals who, while primarily resident in a town, were described by contemporaries, or chose to describe themselves, as gentlemen or esquires. Urban knights are not an issue since knighthoods seem usually to have been conferred on townsmen as a mark of royal favour to the town rather than as an acknowledgement of the individual's status. The paper does not, in other words, seek to impose its own definition of gentility. What is being considered instead is whether contemporaries thought there was an urban gentry, and if so, who they were. This may seem to beg a question. The application of such terms to townsmen could be seen as evidence of a dilution of gentility rather than a comment on the social standing of townsmen. But, even if this were the case, it does not seriously affect the central question addressed here, which is the extent to which townsmen were perceived as part of the same social hierarchy as their rural contemporaries, rather than being, as the traditional view would seem to have it, essentially separate. What matters in this context is not so much the absolute social standing implied by terms such as gentleman (something about which contemporaries themselves were clearly unsure) as the fact that they could be used with equal validity on both sides of the city boundary.

This survey is restricted to provincial towns. London and Westminster have been omitted, primarily because their uniquely large number of resident gentry (many associated with royal service and the inns of court) makes them something of a special case. It is unlikely, however, that their gentry community differed in much but scale from those elsewhere. It was, indeed, swollen by members of the provincial gentry, like John Smith who, in drawing up his will, anticipated the possibility of dying and being buried in London, where he kept a room, but specifically asked to be described on his tomb as John Smith of Coventry, gentleman.[4] At the other extreme, the paper excludes places whose urban status seemed open to question. That apart, the intention has been to cover as wide a range of towns as possible (at the cost of using mainly printed sources) rather than focussing on one or two.

From this survey it is clear that most provincial towns did have resident gentry in the fifteenth century. It is likely, moreover, that the examples so far traced represent only a proportion of the total. The towns' own records are not a particularly fruitful source, often using no distinguishing title at all unless the existence of namesakes demands it. This means that townsmen can often be identified there only in terms of specifically urban criteria, such as their place in the governing structure of town or gild; something which has perhaps contributed to the feeling among some urban historians that the whole concept of an 'urban gentry' is anomalous and that gentry, although useful to towns on occasion, were essentially an alien element in urban society. The apparent silence of many town records is, however, misleading. Where they deliberately set out to record individuals' status, as in the case of the York and Canterbury freemen's lists, they usually yield a significant number of urban gentry, and this picture is confirmed by other, non-urban, sources.[5] Legal records, where some distinguishing title was demanded by statute from 1413, are a rich source, as are wills and royal pardons.

The urban gentry revealed by such sources are sometimes men who took no part in the town's own activities and hence escaped mention in the urban archive. More commonly they are so mentioned, but in terms which give no clue to their assumption of gentility. In the records of Nottingham, John Mapperley is unidentified except as a burgess, but when he had occasion to petition the royal council in a dispute with the town he described himself as a gentleman. Roger Timperley of Ipswich emerges as a gentleman from his wife's will, not from the town records.[6] In such cases, where the source reflects an individual's own perception of his status, there is some risk that an element of self-aggrandizement might be involved. At first sight, a Bristol example would seem to be a case in point. There, the alchemist Thomas Norton, in the course of a long-running dispute with the mayor, consistently described himself as an esquire. The civic official who recorded the dispute, on the other hand, began his account by describing Norton pointedly as a gentleman. But the official letters which follow, including several from the king, always refer to Norton by the higher title, to which, as a royal servant, he was indeed entitled.[7] Even where an individual's claim to gentility receives no independent support, it is unlikely that such assessments were profoundly out of step with contemporary opinion. In legal records it was important to be accurate (or at least plausible) in describing one's status. Pardons, too, needed to be realistic, although here the desire for comprehensiveness tended to produce a scatter of social descriptions, suggesting that the contemporary definition of a gentleman, in particular, was not entirely cut and dried.[8]

The case for an urban gentry does not rest only on an accretion of individual examples. There are also general references which show that contemporaries recognised the existence of such men. In Beverley's *Pater noster* play cycle, in which the eight plays were assigned to specified occupational groups, the gentlemen were given their own play (*viciouse*) in 1441. In a later readjustment, the same play was made the responsibility of gentlemen, merchants, yeomen and clerks.[9] In 1474, Edward IV could write to the mayor of Coventry to summon 'all the gentlemen and other inhabited within this our city and franchise thereof being of the livelihood of £10 by year and above'.[10] Even the towns' attempts to limit gentry interference in their affairs, often taken as indicative of a basic incompatibility between urban and gentry concerns, might draw a tacit distinction between foreign and urban gentry. When in 1460 Northampton ordered that no franchised man dwelling in the town take the livery of any unfranchised lord or esquire except the king, the phrasing left open the possibility of franchised lords and esquires – and the then mayor, William Austyn, was in fact described as an esquire in the same ordinance.[11] In 1516 Newcastle on Tyne stipulated that no freeman was to be retained by, or wear the livery of, any lord, gentleman or other person who was not free of the town. Here again, since urban gentry are known to have existed, it is unlikely that the compilers of the ordinance thought that unfranchised gentry included all gentry.[12]

Urban gentry, then, were a reality. But it remains to discover who they were and to what they owed their gentility. The traditional answer to the second question is, of course, land. Land conferred status, as contemporaries were well aware. John Smith of Coventry, himself a gentleman with land valued at £45, was adamant that the money he bequeathed to his son Henry should be used to purchase land, not to pay off Henry's debts or to buy sheep and cattle.[13] In sufficient quantities, land was the passport to county society, and the figure of the merchant who invests in land and so transforms himself into a country gentleman is familiar from numerous studies of medieval (and later) towns. But such men are not, by definition, *urban* gentry. The assumption, on the contrary, is usually that their gentility is conditional on their leaving the city, and, moreover, that this removal is the object of the whole exercise. They have been seduced, in Bridbury's phrase, by 'the patrician splendours and prospects of county society'.[14] Reality, however, was more complicated. Acquiring gentility through land was not like crossing the Rubicon, with the individual an urban merchant one minute and a country gentleman the next. Contrary to the impression given by some writers, townsmen did not save up their money until they were ready for their social transformation and then go out and buy themselves an estate.[15] The late-medieval land market hardly allowed such tactics. Instead, land was something to be bought piecemeal as opportunity offered. John Smith (whose own land-holding was extremely fragmentary) was clearly aware of this, and put the money to be spent on land for his son into the hands of a trustee until suitable land might become available. In Hooker's words, which are as valid for the fifteenth as the sixteenth century: '[merchants] do attain to great wealth and riches, which for the most part they do employ in purchasing land and *little by little* they do creep and seek to be gentlemen'.[16]

The fact that the transition to landed status was gradual must in practice have helped to blur the distinction between land-owning townsmen and country gentry. Of course, the ownership of small amounts of land was not enough to ensure gentility but it remains far from obvious how much was considered necessary. The turning point may have come when the individual was able to live on the proceeds of his land, but this is difficult to prove. There is not usually enough evidence to allow a detailed correlation of status and land acquisition, and to assume that an individual had reached the stage of living on his rents when he chose to call himself a gentleman is, to say the least, a somewhat circular argument. What is clear, however, is that the point at which gentility was reached was not necessarily marked by an individual's departure from town.[17] Medieval wills and deeds yield numerous examples of townsmen who controlled significant land elsewhere and who, apparently on the strength of that land, described themselves as gentlemen or esquires. William Fisher of

Boston, gentleman, who made his will in 1493, may stand as an example. His description of himself as 'of Boston', together with the range of his bequests, leaves little doubt that he regarded his house in Boston marketplace as his main residence. But he also had interests in Holbeach (where some of his kinsmen lived), Algarkirk, Kirton in Holland and Skirbeck, and left money for forgotten tithes to the parish churches there. In addition he had grazing land in Butterwick, Long Bennington and Wyberton, and, reading between the lines of his will, stockfarming provided much of his income.[18]

Traditionally, the achievement of men like William Fisher has been seen as only second best. The ideal is assumed to be a complete break with town life, even though this was probably always relatively rare. Townsmen who acquired land but remained in the city have accordingly been dismissed as 'failing to achieve the complete transformation they sought'.[19] It is doubtful, however, whether contemporaries saw rural land ownership quite so explicitly as an *alternative* to town life. Land, it is clear, could bring gentility even if its owner remained town-based, and to accept that individuals sought the status conferred by land does not necessarily mean that they also valued land as an escape route from the city. The two are only synonymous if gentility could not be achieved within the urban context. Some of the landowning townsmen, or their sons, did make the transition to country-dweller, but enough did not for the 'escape-route' interpretation to seem simplistic. In some cases, it is true, the urban gentleman may have remained in town from necessity. The acquisition of land piecemeal often produced a scattered estate with no very obvious focus. It seems, for instance, to have been fairly common for townsmen to hold land which, although valuable in total, included no complete manors. In such cases a town provided the obvious base from which to exploit the land. For others, there may have been economic advantages to remaining in town. Fisher, and the other townsmen known to have gone in for large-scale meat production, may have found it useful to maintain a presence in the local market town, for instance.[20] But some men seem simply to have preferred town life, making their home there when it was not strictly necessary. The Baret family of Bury St Edmunds provides one example. John Baret I, who inherited the family land, lived outside the town, while his brother John II pursued a mercantile career in Bury itself. This conforms to the traditional view of medieval expectations, but when John I died childless and his land passed to John II, he apparently did not seize the chance to escape the town, but remained based in Bury, as, later, did his nephew and heir, William Baret.[21] Roger Thornton of Newcastle is a similar case. He was armigerous, and held extensive land outside the town, but his interests remained primarily urban and he chose to be described as a merchant on his tomb.[22] Evidently town life had its own attractions – although some urban historians have been curiously unwilling to admit it. Rather than seeing the abandonment of urban concerns as the ideal, it is more realistic to think of men trying to combine the best of both worlds.[23] This argument is put into perspective by the number of county gentry who evidently valued urban connections, and whose readiness to involve themselves in town affairs in effect endorsed the gentility claimed by town-based families. When county families like the Pastons were discovering the advantages of a town house, it becomes less surprising that native townsmen, having established their claim to gentility, should want to maintain an urban presence.[24] Thus Walter Ingham, gentleman, the son of a former mayor of Norwich, seems to have made his main home at Aylsham (Norf.), but he kept a house in Norwich and at his death in 1485 could still be described as 'of Norwich'.[25] Nor was it only a matter of keeping an urban *pied à terre*. Those urban gentry who remained active in local politics or in the pursuit of trading interests could point to similar involvement by the shire gentry. Members of county families sought the freedom of local towns and joined townsmen as members of the great religious gilds. Some even moved into town permanently. A regional capital like York attracted numerous younger sons of county families. To take just two examples, both from the 1460s: Robert Crathorne, of the parish of All Saints, Pavement, was a kinsman of Sir Ralph Crathorne of Crathorne in Cleveland. He described himself in his will as a gentleman and on his tomb as an esquire. Henry Salvan, an esquire and citizen of York, was the brother of Sir John Salvan of Newbiggin.[26] Smaller towns, too, could attract such men. The Roger Timperley who advanced through the town hierarchy at Ipswich was related to the Timperleys of Hintlesham (Suff.), who themselves acted as advisors to the town.[27] At Cambridge, Clement Cotton, gent., who lived in the Shraggery, was one of the Cottons of Landwade.[28] Clearly, the move to a town did not necessarily entail a loss of class: which helps to explain why some smaller landowners chose to use their land as a springboard to a mercantile career, as Stephen Bramdene appears to have done at Winchester.[29] In some cases the sons of lesser gentry were even put to a trade, like the son of John Preston of Stafford, gent., who was apprenticed to a Coventry grocer in 1494, although in this case his own gentility was probably too precarious to survive the move.[30]

The ownership of land was not, however, the only route to urban gentility. In towns, as in the country at large, service offered a more accessible route to social advancement – and one where there is again no very obvious dividing line between the gentry on either side of the town walls. Townsmen are to be found in the service of the town itself or in that of influential individuals. The two types of service overlapped relatively little, with the latter usually conferring the higher status. Towns did have important men in their service, notably their legal counsel, but these were rarely resident and cannot therefore be regarded as urban gentry – although their existence did contribute to the atmosphere of easy relations between town and country which provides the essential context for the urban gentry themselves. Apart from the occasional resident recorder, like Miles Metcalfe at York, a town's local servants were normally of relatively low standing. Many had no pretensions to gentility, like the waits or scavengers. Mayoral serjeants were usually regarded as gentlemen, although few were able to consolidate what was essentially an honorary status.[31] Town clerks were in an only marginally better position and rarely seem to have risen much further. Those who did, like John Harrington at York or Thomas Audley at Colchester, tended to be men with the backing of non-urban patrons. Both also had the advantage of a legal training, and in general the clerkship carried a higher status when it was seen as a job for a lawyer. York's clerkship, for instance, was filled in 1490 by one of the illegitimate sons of Sir William Plumpton.[32] When the clerk was not much more than a scrivener his gentility was more precarious. Nottingham's clerk, William Easingwold, who seems to have been a scrivener, was at least described as a gentleman in the town records, but an early sixteenth-century town clerk of Cambridge, John Thirleby, described himself only as burgess and scrivener in his will of 1539.[33]

Service to a master other than the town itself offered wider possibilities. Many towns acted as administrative centres for major lordships. Most cathedral towns come into this category and Winchester, for instance, had a number of episcopal servants among its resident gentry.[34] Large religious houses such as Bury St Edmunds could have a similar effect on the composition of local society. Other towns provided a focus for secular lordships. Chester is among the most obvious examples, with a marked gentry presence largely explained by the administrative needs of the county palatine. Lancaster performed a similar role for its county, while towns such as Leicester benefited from the duchy of Lancaster connection. In the 1480s a Leicester draper, John Roberdes, enjoyed the status of esquire as duchy receiver in the region.[35] Boston served as the administrative centre for south Lincolnshire, and was the home of men such as Thomas Tototh esquire, the receiver of the honour of Richmond in the county. The widow of another royal official, Leonard Thornburgh, also chose to settle there. Her son in law was John Brown of Boston, esquire, who was perhaps the lawyer employed by the duchy of Lancaster in the 1480s, although the name is too common for complete certainty. Another Thornburgh associate was John Robinson of Boston, gentleman, who was later active in the service of lady Margaret Beaufort and who, at the time of his death, could ask his 'especial good lord' Richard Fox, bishop of

Durham, to be supervisor of his will.[36] Such coteries of gentlemen-bureaucrats are less common in towns which lacked a regional administrative role. The difference is spelt out in 1419 when royal enquiries were made into gentry eligible for military service in the East Riding of Yorkshire. Hull denied having any gentry (albeit in slightly ambiguous terms) while Beverley, the centre of an ecclesiastical liberty, admitted to several.[37]

The service offered by townsmen was not, however, only administrative. In spite of towns' reiterated hostility towards livery and maintenance, they remained part of the contemporary political nexus and it is relatively easy to find men who enhanced their own standing by looking beyond the town walls for lordship. Richard Clitherow esquire of Newcastle was on sufficiently close terms with the earl of Westmorland for the earl to head his feoffees.[38] The Bridgwater esquire William Gosse probably owed his status to service with the duchess of York.[39] At Norwich the alderman Thomas Wetherby had powerful patrons whose backing must have endorsed, if not established, his claim to gentle status. When Wetherby was in dispute with the city in the early 1440s, the duke of Norfolk described him as 'our right trusty and welbeloved servant Thomas Wetherby esquire', and continued, 'we be his right good lord and will support him in his right'. Wetherby also had links with Ralph lord Cromwell, whom he named supervisor of his will.[40]

But perhaps the most effective route to gentility lay through service to the crown. The numerous *ad hoc* tasks demanded of townsmen did not necessarily confer gentility, but regular employment, for example in the customs, might do so. The career of William Soper, burgess and esquire of Southampton, demonstrates the way in which involvement in royal business could enhance an individual's civic role, and *vice versa*.[41] Townsmen also formed a significant element at the lower levels of the royal household, among the yeomen of the crown and serjeants at arms. In a few cases the urban connection was itself a consequence of royal service. The yeoman of the crown John Ferriby, for instance, who was resident in Beverley in the 1460s, came originally from a very minor county family and owed his town land to a grant by Edward IV.[42] But kings also welcomed native townsmen into their household. The service of merchants seems to have been particularly valued, not only because of their local standing but for their useful access to ships. Edward IV's yeoman John Grauntford, for example, was the son of Babilon Grauntford, esquire and merchant of Rye, and it is possible to find numerous other examples.[43] Such office brought with it the status of esquire, although this strictly lapsed should the individual leave the household. In the records of the Cinque Ports John Crafford of Sandwich is thus described as esquire only as long as he remained a yeoman of the crown.[44] But, as Soper's career suggests, the advantages conferred by royal service could allow an individual to consolidate his status. John Sturgeon of Hitchin (Herts), who rose through the household of Edward IV to end the reign as an esquire of the king's body, was securely established as an esquire in his own right by his death in 1492.[45]

Those urban gentry who achieved their status through service shade into the rather larger group who were regarded as gentlemen by virtue of their occupation. The main group here, and an obvious point of contact with the men so far discussed, were the lawyers. Most medieval towns of any size had their resident lawyers, all but the most humble of whom were regarded as gentlemen.[46] Some were employed to hold local courts, but for others the town was simply a convenient centre from which to maintain business connections in the surrounding region. Robert Rhodes, esquire and lawyer of Newcastle, for instance, was legal advisor to the prior and convent of Durham.[47] Other professions also produced gentlemen – or perhaps it might be more accurate to say that other professions were regarded as compatible with gentility, since it is not always obvious which came first. Scriveners could be gentlemen, particularly if, like John Tilles of Norwich, they combined the job with legal skills. Tilles was made free of the city in 1472 as scrivener and attorney, and by the time of his death eighteen years later could describe himself as a gentleman. Henry Wilton, on the other hand, was already a gentleman as well as a scrivener when he obtained the freedom of the city.[48] Physicians were another group on the edge of gentility. Robert Haridance of Norwich, a doctor of medicine, considered himself a gentleman and was entered as such in the freemen's list, while in 1509 Thomas Hall of Huntingdon was pardoned as a gentleman and physician.[49] Schoolmasters, by contrast, had barely achieved gentility in the fifteenth century although are beginning to appear with the alias gentleman early in the sixteenth century.[50]

Many of these professionals were first generation arrivals in the town which they made their home. Haridance, for instance, is thought to have come from Fakenham by way of study at Cambridge, and freemen's rolls usually show more gentry achieving freedom through marriage or purchase than through paternity. It is usually impossible to tell what attracted an individual to a particular town, although it may often have been a matter of knowing someone already there. This helped to draw Cheshire men to London and there is no reason to suppose that similar motives did not operate at a provincial level.[51] The Barets of Bury St Edmunds, for instance, who came originally from Cratfield in Suffolk, arrived in Bury under the aegis of abbot William of Cratfield.[52] But whatever the exact mechanics of the arrangement, it is clear that towns were exerting a considerable pull. Nor did the lawyers and bureaucrats attracted to towns regard an urban practice as only a temporary stage in their careers. A few did move on, but most spent the rest of their working life in their adopted town, putting down local roots in the process. The lawyer William Eland, for example, was the second son of a northern landed family, who studied at Lincoln's Inn before settling in the East Riding as legal counsel and recorder of Hull (where he lived) and steward of the archbishop of York's lordship of Beverley, eight miles away. He married into the Beverley mercantile elite and put his land into the hands of a group of Hull feoffees.[53] It is even possible to find urban professional dynasties. John Arnold, who arrived in Winchester from Titchfield (Hants) via the diocesan administration, was followed in the city by at least two further generations who were active in episcopal and urban affairs.[54] A slightly more suburban example is provided by the Holands of Cowick in Exeter, three generations of lawyers who acted for the city, the king, local magnates and the cathedral.[55]

As this last example suggests, native townsmen also entered the law, although most who are known to have done so were from a professional or mercantile background – the law, in other words, tended to be a career for those already well established in urban society. Thomas Kebell, for instance, was the grandson of a Coventry artisan, but it was his father who had taken the crucial social step upwards by becoming steward of lady Abergavenney and lord Cromwell.[56] Similarly, Roger Wigston of Leicester, who entered the Inner Temple in 1514 with the backing of the recorder of Leicester, Ralph Swillington, was the younger brother of William Wigston, a leading Leicester landowner and merchant.[57] For some, including Wigston, a legal training proved the prelude to a withdrawal from town life, but, as with the acquisition of land, this was not necessarily the object of the exercise and a legal training could be a way of broadening a family's horizons within a continuing urban context. Thomas Thurland, merchant and burgess of Nottingham, put his son Richard into Lincoln's Inn in the 1450s but the family remained town-based and Richard's son (and Thomas's heir) Thomas junior was mayor of Nottingham in 1484–5.[58] The Osneys of Worcester make the same point particularly clearly. Thomas Osney, an attorney with a county clientele, was followed in the city by his son Richard, gentleman, who was probably also a lawyer. Richard's interests stretched beyond Worcester: he had a study in London where many of his books were stored and his wife was one of the Beaupies of Ludlow, a family active in the central royal administration. However, his will testifies to the reality of the Worcester connection. He sought burial in the cathedral next to his grandfather (possibly the Richard Osney who had been bailiff of the city earlier in the century) and it was Worcester churches which received his charitable bequests.[59]

The types of gentility discussed so far are not exclusively urban. A lawyer and administrator like Robert Rhodes is, apart from his choice of residence, indistinguishable from his county colleagues. The townsmen who acquired gentility through land, even if they then remained town-based, were entering a society which flourished beyond the town walls. They are all, in other words, 'urban' by virtue of their residence rather than because of any explicitly urban dimension to their gentility. It is worth asking whether there was such a thing as a specifically urban form of gentility, to be found only within town walls. In practice, the question is whether it was possible to achieve gentility through a traditional mercantile career, coupled perhaps with a role in town government, or whether it was always necessary to invest in land or develop other non-mercantile pursuits like the law. At one level the question is straightforward. There is no doubt that in the eyes of contemporaries the holding of office at the upper levels of the town hierarchy did confer gentility. A mayor, or his equivalent, was the equal of an esquire. This is reflected in the towns' internal hierarchy. Town clerks, it was suggested above, were normally considered gentlemen and in some cases were drawn from minor gentry families. But there is no doubt that, whatever their professional expertise, they were considered the subordinates of the mayor and council, a relationship nicely displayed in the duty of the Bristol clerk to provide the dice for the mayor and aldermen when they played dice in St Nicholas' church while waiting the arrival of the boy-bishop on St Nicholas' Eve.[60] Even more significant in this context is the status of the mayors' own servants. Most fifteenth-century towns had such officials and they enjoyed the titular status of gentlemen. Normally they were known simply as the mayor's serjeants, but in a few towns, including York and Norwich, they had the title of mayoral esquires – an explicit statement of the superior status attached to the mayor himself.[61] It was not only the towns themselves which thought in these terms. Fifteenth-century courtesy books, in their tables of precedence, accepted that civic officials should be ranked with esquires. Eminent visitors also paid due respect to the mayor. When Henry VI visited Coventry in 1451 it was thought appropriate to send a knight to summon the mayor and aldermen into the king's presence.[62] It was also, by the end of the century, becoming common for the mayor to be knighted on the occasion of a major royal visit, and there is no suggestion that this was thought an improper social leap.

This, however, was gentility conferred by office. The mayoralty did not transform an individual into an esquire in his own right, and town records sometimes distinguish existing esquires who became mayor by describing them as 'N esquire, mayor' – a solecism were the office alone the cause of their status.[63] This social elevation could, however, be made rather more permanent if the individual became an alderman, another post which seems to have conferred the status of esquire. But what about a leading merchant who held no town office? At first sight he was not considered gentle, being usually described simply as merchant, and such men have so far been excluded from this survey. However, the courtesy books set merchants *above* gentlemen in their precedence lists – admittedly only immediately above, but the implication is that a merchant is the equivalent of a gentleman.[64] Townsmen who described themselves as 'merchant' might therefore regard that as tantamount to announcing their gentility. This would explain apparent anomalies like Roger Thornton of Newcastle, who retained the title of merchant but was armigerous.[65] It would also make sense of the fact that merchants appear fairly often in the pardon rolls with the alias gentleman, but that this combination is rare elsewhere: something which suggests that the dual appellation was considered unnecessary (except, as in pardons, where comprehensiveness was at a premium) rather than contradictory.[66] More specifically, a tacit equation of gentlemen and merchants would explain why Hull, faced with an enquiry about gentry eligible for military service, chose to respond by pointing out that its merchants had provided ships.[67]

Of course, this did not mean that a merchant need have no further social ambition. What it probably does mean is that for a merchant to start describing himself as gentleman does not imply a major social advance. In fact, it is difficult to find cases of merchants who abandoned that designation for that of gentleman, which perhaps implies that the service implications of the term 'gentleman' made it unpopular with merchants accustomed to running not only their own business but their own city.[68] The real step forward was recognition as esquire, and examples of this transition are easier to find.[69] It follows that the merchant sons who entered the law probably did not see themselves as making a social leap, although no doubt they hoped that the law might lead to further advancement. The law was, rather, recognized as an appropriate opening for someone of a mercantile background just because the two careers occupied a similar place in the social scale. In this context it is worth noting that in the Norwich Corpus Christi day procession the mercers, drapers, lawyers and scriveners marched under one banner, suggesting at least an approximate equation of social status.[70] In Canterbury it was thought that clothiers could properly be regarded as living like gentlemen, and although the statement was made with an ulterior motive it was presumably considered plausible.[71]

In theory, therefore, an explicitly urban gentry did exist. In practice it is almost impossible to separate a mercantile career from the other elements conducive to gentility, which leaves open the question of how far trade itself had increased in status by the late middle ages, or whether the gentility of merchants was in recognition of their wider functions. Most merchants invested in land and played a role in local government, many had dealings with the crown, a few combined mercantile interests with a legal training.[72] It is probably unrealistic in such cases to argue that one element rather than another was the crucial one for achieving gentility: the overall pattern was what mattered. Similarly the other categories of urban gentry discussed above were not entirely self-contained. Many men combined a professional career with investment in land, for instance. The Canterbury gentleman and lawyer Roger Brent was able to buy local land, including the manors of Shelford near Sturry and Dungeon near Canterbury.[73] One consequence of this blurring of interests is that the urban gentry, with only a few exceptions, were men who straddled town and country. Many, as we have seen, owned land or had professional contacts beyond the town walls. Some were drawn into local government at a county level, and urban gentry can be found acting as commissioners, escheators and under-sheriffs.[74] A very few were even chosen to represent their county in parliament, like John Bell of Boston.[75] Against this background, the numerous marriage alliances between urban and county gentry look less like a cynical exchange of money for gentility (the later literary model) and more like a straightforward recognition of shared interests and acquaintance. Thus Thomas Wetherby, who had the backing of the duke of Norfolk in his dispute with Norwich, married his heiress to one of Norfolk's servants, John Jenny, the third son of Sir John Jenny of Dilham.[76] Other urban gentry achieved more spectacular matches. The daughter of Lawrence Acton esquire of Newcastle married Sir Ralph Percy and, after his death, returned to Newcastle to marry another urban esquire, John Carliol. The eldest son of Roger Thornton of Newcastle married a daughter of lord Dacre. Philip Mede of Bristol, alderman, merchant and esquire, made a gentry marriage himself and married his daughter Isabel to Sir Maurice Berkeley.[77]

But although it could thus be argued that many of the urban gentry, including the merchants, derived that gentility at least in part from their non-urban interests, it should also be emphasized that they were at the same time indisputably urban figures, fully integrated into urban society. Many were gild members, choosing not only the 'great' gilds like Corpus Christi at Boston which combined an urban and county membership, but more explicitly urban gilds like St Christopher at York which had close links with the city corporation.[78] They worshipped in town churches and supported local charities.[79] Many of them were involved in local government, not only as professional employees but as members of the ruling oligarchy itself. Richard Smith of Reading, gentleman, a wardrobe servant of Henry VII and his queen, was mayor in 1504, while Piers Curtis of Leicester is a better known example of the same combination.[80] As with the urban gentry's activities outside the town, these contacts were often reinforced by family connections. Those gentry who came from local families might have brothers or other kinsmen in business within the town. John Brown of Boston esquire left a bequest to John Brown of

Boston, innholder (presumably a relation) for his true and diligent service.[81] Gentry daughters forged further alliances with the urban community. The daughter of Edmund Chertsey of Rochester, gentleman, married a goldsmith. At Canterbury the daughter of Roger Leybourne esquire married a taverner, and the daughter of the notary Andrew Russell married a glover.[82] A few gentry sons took up a craft. The York freemen's lists, which chart the rise to gentility of numerous craftsmen's sons, also contain one example of movement in the opposite direction. John Scalby, saucemaker, admitted to the franchise in 1455, was the son of William Scalby, gentleman, who had been admitted as a man of law [*homo legis*] in 1423.[83]

The urban gentry thus spanned what have traditionally been seen as two societies, and in so doing they challenge the assumption that the social hierarchies of town and country can be treated as though they were separate. The tacit belief in the separateness of town and country is closely bound up with the view that gentility is somehow alien to towns. On the one hand it is thought that men could achieve 'real' gentility only by leaving the town. On the other, the involvement of gentry in towns is presented as contrary to a town's best interests. Those interests are taken to be the pursuit of trade and industry: an assumption which explains the tendency of some parliamentary historians to equate the 'true burgess' with the merchant.[84] Neither assumption is true. Although towns disliked blatant interference in their internal affairs, they recognized the value of backing from the gentry in their own dealings with the outside world.[85] Moreover, as this paper has shown, towns had their own gentry: men who were in all senses urban figures and whose activities were *ipso facto* part of town life. It is taking too limited a view of urban function to deny resident lawyers or bureaucrats the status of true burgesses. For the same reason, it is misleading to see the medieval townsman's country interests as something which weakened his sense of urban identity – an argument which again makes the tacit assumption that such interests were a distraction from the 'real' concern of townsmen.[86] It is clear that such interests did not necessarily reduce the individual's urban involvement. Service to an outside body was at least as likely to strengthen a man's hold on local affairs as to divert him from them. At a more personal level, some of the townsmen with the strongest gentry connections produced wills which display a continuing loyalty to, and concern with, their home town. Many of them sought burial in their town church, or wished to be commemorated there, even if they held land elsewhere. In some cases, it is clear that the urban church had become the focus of dynastic loyalties. Thus Robert Blickling, esquire, common speaker and alderman of Norwich, asked for burial at Carrow, but stipulated that a marble slab should also be placed in the Norwich church of St Mary in the Field, near the tomb of his grandfather Simon.[87] Most urban gentry also made bequests to town charities which, although by their very nature often conventional, sometimes reveal an informed awareness of local needs. John Sturgeon esquire of Hitchin, for instance, turned his attention to ways of improving the standard of singing in his parish church.[88] A few, including John Smith of Bury and Robert Rhodes, effectively made the town their heir.[89] Nor was this merely death-bed sentiment. Many had already shown themselves happy to maintain urban connections alongside their wider interests. For medieval townsmen, country involvement did not devalue their urban interests because in their eyes the two things were not regarded as mutually exclusive. Town and country were not separate worlds, between which a choice had to be made, but integrated elements of a single society.

This is not to say that the position of the urban gentry never gave rise to social tensions. Such evidence as survives, however, suggests that those tensions were neither as great, nor arose from quite the same causes, as later literary conventions would lead one to expect. There was a school of thought which held that gentility was essentially an attribute of birth, a view which receives literary expression in Malory's story of Torre, the putative son of Aries the cowherd whose true, knightly, paternity was revealed by his childhood passion for military things.[90] In practice, however, contemporaries accepted that gentility could be acquired as well as inherited, although they may well have harboured a sense that gentility by birth was the best sort of gentility. Certainly, in an age where political effectiveness was so closely tied up with perceptions of an individual's 'worship', a man's background was something about which he might worry, or from which his enemies might derive ammunition, and former townsmen could be made to feel that their origins counted against them.[91] But social anxieties of this sort were not confined to townsmen, and established knightly families were as catty about each other as about men who could be considered outsiders.[92] There is no real sense of the English county gentry or nobility closing ranks against newcomers. There is no sense, either, that new arrivals among the gentry had to cross a significant mental or cultural divide – the successful merchant who makes a fool of himself in adopting a gentle lifestyle is not yet a stock literary character, at least in England. Of course differences in status and wealth brought differences of outlook, but there is no reason to assume that these differences coincided with city boundaries.[93] It is always possible to find men outside towns wealthier and more influential than any within, something recognized by the towns themselves, who, as well as exploiting their own gentry in lobbying for favours, still felt the need to enlist the support of the county gentry and aristocracy. But there are plenty of rural gentry who compare unfavourably in wealth and influence with townsmen. As a result, one should be wary of talking too readily of an urban elite 'copying' the culture and attitudes of the land-owning gentry of the shires. Similarities may well be a matter of shared outlook rather than conscious emulation.[94]

If one is looking for a social divide around which tensions could develop it may be more fruitful to look below, rather than above, the urban gentry. If, as has sometimes been suggested, urban society was becoming more polarized in the later middle ages, the urban gentry can be seen as constituting one side of the divide. When internal tensions erupted into overt hostility in 1381, the victims were the men categorized here as the urban gentry (although the term itself is an anachronism in 1381): townsmen whose urban role was combined in many cases with county connections. In Canterbury, several of the men attacked by the rebels were identified with royal and ecclesiastical administration in the region.[95] The towns' employees also felt threatened, and at Colchester the town clerk was 'in very great fear both for himself and his friends'.[96] Most vulnerable of all, perhaps, were the urban lawyers with a county clientele, men like Roger Harleston of Cambridge, whose house at Cottenham was attacked. Harleston escaped unscathed but his doves were suffocated in their dovecote.[97] This does not mean that one should revive the old town/country divide in a new format and present the urban elite as essentially 'country' in their outlook, as opposed to the rest of the townsmen. The distinction is meaningless. As far as contemporary opinion was concerned, the town, in a very literal sense, was the urban elite.[98] But the tensions which become apparent in 1381, and intermittently throughout the next century, do serve to emphasize the difficulties in seeing medieval towns as social organisms united by a shared mentality which at the same time set them apart from the wider world.[99]

This discussion of the urban gentry has been concerned with the fifteenth century as a whole. Within that period the number of townsmen designated 'gentleman' or 'esquire' increased dramatically. Chronologically-arranged sources such as wills or freemen's lists make this very plain. In part this may represent real growth. There is likely to have been some increase in the number of urban lawyers and lay administrators in the course of the century, as there certainly was in the number of civic employees. But much of the apparent growth is explained by the major change in terminology charted by Professor Storey.[100] The use of the term gentleman as a social definition was a fifteenth-century development, spurred by the 1413 statute of additions. Alongside this development, and no doubt influenced by it, the longer-established term esquire seems to have been achieving wider currency. Both usages took time to catch on in towns, and it is probably no coincidence that some of the earliest provincial users of 'gentleman' were men who had dealings with London, where the gentleman bureaucrat was a familiar animal. The result is the apparent emergence of a new group, but there is no doubt that, although there may have been some genuine growth, the new terminology was being applied to an existing element in urban society. The fourteenth century provides plenty of examples of townsmen who, except in the terms applied to them, are indistinguishable from the urban gentry discussed above. In Boston, for instance, the career of William Spayne in the 1360s and 1370s would have earned him the title of gentleman, if not esquire, a century later, and the same could be said of Richard de Morton, active in Canterbury in the 1330s and 1340s.[101] The fourteenth century also produced the de la Poles, who went beyond urban gentility, but whose early careers display many of the characteristics discussed above.[102]

Such men may not have been new even then. As far back as one can see townsmen were acquiring land in the country.[103] Service, too, had deep roots. Winchester townsmen were benefiting from the proximity of the royal court in the thirteenth century, for example.[104] The urban professional and gentry class which writers such as Clarke and Slack have seen as characteristic of the early modern period was certainly more visible then, and may genuinely have been getting bigger, but it was not new.[105] It can be projected back well into the middle ages and was perhaps to some extent always there. Medieval men seem to have been less interested than some modern writers in erecting mental and social walls around their towns.

Notes

I am most grateful to Dr Richard Britnell for reading this paper in draft, and to members of the Cambridge seminar in medieval economic history for their comments.

1   W.T. MacCaffrey, *Exeter, 1540–1640: the growth of an English county town* (Harvard, 2nd ed, 1975) p. 260; J.I. Kermode, 'The merchants of three northern English towns' in C.H. Clough (ed), *Profession, Vocation and Culture in later medieval England* (Liverpool, 1982) p. 37.

2   MacCaffrey, *Exeter* pp. 276, 279. In 1433 John Stafford's tripartite division of society equated merchants with knights and esquires as the administrators of justice: J.P. Cooper, 'Ideas of gentility in early-modern England' in *Land, Men and Beliefs: studies in early-modern history* (1983) p. 49.

3   D.A.L. Morgan, 'The individual style of the English gentleman' in M. Jones (ed), *Gentry and Lesser Nobility in Late Medieval Europe* (Gloucester, 1986).

4   PRO Prerogative Court of Canterbury wills, Prob 11/13 fo. 47v. Among similar examples are John Cogan of Tewkesbury, gent., who sought burial in London, and John Brown of Boston, esq., who made plans for burial in either London or Boston: Prob 11/11 fo. 258v, /6 fo. 263.

5   *Register of the Freemen of the City of York, 1272–1558*, Surtees Soc. 96 (1897 for 1896); J.M. Cowper (ed), *The Roll of the Freemen of the City of Canterbury* (Canterbury, 1903). Such lists also include numerous county gentry admitted to the franchise, but they have been excluded from discussion.

6   W.H. Stevenson (ed), *Records of the Borough of Nottingham* II (1883) p. 395; W.H. Richardson (ed), *The Annalls of Ipswiche by Nathaniell Bacon* (Ipswich, 1884) pp. 151, 152; Prob 11/13 fo. 249v.

7   E.W.W. Veale (ed), *The Great Red Book of Bristol* IV, Bristol Record Soc. 18 (1953) pp. 57–93. It could be argued that gentleman was Norton's inherited, as distinct from honorary, status, compare *ibid* III, Bristol Rec. Soc. 16 (1951) p. 139.

8   For some examples see R.L. Storey, 'Gentlemen-bureaucrats' in *Profession, Vocation and Culture* p. 95. Pardons may, however, exaggerate the degree of social uncertainty involved. Where a range of evidence survives it seems clear that the title gentleman, once adopted, would be used fairly consistently. Thus William Baret of Bury St Edmunds, who described himself as a gentleman in his will of 1502, had been so described when he acted as feoffee for a townswoman ten years previously: S. Tymms (ed), *Wills and Inventories from the registers of the commissary of Bury St Edmunds*, Camden Soc. 49 (1850) pp. 79, 93. Such examples suggest some measure of agreement on what constituted gentility. Compare the nice social distinction made by Sir John Aske, speaking of William Harrington: 'a poor gentleman born, though he never were taken here but for a yeoman': A. Raine (ed), *York Civic Records* I, Yorks Archaeol. Soc. Record Series 98 (1938) p. 169.

9   Beverley Borough Records, BC II/7/1 fos 49v, 204v.

10 M.D. Harris (ed), *The Coventry Leet Book*, EETS (1907–13) p. 413.

11 C.A. Markham (ed), *The Records of the Borough of Northampton* (2 vols, Northampton, 1898) I pp. 297–8. This loophole was stopped, whether by accident or design, by Richard III's ordinance of 1483: R. Horrox and P.W. Hammond (eds), *British Library Harleian MS 433* (4 vols, 1979–83) II p. 10.

12 John Drake, *The History and Antiquities of the Town and County of the Town of Newcastle upon Tyne* (2 vols, 1789) II p. 179.

13 Prob 11/13 fo. 48.

14 A.R. Bridbury, 'English provincial towns in the later middle ages', *EcHR* 2nd ser. 34 (1981) p. 19.

15 A view most forcefully expressed by Bridbury, *ibid.*

16 Quoted by MacCaffrey, *Exeter* p. 260. The italics are mine.

17 This is also true elsewhere in Europe, in spite of the often-expressed noble disdain for the urban *milieu*: M. Keen, *Chivalry* (Yale, 1984) p. 147.

18 Prob 11/10 fo. 15 – v.

19 MacCaffrey, *Exeter* p. 261.

20 For other urban graziers see A.F. Butcher, 'The origins of Romney freemen, 1433–1523', *EcHR* 2nd ser. 27 (1974) p. 18; C. Dyer, *Warwickshire Farming 1349-c1520*, Dugdale Soc. occasional paper 27 (1981) pp. 17–18. Not all these men, it is clear, were considered gentlemen, but some, like John Lichfield of Coventry, may have been on the borders of gentility. I am grateful to Dr Christine Carpenter for her advice on this point.

21 R.S. Gottfried, *Bury St Edmunds and the Urban Crisis: 1290–1539* (Princeton, 1982) pp. 156–8.

22 Richard Welford, *History of Newcastle and Gateshead I: fourteenth and fifteenth centuries* (1884) pp. 280–8. For Thornton's use of the title merchant see further below.

23 For a more general discussion of the fluidity of late medieval society, and the range of interests possible to an individual, see M.J. Bennett, 'Sources and problems in the study of social mobility: Cheshire in the later middle ages', *Trans. Hist. Soc. of Lancs. and Ches.* 128 (1978).

24 N. Davis (ed), *Paston Letters and Papers of the fifteenth century* (2 vols, Oxford, 1971–6) I pp. xlviii, 545. John Paston III became a freeman of Norwich as esquire and mercer: John L'Estrange, *Calendar of the Freemen of Norwich, 1317–1603* ed W. Rye (1888) p. 106.

25 Prob 11/7 fos 155v–156; B. Cozens-Hardy and E.A. Kent, *The Mayors of Norwich 1403–1835* (Norwich, 1938) pp. 19–20.

26 York, BIHR Probate Register 3 fos 299, 301; Mill Stephenson, *A List of Monumental Brasses in the British Isles* (1926) p. 564.

27 *Annalls of Ipswiche* p. 148; G.H. Ryan and L.J. Redstone, *Timperley of Hintlesham* (1931) pp. 5, 14, 22–3.

28 Prob 11/13 fo. 77v; W.M. Palmer, *Cambridge Borough Documents* I (Cambridge, 1931) pp. 61, 149. The Shraggery is the modern Wheeler Street: *ibid* p. 143.

29 D. Keene, *Survey of Medieval Winchester*, Winchester Studies 2 (2 vols, Oxford, 1985) I pp. 227–8.

30 *Leet Book* p. 560.

31 Mayoral serjeants admitted to the York franchise as gentlemen include Thomas Wandesford, Edmund Barwyk, John Eglesfield, Humphrey Manners and John Seiston: *York Freemen* pp. 174, 184, 196, 212, 213; R.B. Dobson (ed), *York City Chamberlains' Account Rolls, 1396–1500*, Surtees Soc. 192 (1980 for 1978–9) *passim*. Although three (Wandesford, Eglesfield and Manners) have northern 'gentry' names it has not been possible to identify them conclusively with the families concerned.

32 Harrington: R. Horrox (ed), *Richard III and the North* (Hull, 1986) p. 88. Audley: W.G. Benham (ed), *The Red Paper Book of Colchester* (Colchester, 1902) p. 26; S.T. Bindoff (ed), *The House of Commons 1509–58* (3 vols, 1982) I p. 350, now amplified by R.H. Britnell, *Growth and Decline in Colchester, 1300–1525* (Cambridge, 1986) p. 259. Plumpton: *York Freemen* p. 213; *Testamenta Eboracensia* IV, Surtees Soc. 53 (1869 for 1868) pp. 258–60.

33 Stevenson, *Nottingham* II pp. 304, 340; Palmer, *Cambridge* pp. 119, 157.

34 Keene, *Winchester* I pp. 228, 323.

35 PRO Duchy of Lancaster Misc. Books DL 42/19 fos 28v-9, 149; Mary Bateson (ed), *Records of the Borough of Leicester* II (1901) pp. 268, 305, 306; A. Hamilton Thompson (ed), *A Calendar of Charters and other documents belonging to the Hospital of William Wyggeston at Leicester* (Leicester, 1933) nos 654–5, 669.

36 Prob 11/10 fo. 29v, /11 fo. 258v, /12 fo. 39. Tototh: *Harleian Ms 433* II p. 71. Thornburgh: *ibid* I p. 98; *CPR 1476–85* p. 403; he came originally from Carlisle, PRO Pardon Rolls C 67/53 m. 10. Brown: PRO Duchy of Lancaster Council Minutes DL 5/2 fo. 15; R. Somerville, *History of the Duchy of Lancaster* I (1953) p. 454. Robinson's career is discussed in M.K. Jones, 'Lady Margaret Beaufort, the royal council and an early Fenland drainage scheme', *Lincs History and Archaeology* 21 (1986), p. 14. This particular circle of urban gentry was given a more formal identity by their involvement in the Boston fraternity of St Mary: *CPR 1476–85* pp. 272–3, 329–30.

37 A.E. Goodman, 'Responses to requests in Yorkshire for military service under Henry V', *Northern History* 17 (1981) p. 242. For Hull's reply see further below, note 67.

38 *Early Deeds relating to Newcastle upon Tyne*, Surtees Soc. 137 (1924) pp. 187–9. For a glimpse of his life-style see Welford, *Newcastle* I p. 274. The family was one of the major trading and administrative dynasties of the century and deserves fuller study. They were also active in Hull and the Cinque Ports, although the exact relationship of the various branches has not been traced.

39 T.B. Dilkes (ed), *Bridgwater Borough Archives, 1445–1468*, Soms Record Soc. 60 (1948 for 1945) pp. 52, 123, 130, 136; R.W. Dunning and T.D. Tremlett (eds), *Bridgwater Borough Archives, 1468–1485*, Soms. Rec. Soc. 70 (1971) p. 68.

40 W. Hudson and J.C. Tingey (eds), *The Records of the City of Norwich* (2 vols, Norwich, 1906) I p. 347; W.J. Blake, 'Thomas Wetherby', *Norfolk Archaeology* 32 (1958–61); F. Blomefield, contd by C. Parkin, *An Essay towards a Topographical History of the County of Norfolk* (5 vols, 1739–75) II p. 551.

41 A.B. Wallis Chapman (ed), *The Black Book of Southampton*, Southampton Record Soc. (2 vols, 1912) II p. 98; C. Platt, *Medieval Southampton* (1973) pp. 257–8.

42 Beverley Borough Records, BC II/7/1 fo. 171-v; *Testamenta Eboracensia* III, Surtees Soc. 45 (1865 for 1864) pp. 178–81.

43 *HMC, appendix to 5th report* (1876) pp. 489, 493, 495; CPR 1467–77 p. 448 (yeoman of the crown), he later became an usher of the chamber, PRO Exchequer Warrants for Issues E 404/77/1/24. John himself was a ship-owner, whose ship, the *Agnes* of Rye, was used on royal business: E 404/77/3/60.

44 Felix Hull (ed), *A Calendar of the White and Black Books of the Cinque Ports*, Kent Records 19 (1966) pp. 83 (esq, April 1482), 86 (esq, April 1483), 88 (no designation, Oct. 1483). Crafford was in Edward IV's household, but there is no evidence that he made the transition to Richard III's. See also Storey, 'Gentlemen-bureaucrats' p. 92.

45 Prob 11/9 fo. 143; BL Harleian MS 1546; Somerville, *Lancaster* p. 593. His will pays explicit tribute to the role of royal service in his rise.

46 Lesser members of the legal profession were generally regarded as yeomen: E.W. Ives, 'The Common Lawyers in pre-Reformation England', *TRHS* 5th ser. 18 (1968) p. 148.

47 C.H. Hunter-Blair, 'Members of Parliament for Newcastle upon Tyne', *Archaeologia Aeliana* 4th ser. 14 (1937) pp. 44–5; R.B. Dobson, *Durham Priory, 1400–1450* (Cambridge, 1973) pp. 44–5, 129–31.

48 L'Estrange, *Calendar* pp. 138, 153; Prob 11/8 fos 301–2.

49 Haridance: L'Estrange, *Calendar* p. 68; Bindoff, *Commons* II p. 313. Hall: C.H. Talbot and E.A. Hammond, *The Medical Practitioners in Medieval England: a biographical register* (1965) p. 346.

50 J.H. Moran, *The Growth of English Schooling 1340–1548* (Princeton, 1985) p. 73; N. Orme, 'Schoolmasters' in *Profession, Vocation and Culture* pp. 226–9; *Letters and Papers, foreign and domestic, of the reign of Henry VIII* I pt 1 p. 254 (a reference I owe to Professor Storey).

51 R. Cunliffe Shaw, 'Two fifteenth-century kinsmen: John Shaw of Dukinfield, mercer, and William Shaw of Heath Charnock, surgeon', *Trans. Hist. Soc. of Lancs. and Ches.* 110 (1958) pp. 19, 21. More generally, see M.J. Bennett, *Community, Class and Careerism* (Cambridge, 1983) pp. 125–6.

52 Gottfried, *Bury* p. 154.

53 W.H.D. Longstaffe (ed), *Heraldic Visitation of the Northern Counties*, Surtees Soc. 41 (1863 for 1862) p. 69; York Prob. Reg. 5 fo. 364; R. Horrox, 'Urban patronage and patrons in the fifteenth century' in *Patronage, the Crown and the Provinces* ed R.A. Griffiths (Gloucester, 1981) p. 159.

54 Keene, *Winchester* I p. 228, II pp. 1148–9.

55 M.M. Rowe and A.M. Jackson (eds), *Exeter Freemen 1266–1967*, Devon and Cornwall Record Soc., extra series 1 (1973) p. 47; J.C. Wedgwood, *History of Parliament: biographies of members of the commons house, 1439–1509* (1936) pp. 461–2.

56 Ives, *TRHS* 1968 p. 159. The career of Thomas' father is treated more fully in E.W. Ives, *The Common Lawyers of Pre-Reformation England* (Cambridge, 1983) chapter 2.

57 Hamilton Thompson, *Wyggeston Charters* pp. xiv-xv, nos 697, 712; Bindoff, *Commons* III p. 612.

58 Wedgwood, *Biographies* pp. 853–4; Stevenson, *Nottingham* II pp. 421, 432.

59 Prob 11/10 fos 62–3. Richard Osney was a member of the Inner Temple, but his professional standing in the law remains uncertain. I am grateful to Dr John Baker for advice on this point.

60 L. Toulmin Smith (ed), *The Maire of Bristowe is Kalendar*, Camden Soc. new series 5 (1872) p. 80. In the early sixteenth century one Bristol clerk (turned out for extortion) was himself an esquire: William Barrett, *The History and Antiquities of the City of Bristol* (Bristol, 1789) p. 116.

61 Dobson, *York Accounts* p. xxxiii; Hudson and Tingey, *Norwich* II pp. 54, 71. The York mayoral serjeants were regularly admitted to the franchise as esquires, rather than gentlemen, sometimes without it being made clear that the title was an official one,

e.g. *York Freemen* p. 114 (John de Kirkeby). See also the Norwich admission of Thomas Trewe as 'yeoman, armiger': L'Estrange, *Calendar* p. 140.

62 F.J. Furnivall (ed), *The Babees Book*, EETS 32 (1868) pp. 187, 189; *Leet Book* p. 263. In this context it should be added that MacCaffrey's example of servants of an earl knocking down an alderman does not bear the weight of interpretation placed upon it: *Exeter* pp. 276–7.

63 For example, J.H.E. Bennett (ed), *The Rolls of the Freemen of the City of Chester, 1392–1700*, Lancs. and Ches. Record Soc. 51 (1906) p. 11; R.H. Morris, *Chester in the Plantagenet and Tudor Reigns* (Chester, n.d.) p. 275n (Richard Goodman esq.); Bateson, *Leicester* II pp. 305, 306 (John Roberdes esq.).

64 *Babees Book* pp. 187, 189, 285, 381. The merchants in two cases (pp. 187, 285) were specifically described as 'worshipful', which may be intended to imply the exclusion of all but the most eminent.

65 For Thornton see Welford, *Newcastle* I pp. 280–8; a similar example is Thomas Elys alias Smith of Norwich, described on his tomb in St Peter Mancroft as *prudens mercator* and shown in the east window in his mayoral gown, with his coat of arms: Cozens-Hardy and Kent, *Mayors of Norwich* pp. 28–9. At a time when heralds were asserting their right to regulate the possession of arms this perhaps implies some official sanction of urban gentility, although surviving grants of arms to townsmen are very rare and one cannot discount the possibility that some arms were assumed without authorization. For grants of arms see: Morgan, 'Style of the English gentleman' pp. 17–18; W.H. Rylands (ed), *Grantees of Arms*, Harleian Soc. 66 (1915), a reference I owe to Peter Hammond. Rylands includes several fifteenth-century grants of arms to Londoners (e.g. pp. 8, 23, 169, 247) and a sprinkling of provincial urban grantees. Among them are Robert Cromer of Yarmouth (p. 66), Robert Royden of Exeter (p. 218), William Skipwith of St Albans esq. (p. 230) and Robert Thorne of Bristol (p. 252). The latter two are early sixteenth-century, and numbers increase markedly later in the century.

Other urban gentry known to have borne arms include: John Ludlow of Southampton, gent. (bequeathed plate with his arms: Prob 11/8 fo. 70v); John Ypres of Rye, esq. (used an armorial seal: HMC, *appendix to 5th report* p. 499); Philip Mede of Bristol, esq. (shown in armour with an heraldic tabard on his brass: Stephenson, *Brasses* p. 146); Robert Rhodes of Newcastle, esq. (arms in three Newcastle churches: Hunter-Blair, 'Newcastle MPs' p. 45); William Innyngh of Bristol, burgess and esq. (owned a gold ring with his arms: *The Great Red Book of Bristol* II, Bristol Rec. Soc. 8 (1938) p. 205).

66 Morgan, 'Style of the English gentleman' pp. 23–4; Storey, 'Gentlemen-bureaucrats' p. 95 offers another explanation for the dual appellations in the pardon rolls. The other main source for such aliases are freemen's lists, e.g. L'Estrange, *Calendar* p. 137; *York Freemen* pp. 217, 222.

67 Goodman, 'Yorkshire Responses' p. 242. After mentioning a Holderness esquire temporarily in the city, the Hull return continued: 'other gentlemen they know none there, but men that live by their merchandise and by their ships, the which ships are in the king's service. . . .'

68 For an apparent preference for the title of merchant see William Vescy of York, admitted to the franchise as a gentleman in 1439, who described himself as a merchant in his will of 1477: *York Freemen* p. 156; York Prob. Reg. 5 fo. 196v.

69 For example, Philip Mede of Bristol (Wedgwood, *Biographies* p. 583; Stephenson, *Brasses* p. 146); John Smith of Bury St Edmunds (Gottfried, *Bury* p. 141; Tymms, *Bury Wills* p. 55); John Carliol of Newcastle (Hunter-Blair, 'Newcastle MPs' pp. 53–4; Drake, *History of Newcastle* I pp. 342, 363, 448).

70 Hudson and Tingey, *Norwich* II p. 313.

71 HMC, *appendix to 9th Report* (1883) p. 174. Here victuallers, bakers and brewers were,

by implication, considered not to be gentlemen but it is possible to find examples of gentlemen in such trades. Norwich yields a glazier who was also a gentleman of coat armour, although this was evidently thought anomalous: Blomefield, *Norfolk* II p. 555. See also *York Freemen* pp. 224 (gent. and miller), 226 (gent. and haberdasher).

72 Roger Wigston (see note 57, above) maintained his family's trading interests after his legal education, although he left Leicester. Richard Osney of Worcester may have had a foot in both worlds since his London study contained a 'new carven box from beyond the sea' and a set of weights and balances for gold: Prob 11/10 fo. 62v.

73 Prob 11/8 fo. 43-v.

74 Urban escheators include Robert Rhodes (Northumbs, 1434–6: Wedgwood, *Biographies* p. 720) and John Bell of Boston (Lincs 1404–5: see note 75 below). Roger Brent of Canterbury was under-sheriff of Kent in 1470: Wedgwood, *Biographies* p. 108. Roger Thornton junior was sheriff of Northumberland in 1457 but by this date was barely an urban figure: Welford, *Newcastle* I p. 385.

75 J.S. Roskell, 'The parliamentary representation of Lincolnshire during the reigns of Richard II, Henry IV and Henry V', *Nottingham Medieval Studies* 3 (1959) pp. 72–3.

76 Cozens-Hardy and Kent, *Mayors of Norwich* p. 22.

77 Wedgwood, *Biographies* pp. 157, 583; Welford, *Newcastle* I pp. 295, 385; Stephenson, *Brasses* p. 146.

78 D.M. Palliser, *Tudor York* (Oxford, 1979) pp. 48–9. Fifteenth-century gentry members of St Christopher's Gild included John Wyman gent. (York Prob. Reg. 3 fo. 350v) and Richard Torald esq. (*ibid* fo. 583v). Other gentry founded their own urban gilds, among them Richard Smith, gentleman and burgess of Reading, a founder of the Brethren of the Mass of Jesus there in 1493: Wedgwood, *Biographies* pp. 777–8; J.M. Guilding (ed), *Reading Records: Diary of the Corporation* I (1892) p. 97. For a Boston example, see note 36 above.

79 See, for instance, Adam Oxenbridge of Rye, esquire, who wished to be buried before his seat in the lady chapel in the church of Rye: Prob 11/11 fo. 59.

80 Prob 11/14 fo. 179; *Reading Records* I p. 110; Wedgwood, *Biographies* pp. 244–5, 777–8. Some urban gentlemen were less enthusiastic. William Debenham, gent., of Colchester refused election as an alderman, but he had previously been a bailiff and responded angrily to the suggestion that he 'never did good to this town': Britnell, *Colchester* p. 231. Of course, non-gentry townsmen might also choose not to become involved in local government.

81 Prob 11/11 fo. 258v.

82 *Ibid*/6 fo. 110v; *Freemen of Canterbury* cols 100, 114, 134.

83 *York Freemen* pp. 134, 176.

84 J.S. Roskell, *The Commons in the Parliament of 1422* (Manchester, 1954) pp. 126–7, 130; P. Jalland, 'The revolution in northern borough representation in mid-fifteenth-century England', *Northern History* 9 (1975) *passim*.

85 Horrox, 'Urban patronage'. The argument in the present paper that towns had their own gentry (even if they did not necessarily return them as parliamentary representatives) reinforces my earlier suggestion that the gentry chosen as borough members should not be seen as an alien element in urban affairs. The gentry chosen may well have shared the attitudes of many of the leading men in the city.

86 For example, C. Platt, *The English Mediaeval Town* (1979 ed.) pp. 121–2, 230.

87 Hudson and Tingey, *Norwich* I pp. 282, 325; Blomefield, *Norfolk* II p. 614.

88 Prob 11/9 fo. 143. His plan included inducing a mercer with a good voice to move from Shillington to Hitchin.

89 Gottfried, *Bury* p. 141; Hunter-Blair, 'Newcastle MPs' pp. 44–5.

90 Thomas Malory, *Works* ed E. Vinaver (Oxford, 2nd ed., 1971) pp. 61–2.

91 Morgan, 'Style of the English gentleman' p. 23. Compare also the taunt levelled at Michael de la Pole, earl of Suffolk, the son of a Hull merchant, that he was more suited

for mercery than the martial life (*vir plus aptus mercimoniis quam militiae*): Thomas Walsingham, *Historia Anglicana* ed H.T. Riley (2 vols, 1863–4) II p. 141.

92   See, for instance, Sir Robert Hilton's comment in the 1340s about Richard lord Scrope: 'I have heard that he is not a *grand gentilhomme*': N.H. Nicholas (ed), *The Scrope and Grosvenor Controversy* (2 vols, 1832) II p. 37.

93   One difference which is sometimes cited is that the townsman saw his land primarily as an investment, while for the country gentleman it embodied his dynastic identity. Recent work, however, suggests that country gentlemen were as pragmatic in this matter as their urban fellows: Britnell, *Colchester* p. 260; Christine Carpenter, 'The fifteenth-century English gentry and their estates' in Jones, *Gentry and Lesser Nobility* pp. 45, 54–5.

94   The blurring of 'court' and 'urban' literary tastes is one of the themes of A.I. Doyle, 'English books in and out of court' in *English Court Culture in the Later Middle Ages* ed V.J. Scattergood and J.W. Sherborne (1983). This blurring is exemplified in the will of John Morton esq. of York (d. 1413), who bequeathed a Latin text of Higden's *Policronica* to his rector, a book in English called *Gower* to the countess of Westmorland and a book *de gestis Romanorum* to its scribe, John Alne, the brother of a former mayor of York: York Prob. Reg. 2 fos 653v–4; printed in *Testamenta Eboracensia* II, Surtees Soc. 30 (1855) no. XI. Moran, *Schooling* p. 153, mistranslated *armiger* as knight, and groups Morton with the county gentry. He is probably not the mercer and mayor of York (*York Freemen* p. 101; Dobson, *York Accounts* p. 209) but his will shows that his connections were primarily urban and ecclesiastical and he may have been an administrator associated with the minster.

95   A.F. Butcher, 'English urban society and the revolt of 1381' in *The English Rising of 1381* ed R.H. Hilton and T.H. Aston (Cambridge, 1984) pp. 108–9.

96   Britnell, *Colchester* pp. 124–5.

97   *Victoria County History of Cambridgeshire* III p. 10. In this context it is worth remembering that one of the most eminent victims of the unrest, the chief justice Sir John Cavendish, had a town house in Bury and that it was to Bury that his head was sent: Gottfried, *Bury* p. 233. For the attack on London-based lawyers see A. Prescott, 'London in the Peasants' Revolt: a portrait gallery', *London Journal* 7 (1981) pp. 133–5.

98   There is also the question of how far the lower levels of urban society had retained rural connections and attitudes, a subject which needs further investigation.

99   Butcher, 'Urban society' p. 110. For an extreme expression of the separateness of towns see MacCaffrey, *Exeter* pp. 1–2, 279–80.

100   Storey, 'Gentlemen-bureaucrats'.

101   Roskell, 'Parliamentary representation' pp. 63–4; Butcher, 'Urban society' p. 96.

102   R. Horrox, *The de la Poles of Hull* (Hull, 1983) pp. 36–7.

103   Platt, *Mediaeval Town* pp. 122–3. For some thirteenth-century examples see E. Miller, 'Rulers of thirteenth century towns: the cases of York and Newcastle upon Tyne' in *Thirteenth Century England* 1 ed P.R. Coss and S.D. Lloyd (Woodbridge, 1986) pp. 137–9, where the thirteenth-century urban elite is discussed in 'gentry' terms.

104   Keene, *Winchester* I p. 322.

105   P. Clark and P. Slack, *English Towns in Transition, 1500–1700* (Oxford, 1976) pp. 120–1; Platt, *Mediaeval Town* pp. 226–30, sets the beginning of this development earlier, in the mid-fifteenth century, but this is when it becomes clearly visible rather than when it gets under way.

3

London and Westminster:
The Suburb in the Urban Economy
in the Later Middle Ages

Gervase Rosser

University of Birmingham

The medieval city has tended to appear, in the writings of recent historians, in a peculiarly negative light. Not only has it been (and rightly) denied any distinctive status within feudal society at large, of which it is seen to have formed an integral part;[1] but its role within that society has been felt to be reactionary to a degree. Like a collective great seigneur, the city battened upon its own population and upon the surrounding countryside, gathering the surplus produce of both into the hands of an elite of merchant oligarchs. Meanwhile the accumulation, from these sources and from the proceeds of long-distance trade, of merchant fortunes never led in turn to new investment such as could transform existing social relations. The vitality of the city as a cultural centre is allowed; but economically, socially and politically it is identified with the most unenlightened and intolerable of feudal lords.[2] Consequently those historians who have looked for the forces within feudal society which could act upon it as a solvent, preparing the way for capitalist development, have increasingly turned away from the old-established cities to find the quarry elsewhere. Following Marx, they have looked to newly emergent 'factory towns' growing up in the countryside, free of the constraining guild controls and patrician monopolies of the older cities: the glory of industrial Birmingham is attributable to its unchartered liberty.[3] Changes in farming methods have been stressed: the economic conditions of the later middle ages provided the opportunity, as Christopher Dyer has shown, for enterprising *kulaks* to turn themselves into early agrarian capitalists.[4] And Rodney Hilton has drawn attention to the numerous small market towns, where peasants could profitably exchange such of their surplus produce as they could withold from their lords.[5] Each of these approaches has been, and promises to continue to be, rewarding. But if the city may be brought back into view, it may yet be found itself to have taken part in the wider developments identified elsewhere. The fat merchant was indeed often first cousin to the least adventurous of rural landlords. But the merchant's command of the urban situation was not complete. The suburbs and hinterland of a city were sectors of the urbanised area over which the mercantile hold was never more than partial. These sectors merit attention as a fresh potential context of economic change. The case considered here, that of the relationship between London and Westminster, was in some respects untypical: the size and political importance of the capital obviously set it apart from other English towns. Yet these factors were largely matters of degree; and the metropolitan experience may be a more valid indicator of developments in the wider urban economy than is often assumed.

It was only scale, for example, which distinguished the most prominent economic function of the late medieval metropolis from the otherwise comparable role of lesser towns: the provision of a complex of services, to both visitors and residents. Country dwellers regarded the city with an ambivalence which is still familiar. In the fifteenth century, the Pastons of Norfolk repeatedly exclaimed to one another at the costliness of London living, at the obstructiveness and corruption of its officialdom or at the urgent necessity to escape to the country from the lethal clutches of London doctors. Yet for the Pastons London and Westminster, together, were a vital and inescapable resort, not only as the unique source of supply of such luxuries as almonds, gold thread and news of the war abroad for which the women at home continually badgered the husband or son currently in town, but as a lifeline to legal aid and political support in the troubled affairs of their own county.[6] The capital was well provided to cater hospitably for such transients as the Pastons. The suburban district of Westminster alone offered the late medieval visitor a choice of at least sixty alehouses, amongst which one called the Bull was so regularly patronised by the Pastons that messages could be left there with the alewife for their business and legal contacts.[7] At the period, in the late 1460s, when the Pastons were pursuing at law their claim to Caister Castle, their rival in the case, the duke of Norfolk, would himself, on his own visits to Westminster, resort for refreshment either to the Bell or to the Swan in King Street.[8] The metropolitan watering-places of the country gentry and aristocracy may seem a trivial starting-point to a discussion of the economy of London and Westminster in the fifteenth century. Yet the urban inn is arguably the very best place from which to begin. Together with the professional legal advice and the specialised tailoring jobs which they commissioned in Westminster and London, the ale drunk by the Pastons in Westminster taverns was a component of the capital's economy of services. It would be premature, pending the results of Derek Keene's Social and Economic Study of Medieval London, to assert that the provision of such services was the most important dimension of the economy of the late medieval city. But although London boasted a wide range of artisanal crafts, evidence for industrial production beyond local needs is yet largely lacking. The present review will give prominence to the service sector, highlighting the distinctive role within that sector of the suburban areas. First, however, it will be well to emphasise the wider unity of the total urban economy, with particular reference to relations between the city and its western suburb (see illustration, p48).

To a greater degree than the other London suburbs, Westminster developed in the later middle ages an identity of its own;[9] yet the interdependence of the city and Westminster was vital to the history of each. When the Norman kings departed, after the mid-twelfth century, from their former capital of Winchester, the consequent effect upon that city, deprived of its chief *raison d'être*, was catastrophic. After the prosperity described, at the close of the period of greatness, in the early twelfth century Winton Domesday, Derek Keene's account of the later medieval town reads as an extended anti-climax.[10] The selection as the new capital of Westminster, where in the course of the following two centuries the departments of royal government successively fixed their permanent homes, was undoubtedly determined by the pre-existing and continuing importance in its own right of London.[11] The gain from this alliance was, however, mutual, and was crucial to London's subsequent development, as late medieval records make explicit.

At this period Londoners evinced, together with the inhabitants of Westminster itself, a marked sensitivity to the movements of the royal court. Householders in the metropolis at large expressed resentment when livery was taken of them for the accommodation of the royal entourage; but retailers of all kinds, as London ordinances show, relished the opportunity to increase their prices to visiting courtiers and provincials. When the king's court, together with the offices of government, were removed from Westminster, as they were for a few months in 1392, the traders of London protested as loudly as did those of Westminster. To the market comprised by the citizenry themselves, the superaddition of the army of ministers of the royal government was clearly a factor of importance.[12] The precise worth of the Westminster market to London's retailers cannot be quantified, but the indications are that the value was high. Those who profited from suburban commerce ranged from wealthy barons of trade to the humblest hawkers and stall-holders. City manufacturers and merchants regularly sought outlets through local retailers in the suburb. In Richard II's reign the London governors were concerned that ale was being exported from the city for resale by hucksters in Westminster.[13]

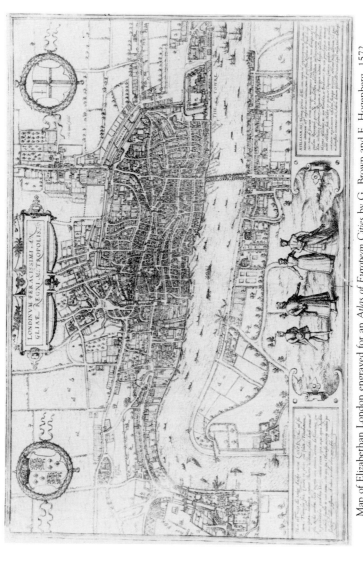

Map of Elizabethan London engraved for an *Atlas of European Cities* by G. Brown and F. Hogenberg, 1572 (*Museum of London*)

Westminster's many tavern-keepers were likewise supplied by London vintners. In 1394 William Bromley, a modest taverner of Westminster and Hugh Short, vintner of London, conspired to sell at Westminster bad La Rochelle wine which they had sweetened with honey (and for which they naturally charged an inflated price).[14] Also at a relatively minor level of operation, a fishmonger who moved from the city to Westminster around 1475 continued to buy large quantities of stockfish, salt fish, fresh fish and herrings from middlemen in London.[15] Bulk orders might be supplied directly from London-based citizen suppliers, from whom, for example, the Westminster monks purchased quantities of wax, oil and fish.[16] The abbey had also more costly requirements. The abbot of Westminster in the 1460s, admittedly a financial incompetent, ran up debts with the city draper Ralph Josselyn, for merchandise and perhaps also for financial loans, totalling £1,000.[17] Westminster contained in addition the attraction of the kingdom's wealthiest and most ostentatious shopper. King Richard II was capable of spending, on saddlery, mercery, skins and drapery supplied by London merchants, in the space of just two years, over £11,000.[18] Moreover cash loans from the city's mercantile elite continued in the fifteenth century as in the fourteenth to be a major service provided by London to the monarch at Westminster.[19]

Certain London traders, while usually retaining their head offices in the city, chose themselves to rent premises in Westminster, the better to command the lucrative local market. The majority of Londoners in this category, who may thus have been opening 'West End branches', dealt in luxury goods: they were goldsmiths, mercers and grocers, haberdashers, drapers and tailors. Property records of the fifteenth century reveal the presence in Westminster of about fifty Londoners bearing these designations, each of which meant effectively, 'high class provision merchant'.[20] Their characteristic stock would have been similar to that of an Italian also trading at Westminster towards 1400, who was robbed there of six pieces of Cyprus cloth of gold (valued at £32), half a bale of cloves (£12) and gold to the value of £20.[21] These Fortnums and Masons of the fifteenth century belonged to the trading community which dominated London's government in the later middle ages. Their wealth and social affectations (the coat of arms, the country house at Hendon or Staines) set them virtually on an equal footing with the quality whose custom they went to Westminster to seek. The class may be exemplified by the tailor, James Fytt. It was no wonder that a tailor of London should be drawn to Westminster where, in the orbit of the court, as a satirist remarked around 1400, a practitioner of that craft might charge twenty times the cost of his material.[22] A citizen of London, where he was admitted to the tailors' fraternity in 1459 and where he continued to be active, Fytt yet became at the same time sufficiently a Westminster figure to serve as a churchwarden

of the local parish church of St Margaret in 1458–60 and as a constable of
the liberty of Westminster in 1464. He buried his father, a wife and an
apprentice in St Margaret's, where he chose to seek his own grave in 1500.
By an act of patronage which expressed his elevated standing in Westmin-
ster, Fytt paid for one of the glass windows set in the newly rebuilt St
Margaret's in 1499. Houses which he owned in the London parish of St
Mary Aldermary Fytt gave to the prominent Westminster guild of the
Assumption of the Virgin Mary. In return, the guild undertook to provide
Fytt's funeral at St Margaret's church and also to keep an obit there for
him and for 'his wives and friends'.[23]

Westminster was separated from London by a short boat-ride;[24] the
river, which was probably always preferable to the route by land, may have
created a psychological distance between these two parts of the metropolis. Nevertheless the examples which have been cited of both large- and
small-scale exchange, together with other indicators such as the recruitment of Londoners to the fraternities of Westminster[25] and the attendance
of London boys at Westminster school,[26] are reflections of the essential
unity of the wider urban area. Westminster was an integral and vital part
of London's consumer economy.

In one important respect, however, Westminster, together with the
other suburbs, was set apart from London. For the jurisdiction of the
mayor of the city did not extend over the suburban liberties, of which that
of the abbot of Westminster, extending from south of the abbey north-
wards and westwards to the Strand, was the largest.[27] Moreover, within
the ambit of the liberty of Westminster lay a smaller area of still greater
privilege: the sanctuary itself. The Westminster sanctuary, like the other
notable case of St Martin-le-Grand within the city walls, enjoyed the very
fullest rights of ecclesiastical immunity.[28] All medieval towns contained
such pockets of more or less complete jurisdictional independence, whose
existence vitiated attempts by urban governments to control the
economy.[29] The sanctuary at Westminster, which was defined by the
precinct wall of the abbey, was by the early fifteenth century crowded with
the premises of shopkeepers and other retailers. The sole authority
recognised within this hallowed commercial enclave was that, under the
abbot, of the monk-archdeacon of Westminster.[30] The retailers who
congregated here were therefore drawn by the dual attraction of the
proximity of good custom and of freedom from control. Among them,
indeed, were some evidently grateful to leave behind them in the city
what might politely be termed 'business difficulties'. One day in 1477, the
wardens of the Mercers' Company of London 'marvelled greatly' to receive
a letter from one of their fellow-members, John Baron, which was
unconventionally delivered by the hand of his wife. Baron, as it
transpired, had taken sanctuary at Westminster, and being therefore 'not

at large', begged the company to act on his behalf with regard to 'diverse articles grievous and great complaining [against] John Fyssher the elder'. The outcome of the dispute with Fyssher is unknown, but it may be that Baron had not expected to prevail, for in August the previous year, shortly before his disappearance from London, he had transferred all his goods to trustees; and by 1479, when he reserved a pew for his wife in St Margaret's church (which itself stood within the precinct of Westminster Abbey), he was well settled in the Westminster sanctuary. Husband and wife rented a succession of tenements here until they died, in c. 1503. Safely ensconced, Baron could ignore the indignant cries of his creditors, and even emerge periodically from the sanctuary to travel, with royal safe-conducts, on the king's business.[31] For the likes of John Baron, the sanctuary represented a tax haven. For the many humbler tradespeople who operated there, meanwhile, the area was simply an island of ungoverned commerce, where no questions could be asked about guild membership, quality standards or price fixing. The sanctuary also attracted a class of professional criminals, who made predatory sorties from this stronghold. Evidently, as hostile critics pointed out, its privileges were open to abuse.[32] But the monks, who collected in rents from the sanctuary over £100 a year, held on righteously to their ancient franchise. Indeed, when, in 1566, it was moved that sanctuaries should finally be abolished, the dean and chapter of Westminster rested their objection on the ground that the privilege brought tenants to the neighbourhood.[33]

If its unusual situation and privileges were especially appealing to those who settled in the sanctuary, the wider liberty of Westminster shared with London's other suburbs an attraction for those – and they were many – who wished to be in London but, in terms of jurisdiction and taxation, not of it. Their immunity from craft controls and civic legislation gave London's medieval suburbs a character distinct from that of the city proper. In view of the links which have been noted, however, the suburbs must be seen as playing a partially differentiated role within a single urban zone.

The most critical function performed by the suburban economy was the provision of food. This was obviously vital to the entire urban population, which operated collectively as a stimulus to supply and suffered together in times of shortage. Thus the Westminster Chronicler observed of a dearth in the region in 1391:

If people outside (*extrinseci*) had not lent their aid, the whole London area and its neighbouring districts (*tota plaga Londoniensis cum suis adjacentibus*), deprived of their food supply, would have wasted away from the deadly effects of hunger and starvation.[34]

The most productive areas of supply, meanwhile, were the urban fringes. By the later middle ages, a degree of diversification had developed, much of London's bread coming from its eastern hinterland around Stratford-at-Bow,[35] while meat was being produced on a large scale by graziers and butchers on the northern and western edges of the built-up area. Meat consumption seems to have increased in the late fourteenth and the fifteenth centuries, when personal living standards rose in proportion to losses in population; certainly butchers were prominent figures in fifteenth century Westminster and its surrounding fields. This particular suburban trade was promoted by the London ordinance, first promulgated in 1361 and reiterated thereafter, which (albeit without complete success) banished slaughter-houses from the city.[36] In Westminster, in the absence of such environmental controls, butchering could be practised in the midst of a residential area. Even without the London end of the urban market, the provision of banquets at the royal palace would have gone some way to account for the herds of cattle, sheep and pigs which populated the meadows of Westminster. John Waryn, however, a butcher who in the 1380s bought fifty-seven oxen from the cellarer of Westminster Abbey, who leased a flock of three hundred sheep belonging to the monks and who was unsurprisingly summonsed for overcrowding the common pasture on nearby Tothill with his animals, did have a trading connection with London.[37] Londoners themselves were drawn out to invest in this lucrative suburban occupation, as was William Gryffen, a London butcher who in 1500 leased from the abbot of Westminster extensive grazing fields in the abbey's manor of Belsize Park.[38] To those with cash to invest, capitalist grazing close to town evidently offered good returns in the late middle ages.

Many suburban dwellers of more modest means were encouraged to engage in horticultural production for the urban market. Westminster itself at this period contained professional gardeners. In the fourteenth century the gardeners to 'earls, barons and bishops' claimed a traditional right to retail their surpluses near St Paul's in London; no doubt some of their 'cherries and vegetables' were nurtured in the gardens of lay and ecclesiastical magnates in Westminster, such as were concentrated along the Strand.[39] Once again, however, heavy consumption in the suburb itself outran local sources of supply, which were supplemented by mongers from the surrounding countryside. Robert White of Kensington and Juliana Combe of Hammersmith were two such 'common victuallers, retailers of beans, peas, oats, cheese and butter'. As they plied to London from these outlying villages with their produce in 1410, they were intercepted by a forestaller, one Margaret Neuport, who bought out their stock in order to sell it again in Westminster; for demand there was such that she could mark up her prices by a half.[40] These small-scale market gardeners recognised that the entire urban area, city and suburbs together, represented a single pitch for the retail of their wares. Not yet the great wen, late medieval London was already a wide and hungry maw. Professor Wrigley has argued that the massed market of London's population in the sixteenth and seventeenth centuries acted as a stimulant upon the hinterland to greater production of basic foodstuffs and other goods.[41] It is an argument which could be pushed back in time.

In addition to provisioning, another aspect of London's economy which offered scope to even the humblest householder was hospitality. The ale-drinking Pastons have already been indicated as symptomatic of a large market for such refreshment among visitors to the capital. Taverns apart, the streets of medieval Westminster were crowded with the simple stalls of ale-hucksters and the take-away stands of baked meat vendors, vying for the custom of the pilgrim or the suitor at the courts.[42] Temporary accommodation was also in demand, below the level of the aristocracy who sometimes maintained their own town houses in the city or suburbs. Specialist innkeepers flourished along the approaches to London;[43] but it was also normal for private householders to turn a penny by offering 'bed-and-breakfast' accommodation or by taking in longer-term paying guests during peak times, such as the legal terms. When John de Whalley, a monk of the Cistercian abbey of that name in Lancashire, came in Lent 1404 to prosecute certain cases in the courts (*ad diversa negocia et sectas faciendum et prosequendum*), he stayed in the house (*hospitabatur in domo*) of Alice Hulle. The night was an eventful one for Brother John, who (by a ruse, according to his account) was found naked in bed with Alice by her friend and pretended husband, Thomas Worsopp. Crying 'False monk and traitor!' Worsopp dragged the hapless visitor by his legs out into the street, where he spent three cold hours before a payment of 5s. 8d. was exacted for his readmittance.[44] As John de Whalley, once gratefully returned to his monastery, might have put it to his prior when accounting for his costs, lodgings in the capital could be fearfully expensive.

Modesty of scale once again characterised most of the crafts known to have been practised in the suburbs. The typical suburban crafts were those which had been driven there either (as the Common Council of London acknowledged after 1450 to be true of some) by the excessive costs of taking up and maintaining the freedom of the city,[45] or else by deliberate exclusion from the walled area under city law. Practitioners in the latter category, in addition to the butchers already mentioned, included tanners, documented in Southwark and along the streams to the north of the city, and potters and bell-founders identified to the east, around Aldgate.[46] Environmental pollution was the common ground of objection to these crafts within the city. While the local importance of London's artisans, including those of the suburbs, is unquestionable, the evidence currently available does not support a picture of London as major producer of goods for export within the country or abroad.[47]

Westminster, therefore, was broadly typical of London as a whole in the fifteenth century in that the particular crafts concentrated in this western district were concerned with the production, on a small scale, of finished goods, ready for immediate sale to the consumer. It was another feature which Westminster shared with the suburbs in general that some of these crafts were largely in the hands of foreign immigrants, who were excluded by the protectionism of the city companies from the sphere of the latter's jurisdiction. The Flemings and Germans who made up the bulk of the immigrant community were adept at the kind of small-scale artisan crafts which flourished in London at large and Westminster in particular. They were, for instance, tailors, hatters, pointmakers, pouchmakers and cob-blers. A native *forte* was metalworking, and the art of continental goldsmiths who set up their workshops here met with appreciation in the extravagant environment of Westminster.[48] New skills and new commo-dities were introduced to the London market by these suburban-based immigrants. For instance, Westminster's expensive gift trade drew here Anthony Tresylyan, clockmaker, whose craft and whose personal connec-tions both evince Teutonic origins. From 1513 until his death in 1532, Tresylyan kept a shop in King Street; at his death his stock included a gilded cuckoo-clock (*horologium cucum*), valued at £10.[49] 'Doche' spectacle-makers, too, found some of their first English customers among the blear-eyed clerks of Westminster. The Flemings would gather in Palace Yard like an expectant flock of starlings, waiting to swoop chattering down upon one, like the London Lickpenny, leaving the hall:

> Without the doors [*sc.* of Westminster Hall]
>   were Flemings great wone [in great numbers],
> Upon me fast they gan to cry,
> And said, 'Master, what will ye copen or buy,
> Fine felt hats, spectacles for to read
> Of this gay gear? – a great cause why
> For lack of money I might not speed.[50]

Londoners also turned to the suburbs for amusement; another commo-dity which, like food and drink, offered to the purveyor a profitable return on even a small investment. Leisure activities banned from the city within the walls for either practical or moral reasons burgeoned in the late medieval suburbs. Archery butts were set up in the infirmary garden at Westminster Abbey in the 1460s;[51] bowling alleys began to appear in Westminster, as also in Southwark and in the eastern suburb, around 1500;[52] the professional gambler, deluding the greenhorn with high stakes and loaded dice, was a figure of fifteenth century Westminster, even as the three-card tricksters still con the tourists on Piccadilly.[53] Dicing, bowls and tennis (which was also played at Westminster) were all proscribed within the city.[54] On special occasions, such as royal coronations, Westminster was capable of staging the very best entertainment in town. For the coronation of Queen Margaret in 1445, as at other royal events later in the century, splendid jousts were held in the precinct of the abbey. Stands for the crowds were erected in the sanctuary, and viewing places were even created on the roof of the abbey nave. The monks charged their tenants within the sanctuary a supplementary levy for the valuable privilege of continuing to trade there during the festivities.[55] Another branch of the business of hospitality and entertainment which was particularly concentrated in the suburbs, being officially banned from the city centre, was prostitution. The famous stews of Southwark were subject to elaborate controls, one of which prohibited trade while parliament was meeting at Westminster.[56] But MPs in town for the session were not thereby saved from temptation, for whores were freely available in the other suburbs (including male as well as female prostitutes, at least in one case of 1480 outside Aldgate).[57] Prostitution was a major business for some, like William Chamber, clerk, reputed in 1407 to let his houses at Charing exclusively to whores, and John Norton of London, clerk, who around 1500 managed suburban brothels at Westminster, Shoreditch and elsewhere on London's fringes.[58] Marx would have recognised these operators as capitalist entrepreneurs.[59] Others, such as Elizabeth, wife of John Waryn, skinner (possibly identical with the butcher of the same name encountered earlier), and Stephen Essex's wife, who together kept a 'bordelhouse for monks, priests and others' at Westminster in 1409, evidently ran a more modest domestic sideline.[60] These varied diversions offered a career, or at least a profitable by-employment, to large numbers of suburban Londoners in the later middle ages.

Within the consumer-oriented, service economy which it is suggested characterised fifteenth century London as a whole, the proportionate contribution of the suburbs may have increased in the later fifteenth and early sixteenth centuries, as a result of demographic developments which are only now beginning to be studied.[61] Recent research on the Cheapside area, at the heart of the walled city, has revealed a decisive and major reduction in the density of occupation after 1400. This demographic down-turn at the centre was not reversed for well over a century and a half, until 1580 or even later.[62] The indications which are becoming available from the suburbs, however, present a partially contrasting picture. After an equivalent contraction in the early fifteenth century, Westminster,[63] Southwark[64] and the suburb without Aldgate[65] each experienced a fresh phase of population growth from between the late fifteenth and the mid-sixteenth century, reflected in the recovery of rent-values and speculative building.[66] The reasons for this are not simple, but the attractions of the suburbs to an immigrant from the countryside or abroad have been indicated, and the same factors continued to operate when migration from the countryside to the capital began to gather momentum around 1500. Very many of the migrants who swelled the suburban population in the sixteenth century were poor.[67] Both civic and royal authorities found cause for alarm in the concentration of poor people in areas just beyond the control of the city government. Their worries related in part to the impossible strains imposed on poor relief and to the spread of disease in the crowded suburban alleys. But while fears of social disorder were paramount in the Tudor royal proclamations,[68] the evident anxiety of the citizen elite stemmed also from economic causes.

There is a reflection of developments on the urban fringes in the expressed attitudes of London's rulers, who themselves appear to have sensed that in the late fifteenth and early sixteenth centuries a growing element of the city's economic life was eluding the control of the Aldermen and Common Council. An earlier ordinance of 1420 was effectively reversed in injunctions of the 1450s, 1470s and 1510s whereby out-of-town residents claiming to possess the freedom of London with its attendant privileges were now to be deprived of their status, if they would not compound for city taxes or, by a more radical provision introduced in 1454 and reapplied in the 1470s and in 1516, if they refused to move almost immediately, with their families, to within the area of the city's jurisdiction.[69] The same concern seems to lie behind contemporary agitation in such companies as the Mercers'[70] and Goldsmiths',[71] giving rise in turn to Common Council petitions to the crown through parliament for the suppression of the franchises with which the city and suburbs were riddled, which together bore fruit in mid-Tudor legislation restricting such immunities and empowering the city crafts to make searches of goods and workshops in the suburbs.[72]

These concerns, which would continue in the later sixteenth century to preoccupy the city governors,[73] had in fact typified the attitude of London's guild masters throughout the late middle ages. The semblance of legal unity and monopolistic control which they propounded could not, however, be sustained in practice. The immunity of the suburbs endowed the total urban economy with a greater diversity than at first appears. Among those who took advantage of this diversity were, as has been seen, the great merchants in luxury goods who dominated the city proper. In addition, however, the concentrated market of London's population provided an outlet and an incentive to manufacturers and purveyors of all kinds of goods. To many of these operators, the suburbs offered a particularly congenial environment. Relatively free from jurisdictional constraints and yet poised to capitalise on a vast and varied market, the suburbs offered scope for enterprising speculation by a burgeoning class of commodity producers. Their scale of operation tended to be small; and indeed the artisan crafts of London seem to have continued, even in the early modern period, to be confined to the domestic mode of production. Yet the orientation of London's economy in the later middle ages towards the servicing, in a myriad ways, of the individual customer created the ideal context for the spread of that petty commercialisation which was a precondition of the development of a capitalist society. Late medieval London was the ultimate market, the consumer's dream. It furnished him on demand with financial assistance, professional advice, cultural exchange, entertainment, clothing, food – and drink. Which brings us back to the urban inn where we began. It was not of the froth but of the essence of London life in the fifteenth century that Thomas Hoccleve, a clerk who *c.* 1400 lodged 'at Chestres Yn right fast by the Stronde' and who commuted daily from there to the privy seal office in Westminster Palace, passed on his way so many taverns, distinguished by their inviting sign-boards, that it was quite impossible to avoid them:

> The outward signe of Bachus and his lure
> That at his dore hangith day by day,
> Exciteth folk to taaste of his moisture
> So often that man can nat wel seyn nay.[74]

Notes

1 R.H. Hilton, 'Towns in Societies – Medieval England', *Urban History Yearbook* (1982), 14–23. The dangers of identifying particular economic phenomena with 'towns' are underlined by P. Abrams, 'Towns and Economic Growth: Some Theories and Problems', in P. Abrams and E.A. Wrigley, eds, *Towns in Societies* (Cambridge, 1978), 9–33. The present essay seeks not to identify suburbs with primitive capitalism, but rather to show how suburbs provided a congenial environment for small-scale commercialisation, a process by no means confined to towns or to their fringes.

2 R.H. Hilton, 'Capitalism – What's in a Name?', repr. in *The Transition from Feudalism to Capitalism*, with introduction by R.H. Hilton (London, 1976), 145–58, esp. 151–2; J. Merrington, 'Town and Country in the Transition to Capitalism', in ibid., 170–95, esp. 180–1; D.M. Nicholas, *Town and Countryside: Social, Economic and Political Tensions in Fourteenth Century Flanders* (Bruges, 1971), 345–6, 351.

3 J.L. Bolton, *The Medieval English Economy 1150–1500* (London, 1980), 252–3; P. Clark and P. Slack, eds, *Crisis and Order in English Towns 1500–1700* (London, 1972), 11, 33–4.

4 C.C. Dyer, 'A Small Landowner in the Fifteenth Century', *Midland History* i, 3 (1972), 1–14.

5 R.H. Hilton, 'The Small Town and Urbanisation – Evesham in the Middle Ages', *Midland History* vii (1982), 1–8; idem, 'Lords, Burgesses and Hucksters', *Past and Present* 97 (1982), 3–15; idem, 'Medieval Market Towns and Simple Commodity Production', *Past and Present* 109 (1985), 3–23.

6   *Paston Letters and Papers of the Fifteenth Century*, ed. N. Davis (Oxford, 1971-), i. 26, 27–8, 226–7, 236, 255, 291, etc.
7   *Paston Letters*, i. 430; *Middlesex County Records*, ed. J.C. Jeaffreson, i (London, 1886), 11; W.H. Manchee, *The Westminster City Fathers* (London, 1924), 215.
8   B. Botfield, ed., *Manners and Household Expenses of England in the Thirteenth and Fifteenth Centuries* (London, 1841), 377, 378, 380.
9   A.G. Rosser, 'The Essence of Medieval Urban Communities: The Vill of Westminster 1200–1540'. *TRHS*, 5th ser. xxxiv (1984), 91–112. A book on medieval Westminster by the present author is in course of preparation.
10 M. Biddle, ed., *Winchester in the Early Middle Ages: An Edition and Discussion of the Winton Domesday*, Winchester Studies i (Oxford, 1976); D. Keene, *Survey of Medieval Winchester*, Winchester Studies ii, 2 vols (Oxford, 1985).
11 C.N.L. Brooke and G. Keir, *London 800–1216: The Shaping of a City* (London, 1975), 362–5; T.F. Tout, 'The Beginnings of a Modern Capital: London and Westminster in the Fourteenth Century', *Proceedings of the British Academy* x (1921–23), 487–511.
12 *CPR, 1330–34*, 219; *CCR, 1337–39*, 552–3; *CCR, 1341–43*, 89; *Cal(endar of) Letter-Book(s preserved among the archives of the City of London, 1275–1498)* ed. R.R. Sharpe, 11 vols (London, 1899–1912), *Cal. Letter-Book I*, xxviii, 160–1 and n.2; *Acts of Court of the Mercers' Company, 1453–1527*, ed. L. Lyell and F.D. Watney (Cambridge, 1936), 107, 183–4. See also C.M. Barron, 'The Quarrel of Richard II with London 1392–7', in F.R.H. Du Boulay and C.M. Barron, eds, *The Reign of Richard II* (London, 1971), 173–201, at 181–2, 193; idem, 'The Government of London and its Relations with the Crown', Ph.D. thesis, Univ. of London (1970), 341–2.
13 *Cal. Letter-Book H*, 215.
14 PRO, KB9/172/1/23.
15 John Maxfeld: PRO, C1/157/25–6; CCR, 1468–76, 97; WAM -50764–5; WCL, Churchwardens' Accounts of St Margaret's, Westminster, I, 140.
16 WAM 5784, 17767; WAM Register Book I, ff. 72v–73.
17 WAM 5668; CCR, 1461–68, 199–200; B.F. Harvey, *Westminster Abbey and its Estates in the Middle Ages* (Oxford, 1977), 67, 99–100.
18 Barron, 'Quarrel of Richard II with London', 197.
19 Barron, 'Government of London', 451–4; and C.M. Barron, 'London and the Crown 1451–1461', in J.R.L. Highfield and R. Jeffs, eds, *The Crown and Local Communities in England and France in the Fifteenth Century* (Gloucester, 1981), 88–109.
20 Leases and rentals in the Westminster abbey archive have been correlated with printed and some unpublished records of the City of London. I am grateful to Caroline Barron for advice on the London records.
21 *CPR, 1388–92*, 313.
22 G. Mathew, *The Court of Richard II* (London, 1968), 25–7.
23 London, Guildhall Library, Wardens' Accounts of the Merchant Tailors' Company, vol. 2 (microfilm; original at Merchant Tailors' Hall), f. 152 (1458/9); WCL, Churchwardens' Accounts of St Margaret's, Westminster, I, 8, 20, 76, 132, 174, 376, 394; WAM 50757; Cambridge, Trinity College, MS. 0.9.1, ff. 230–1; *Cal. Letter-Book L*, 211, 268.
24 Boatmen might charge 2d. or 3d. for the hire of an entire boat over the distance. *Munimenta Gildhallae Londoniensis*, ed. H.T. Riley, Rolls Series, 3 vols (London, 1859–62), i. 580.
25 WAM, Accounts of the Guild of the Assumption of the Virgin Mary (unnumbered), s.a. 1477, 1515–18. For a Westminster member of a London guild, see *Parish Fraternity Register: Fraternity of the Holy Trinity and SS. Fabian and Sebastian in the Parish of St. Botolph without Aldersgate*, ed. P. Basing, London Record Society xviii (1982), 13.
26 WAM 33301.
27 M. Carlin, 'The Urban Development of Southwark c.1200 to 1550', Ph.D. thesis,

Univ. of Toronto (1983); Barron, 'Government of London', 170ff.; A.G. Rosser, 'Medieval Westminster: The Vill and the Urban Community 1200–1540', Ph.D. thesis, Univ. of London (1984), fig. 2.

28 M.B. Honeybourne, 'The Sanctuary Boundaries and Environs of Westminster Abbey and the College of St. Martin-le-Grand', *Journal of the British Archaeological Association*, 2nd ser. xxxviii (1932–33), 316-33; I.D. Thornley, 'Sanctuary in Medieval London', ibid., 2nd ser. xxxviii (1932–33), 293–315; Barron, 'Government of London', 393–408.

29 I intend to treat the theme of franchises in medieval towns more fully elsewhere.

30 Rosser, 'Medieval Westminster', 241–5.

31 *Acts of Court of the Mercers' Company*, 98–9; *Calendar of Plea and Memoranda Rolls preserved among the archives of the Corporation of the City of London, 1323–1482*, 6 vols (Cambridge, 1926–61), 1458-82, 173; CCR, 1476–85, 25; WCL, Churchwardens' Accounts of St Margaret's, Westminster, I, 157; WAM 19728–59; WAM Register Book I, ff. 91v-92; CPR, 1485–94, 2, 45, 144; CCR, 1500–1509, 204.

32 *The Complete Works of St. Thomas More*, ii, ed. R.S. Sylvester (Yale, 1963), 30–1.

33 Rosser, 'Medieval Westminster', 245; R. Widmore, *Westminster Abbey* (London, 1743), 141.

34 *The Westminster Chronicle 1381–1394*, trans. and ed. L.C. Hector and B.F. Harvey (Oxford, 1982), 474–5.

35 K.G.T. McDonnell, *Medieval London Suburbs* (London and Chichester, 1978), 77–83.

36 E.L. Sabine, 'Butchering in Medieval London', *Speculum* viii *(1933)*, 335–53; Barron, 'Quarrel of Richard II with London', 175–6; P.E. Jones, *The Butchers of London* (London, 1976), 78–80. For fifteenth century London citizens investing in land to the north of the city around Tottenham, an area of both arable and sheep-grazing, see D. Moss and I. Murray, 'A Fifteenth-Century Middlesex Terrier', *Transactions of the London and Middlesex Archaeological Society* xxv (1974), 285–94; idem, 'Signs of Change in a Medieval Village Community', ibid. xxvii (1976), 280–7.

37 WAM 18866-7, 18869, 5984, 50718; *Cal. Plea and Mem. Rolls, 1364–81*, 270.

38 WAM 16471.

39 H.T. Riley, ed., *Memorials of London and London Life in the XIIIth, XIVth and XVth Centuries* (London, 1868), 228–9; J. Harvey, *Mediaeval Gardens* (London, 1981), 61.

40 PRO, KB9/198/23.

41 E.A. Wrigley, 'A Simple Model of London's Importance in Changing English Society and Economy, 1650–1750', *Past and Present* 37 (1967), 44–70. See also F.J. Fisher, 'The Development of the London Food Market, 1540–1640', *Economic History Review* v, 2 (1935), 46–64.

42 e.g. WAM 50745; PRO, KB9/224/300.

43 The 'Hosteries, and houses for Gentlemen, and men of honor', which in part characterised Westminster were noted in the sixteenth century by John Stow. J. Stow, *A Survey of London*, ed. C.L. Kingsford, 2 vols (Oxford, 1908), ii. 98 and cf. ii. 87.

44 PRO, KB9/193/9. Cf. Rodney Hilton's comment: 'It is clear that in towns large and small, householders were receiving lodgers to such an extent that one wonders whether any houses did not from time to time have (probably short term) lodgers.' R.H. Hilton, *Class Conflict and the Crisis of Feudalism* (London, 1985), 211.

45 CLRO, City Journal 5, f.204 (1454).

46 D.J. Johnson, *Southwark and the City* (Oxford, 1969), 79; J. Schofield and A. Dyson, *Archaeology of the City of London* (London, 1980), 47.

47 The wide range of crafts practised in late medieval London is clearly shown by Elspeth Veale, 'Craftsmen and the Economy of London in the Fourteenth Century', in A.E.J. Hollaender and W. Kellaway, eds, *Studies in London History presented to P.E. Jones* (London, 1969), 133–51. But Lee Beier, having illustrated the same point in relation to the early modern city, pushes the available evidence further than appears warranted in portraying London as a major centre of industrial production. A.L. Beier, 'Engine of

Manufacture: The Trades of London', in A.L. Beier and R. Finlan, Eds, *London 1500–1700: The Making of the Metropolis* (London, 1986), 141–67. Certainly, 'the metropolis was a centre for production as well as trade' (ibid., 150). But the alleged 'shift in the organisation of production' (ibid., 161) is obscured by lack of evidence; and, even in the early modern period, the *scale* of production remained small. At any rate, urban industry in the middle ages was far less complex and less specialised than it later became. See D.J. Keene, 'Some Concluding Reflections', in D.W. Crossley, ed., *Medieval Industry*, Council for British Archaeology Research Reports, 40 (1981), 151–3, at 151. This relative absence of specialisation was the very circumstance which gave opportunity to the casual and 'unofficial' labour which was concentrated in the suburbs.

48 Rosser, 'Medieval Westminster', 226–30.
49 WCL, Peculiar Court of Westminster, Register Bracy, ff. 25v, 49v-50; WAM 23146–8, 23290–311.
50 'London Lickpenny', printed in E.P. Hammond, ed., *English Verse from Chaucer to Surrey* (Durham, N. Carolina, 1927), 238. The earliest recorded spectacle maker in England is a Dutchman active in the London suburb of Southwark in 1458. M. Rhodes, 'A pair of Fifteenth-Century Spectacle Frames from the City of London', *The Antiquaries Journal* lxii (1982), 57–73. Southwark, like Westminster, attracted a substantial population of aliens in this period. See Carlin, 'Urban Development of Southwark', ch.15.
51 WAM 19443.
52 Stow, *A Survey*, ii. 102; Carlin, 'Urban Development of Southwark', 49–50; CLRO Portsoken Ward Presentments, 5–22 Edw. IV, 23 Hen. VII (recurrent references to 'clossch banes', or bowling alleys). On entertainment in Southwark, see also C.L. Kingsford, 'Paris Garden and the Bear-baiting', *Archaeologia* lxx (1920), 155–78. Further references to the proliferation of the suburban bowling alleys in Stow, *A Survey*, i. 126–7, 149, 165, ii. 79–80, 294.
53 PRO, KB9/223/1/52. A set of loaded dice of fifteenth century date recently found in London is published by B. Spencer in *The Antiquaries Journal* lxv, 2 (1985), 451–3 and pl. 99.
54 CLRO, City Journal 8, f. 127v (1476). Only archery, as (naturally) a suburban pastime, was countenanced by the civic authorities. *Cal. Letter-Book G*, 194. An isolated reference to 'le lodge pro le tenyspleyers' near Westminster Abbey occurs in 1447/8. WAM 23513.
55 WAM 19694, 19698, 19711; *Six Town Chronicles of England*, ed. R. Flenley (Oxford, 1911), 120, 172 and n.
56 *Cal. Letter-Book A*, 218 (1276–78); CLRO, City Journal 1, f. 18v (1416); J. Post, 'A Fifteenth-Century Customary of the Southwark Stews', *Journal of the Society of Archivists* v (1974–77), 418–28.
57 CLRO, Portsoken Ward Presentments, s.a. 1480: 'Roger Carpenter, a harlot of his body.'
58 WAM 50738; PRO, C244/161/69.
59 K. Marx, *Theories of Surplus Value*, Part 1, trans. E. Burns (Moscow, n.d.), 160–4.
60 PRO, KB9/198/27.
61 The fifteenth century population of London, with its suburbs, is likely to have numbered between 40,000 and 50,000. For published estimates see C. Creighton, 'The Population of Old London', *Blackwood's Magazine* cxlix (1891), 477–96; S.L. Thrupp, *The Merchant Class of Medieval London* (Chicago, 1948), 41–52. This approximate figure for the fifteenth century represents a marked reduction from that of 1300, currently put at 80,000 (estimate of the Social and Economic Study of Medieval London).
62 D.J. Keene, 'A New Study of London before the Great Fire', *Urban History Yearbook* (1984), 11–21, at 18–19; D.J. Keene and V. Harding, *Cheapside and the Development of London Before the Great Fire* (forthcoming).

63 Rosser, 'Medieval Westminster', ch. 3.
64 Carlin, 'Urban Development of Southwark', 381–2, 610 and Gazetteer, nos 86, 158, 160, 162, 164, 220.
65 Derek Keene, personal communication.
66 The relative rate of suburban compared to city expansion increased still further after 1600. R. Finlay and B. Shearer, 'Population Growth and Suburban Expansion', in *London 1500–1700*, 37–59.
67 For contemporary comment cf. Stow, *A Survey*, ii. 66, 72, 74, 367–8 and references cited. See also M.J. Power, 'The east and west in early modern London', in *Wealth and Power in Tudor England*, ed. E.W. Ives, R.J. Knecht and J.J. Scarisbrick (London, 1978), 167–85.
68 P.L. Hughes and J.F. Larkin, eds, *Tudor Royal Proclamations*, 3 vols (New Haven and London, 1964–69), ii. 46–8, 415–17, 466–8, iii. 245–8.
69 CLRO, City Journal 1, f. 71v; Journal 5, ff. 58, 198, 204, 260; Journal 8, ff. 33v, 124; Journal 10, f. 181v; Repertory Book 2, f. 85; Journal 11, ff. 259, 364; Repertory Book 3, f. 205.
70 *Acts of Court of the Mercers' Company*, 112, 690; J.M. Parker, 'The Ordinance Book of the Mercers' Company of London', Ph.D. thesis, Univ. of London (1980), 172, 330–2.
71 T.F. Reddaway and L.E.M. Walker, *The Early History of the Goldsmiths' Company, 1327–1509* (London, 1975), 108–9, 130–1, 166–7, 251.
72 H. Miller, 'London and Parliament in the Reign of Henry VIII', *BIHR* xxxv (1962), 128–49, at 145–6; I.D. Thornley, 'The Destruction of Sanctuary', in R.W. Seton-Watson, ed., *Tudor Studies presented to A.F. Pollard* (London, 1924), 182–207.; 14 & 15 Henry VIII c. 2.
73 And into the seventeenth century; see a petition addressed by City of London tradesmen to James I in 1609, printed in R. Seymour, *A Survey of the Cities of London and Westminster, & c.*. 2 vols (London, 1735), ii. 692.
74 'La Male Regle de T. Hoccleve', ll. 121–4, and see 'The Regiment of Princes', 1.5; printed in *Selections from Hoccleve*, ed. M.C. Seymour (Oxford, 1981), 15, 31.

4

Urban 'Oligarchy' in Late Medieval England

Stephen Rigby

University of Manchester

I

Students of England's towns in the later middle ages can currently choose between a wide range of assessments of urban fortunes, ranging from buoyancy and resilience to decline, decay and desolation.[1] Much of this debate arises from the vagueness of our concepts and questions and our failure to agree on criteria of 'urban decline', but a central source of disagreement has been the difficulties of interpreting the surviving evidence, such as urban petitions of poverty, the lay subsidy returns and urban building works.[2] However, whilst the evidence available for the study of the urban economy is treacherous, our sources should allow us to establish the nature of urban constitutional change, given that most of the surviving documentation is the product of borough administrations and is concerned, above all else, with the workings of town courts, the election of officers and the collection and expenditure of municipal finances. Indeed, our fifteenth century sources are particularly self-conscious about the nature of town government. Only Bristol may have rivalled London in producing a town chronicle in the fifteenth century but this does not mean that the London chronicles were 'exotic flowers on the soil of urban illiteracy and disinterest.' On the contrary, the fifteenth century was a period of literate civic self-awareness.[3] The Bristol chronicle, compiled by Robert Ricart, the town clerk, in 1479 at the command of the mayor was, after all, only part of a wider compilation of the town's liberties.[4] Towns had always needed the immediate working documents of municipal government (court rolls, chamberlains' accounts and the like) but, increasingly, they were also concerned to codify their franchises and by-laws and to reflect on how town government should be carried out. This civic self-consciousness is not only to be seen in these new forms of town records such as *Ricart's Kalendar*, London's *Liber Albus*, the Lincoln custumal of 1480 (compiled by a former mayor) or the usages and customs recorded in Northampton's *Liber Custumarum*.[5] It is also to be seen in the building and re-building of town halls in the late fourteenth and early fifteenth centuries, in charters of borough incorporation, in the acquisition of civic regalia and in the elaboration of town government.

Yet, despite this abundance of evidence, there is a long tradition of disagreement amongst historians about the nature of late medieval constitutional change. One school of thought, often associated with the case for urban decline, sees urban government as moving from an early popular democracy towards oligarchy and close corporation; another, linked to those who see the period as one of urban growth, sees the late medieval town government as responding flexibly to the challenges of the period.[6] Did the later middle ages see the growth of either 'democracy' or 'oligarchy' in English town life?

II

Before we can answer this question we need to consider Susan Reynolds' important warnings about the use of the word 'oligarchy', for if the debate on urban decline has tended to founder on the meaning of 'decline', then the study of urban government may well founder on the meaning of 'oligarchy'. For many writers the oligarchic nature of medieval English town government is a commonplace[7], but Reynolds objects to the term as a loaded anachronism and asks us to see urban affairs in terms of the townsmen's own values and principles. Is the concept of 'oligarchy' a useful one in helping us to understand political change in the later middle ages?

Reynolds presents medieval urban political life as essentially a consensus based on shared beliefs, sentiments and values; an assumption which has much in common with other models of pre-industrial society (such as those of Mousnier and Fourquin), with Parsonian sociology and, ironically, with certain forms of Marxist theory.[8] She argues that in order to understand urban politics we need to see urban government and political conflict in terms of the preconceptions which underlay political life. In medieval political thought the ideal was one of harmony and civic unity; conflict was seen as the product of sin rather than of inherent structural strains. Conflict tended to revolve around the issue of the virtue and the *personal* corruption of town rulers, rather than abstract issues of principle. It was assumed, in theory and in practice, that social and political inequality was inevitable and that the rich would dominate town government. The rule of the rich was not seen as oligarchic (i.e., rule by the self-interested few) but as aristocratic (i.e., rule by the 'better sort' on behalf of the urban community in general). It was in the countryside, rather than in the towns, that radical views which challenged the prevailing hierarchy of wealth and power were to be found.[9]

The evidence from England's provincial towns certainly confirms the picture of urban political theory which Reynolds established using the London evidence, particularly the excerpts from Brunetto Latini's *Li Livres dou Tresor* which were included in the London *Liber Custumarum*.[10] Such theory simply took it for granted that town government would be by the 'better sort'. As a royal letter to the city of Lincoln put it in 1438, those appointed as mayor or sheriff of the city should be drawn from 'the more worthy, more powerful, more good and true, more discreet and more sufficient, and more befitting to occupy and exercise' such office, rather than from middling persons (*mediocres*) to whom such office would be a burden.[11] In practice, towns such as York were ruled by a mercantile plutocracy who could use the threat of office as a way of raising money from lesser townsmen who were willing to pay for exemption.[12] Richer townsmen were regarded as less likely to succumb to bribery or corruption; more practically, men of property could be distrained to account for their time in office and could afford to help finance town government from their own pocket in the hope of eventual repayment.

The rule of the rich was, of course, supposed to be carried out for the good of the urban community as a whole. The oath of the mayor of Grimsby was typical in its requirement for the mayor to maintain the borough's franchises 'in salvation of the king's people', whilst the town's bailiffs were 'to do right to every person or persons, as well as to poor as to rich, having no reward of any manner of person or persons'. The mayors of Bristol swore similar oaths to do justice, maintain good custom, avoid evil custom and to defend the widows and orphans of the town. Medieval urban political 'theory' was, most definitely, 'against sin'. In return medieval burgesses swore to be true and faithful to the mayor and commonalty, to keep the town's franchises and to obey the mayor's summons.[13] Through these mutual obligations of ruler and ruled the ideal of social harmony and political unity would, it was hoped, be attained. As a fifteenth-century letter patent to the mayor of Northampton pointed out, the good government of each town and city 'first and principally pleases God, establishes perfect rest and tranquility, nourishes and increases love, causes plenty and abundance'; similarly the impartial administration of justice would cause 'universal well' to flourish. Bad government, the neglect of the law and the corruption of justice would, by contrast, lead to 'commotions, strifes, debates, poverty and misery and many other inconveniences'. In the same vein a commission to Sir John Bussy in 1393, to ensure that the mayor of Lincoln should be elected in a manner 'pleasing to God and good for the king and the whole commonalty of the city', claimed that from conflict between 'the high and mighty persons of the city and the king's middling subjects thereof . . .were likely to happen many things not to be borne and perhaps the ruin of the city.'[14]

Harmony in town life was not, however, only thought to arise from the just rule of the better sort and from obedience by the commonalty. It was also seen as the result of town government which was both constitutional and representative. Whilst clerical political theory expressed a *descending* concept of political power in which rulers owed their power to some superior authority, ultimately to God, much day to day political practice embodied an *ascending* concept of power in which the basis of authority lay in some form of popular consent. (This is not to say, of course, that popular consent was conceived of in a modern, egalitarian sense). Medieval towns had much in common with other contemporary communities in their powers of self-government; they were distinguished merely by the permanent and formal expression of this power and of their ascending concept of authority through their councils, elections and common purses. This was particularly true of medieval England where the absence of rural charters of liberty and self-government means that it is town government which provides the clearest bridge between medieval and modern concepts of the basis of political authority.[15] Town mayors made much of the dignity arising from their position as royal officers, and their oaths emphasised their duty to defend the king's peace, his rights and his revenues, but, in practice, mayors obtained much of their authority from their role as municipal *representatives* rather than as crown agents. Indeed, many mayors owed their existence not to any chartered right but simply to the concept of the borough as a self-governing community, free to order its own affairs.[16] Town rulers would, it was assumed, consult their fellow burgesses on matters of policy. As John Shillingford, mayor of Exeter, said in 1448 when the bishop of Exeter offered a solution to a quarrel between himself and the citizens: 'My lorde, if hit please you, ye shall have me excused to answere . . .for thogh me thoght that hit were a mene resonable, I dar not sey yee, thogh I have power, for the mater toucheth a grete comminalte as well as me'.[17]

Restraint by the community on the arbitrary actions of town rulers was implicit in the requirement for them to govern according to town custom since, as Bartolus of Sassoferrato pointed out, it was the tacit consent of the people which gave a legal character to mere practice and usage. John Carpenter's motivation in compiling the *Liber Albus* (1419) was to provide a guide to the city of London's customs for those younger, inexperienced persons elected to office in the place of older men carried off by plague, since ignorance of such customs could lead to perplexity and dispute. It was not only ignorance of custom which could lead to conflict. The Lincoln dispute in 1393 between the rich and middling citizens arose from disagreement over what customs had previously been followed: 'the citizens are of contrary opinions in certain matters and affairs affecting the liberty of the city on account of fraudulent claims of liberties not hitherto enjoyed, of verbal traditions not founded on the solid base of clear conscience.'[18]

If custom involved the tacit consent of the people, then this consent could be given an explicit form through the creation of town by-laws and ordinances. In 1481, when the borough of Grimsby made an ordinance restricting arrest for debt on certain days, it was made by the mayor, bailiffs, coroners 'and all the burgesses of the said town present in the common hall.' Lack of such common assent could provide the justification for resisting the town officers, as in 1389 when Richard Aby of Grimsby refused to pay his 'bustage' assessment since, he claimed, it was wrongly levied by those who did not have authority from election in the borough court. Similarly, in 1508 when Peter Thomson appointed Peter Smyth as his deputy in the office of bailiff of Grimsby, the grant was subsequently cancelled since it was made 'without the assent of the whole commonalty of burgesses.' The same issue arose as a matter of more general principle at Norwich at the beginning of Henry V's reign, when the commonalty discovered that a 1380 charter to the city had omitted the words 'with the assent of the commonalty' from its adoption of a clause from the London charter of 1341, allowing the bailiffs and twenty-four to make ordinances for the city as they saw fit.[19]

Medieval town government was thus a working mixture of popular representation and rule by the rich. York may have been ruled by a mercantile plutocracy yet the commonalty could still justify its participation in political life on the grounds that 'we be all one body incorporate, we think that we be all in like privileged of the commonalty, which has borne none office in the city'.[20]

It has been questioned whether pre-industrial societies, with their lack of mass media, were given a cohesion or consensus by a shared set of values or by the propagation of a 'dominant ideology.'[21] In the medieval town at least there *was* an active attempt to give a legitimacy to the political power exercised by the rich. We can see this legitimation in the emphasis on the dignity of town rulers as royal agents, in the use of religion to underpin urban social and political inequalities, and in the growth of civic ceremonial and regalia.[22] At Grimsby the borough purchased two silver maces in 1402–3, one from Roger de Dale, who had had the mace made when he was common sergeant, and a larger and more expensive mace costing 23s 4d bought from the executor of Richard de Misen (who had been mayor of Grimsby in 1395–6) to be carried by the mayor's sergeant. The common sergeant, mayor's sergeant and bailiffs' sergeant of the borough each had a gown of the same livery whilst in other towns the mayor and aldermen were distinguished by their own gowns, hoods and tabards. Divine legitimation was also invoked. The Grimsby ordinances of 1498 which re-organized the town ferry, regulated the use of the common pasture and so on, were made 'to the laud and joy of our Lord Jesus Christ and the most holy mother and virgin our lady saint Mary and all the holy citizens of heaven.' The burgesses were required to process with the mayor to the chapel of the borough leper hospital on 24th August, although at Grimsby there was not the same emphasis on the town officers' attendance at church services as there was at Bristol or at Coventry.[23] Corpus Christi processions affirmed a similar sense of urban unity in which the harmony of the whole was guaranteed by each social group playing its part. If the medieval town was a stage, then the message of much of its drama was that of social unity within a hierarchy.[24] Consensus, in other words, did not simply exist; it had to be created and maintained.

Nevertheless, it is not sufficient to portray medieval town government as simply a working consensus based on the shared assumptions that 'town government by the few best men . . .would be more good and benevolent' and that town rulers were an aristocracy rather than an oligarchy. Certainly our sources make no attempt to defend oligarchy but, given that oligarchy is defined as government that is self-interested and corrupt, this is hardly surprising.[25] That the documents produced by town governments offer a flattering picture of town rulers is only natural. It was, after all, the aim of these documents to reconcile social and political differences and to emphasise the legitimacy of town government. The problems involved in taking such documents at face value as sources for what medieval townsmen thought can be seen in Reynolds' claim that burgesses had the right of association provided that their actions were lawful.[26] But this begs the question of who defines what is lawful? In 1489 at Leicester, for example, the mayor and the twenty four along with forty eight of the 'wiser' inhabitants of the town elected Roger Tryng as mayor for the coming year 'in the name of the whole community', in accordance with the procedure 'lawfully' laid down in an act of parliament of that year. On the same day the commonalty of the town, described in the act as men of 'little substance and no discretion', met in accordance with past custom and elected Thomas Toutheby as mayor.[27] Doubtless the commonalty considered their election lawful, as did the town rulers theirs. The establishment of what was lawful was, in other words, the product of struggle and power. But this implies that urban political conflicts were about something more than individual sin and corruption.

Urban political conflicts tended to be sparked off by two main issues. As the act of 1489, which re-organized the government of Leicester and Northampton pointed out, it was the election of officers and the 'assessing of lawful charges' which gave rise to 'confederacies, exclamations and headiness.'[28] In a society where political power is hierarchical, the point of entry to authority, election and its accompanying ceremonial, is likely to be a central point of conflict. Attempts to change customary modes of election inevitably generated conflict, as at Leicester in 1489 where the popular movement, typically, took the form of a 'conservative' defence of custom. The rule of the rich was justified in the language of reciprocity: the rich were to rule for the good of society in general. Urban political conflicts, like most movements of popular protest including those of the medieval English countryside, thus rarely challenged hierarchy in general. Social protests normally centred on the alleged failure of the rich to carry out their side of the social contract, rather than rejecting the social contract *per se*.[29] Such protests were often expressed in the claim that custom had been broken or that the rich were not paying their share of the costs of town government. Frequently they resulted in a call for change in how town rulers were elected or supervised.

The twin issues of election and town finances can be seen in the disputes at Lynn in the early fifteenth century, where conflict was sparked off when the annual election of the town's council of twenty-four was replaced by co-option for life. Opposition from the *mediocres* and *inferiores* led to concessions by the town's *potentiores* who agreed to consult the lesser inhabitants about the financial charges made on them and to allow involvement in the election of officers. Conflict continued, however, and in 1416 the *potentiores* obtained royal approval to overthrow the new constitution. Nevertheless, in 1420–1 further reforms were made when a council of twenty seven (three from each of the town's constabularies) was set up to deal with financial affairs but with no part in the election of officers.[30] The shared assumption was still that the town would be ruled by the richer burgesses, the concessions concerning how the mayor was to be elected merely allowed the commonalty to nominate two candidates from the ruling twenty-four. Nevertheless, such disputes do reveal conflicting conceptions about the nature of town government. The lesser burgesses of Lynn may not have had the *word* 'oligarchy' but, in their attempts to prevent the town rulers from becoming a self-perpetuating elite who tallaged without consultation, they certainly had the *concept*, a concept which underlay their actions even it it was not expressed in the explicit manner that the town rulers' conception of urban government tended to be. At Lynn the practical problem of how town rulers were to be supervised spilled over into the wider issues of the degree of popular participation and authority in town government. The burgesses' solution was not, of course, a democratic, egalitarian reform of government, but neither was it to call upon their rulers to have a change of heart and repudiate sin, the means which writers of the rhetorical school such as Brunetto Latini favoured to obtain good government. Like Marsiglio of Padua and the scholastic theorists, they saw good government as not only the product of virtue but also of efficient institutions, of elected officers whose discretionary powers were limited by a series of checks on their actions.[31]

A more radical questioning of the urban social and political hierarchy can be seen at work in the London disturbances of the 1440s which centred on the candidature of Ralph Holland as mayor. Holland was a member of the drapers' guild, the merchants who provided thirty-four aldermen and fourteen mayors between 1327 and 1435, but he had also been master of the tailors' guild, the guild of craftsmen which provided no aldermen or mayors in this period. In the late 1430s a quarrel between the two guilds over the supervision of cloth sales widened into a more general social and political conflict within the city, with Holland as the 'popular' candidate for mayor. Holland himself had been in trouble with the city authorities as early as 1426 when he claimed that a writ of 1315, which the mayor was invoking to restrict attendance at the election of the mayor and sheriffs, was a fabrication. In 1441 Holland stood as mayor for the third time but was defeated by a member of the drapers' guild. Nevertheless, some of the city's tailors claimed that Holland was the rightful mayor and there were disturbances for which various tailors and skinners were imprisoned. The city authorities refused to allow the craftsmen out on bail, the prisoners in turn refused to ask for mercy, hardly an example of ruler and ruled loving each other as contemporary political theory blandly required.

In the following year the mayor and aldermen were commissioned not merely as keepers, but as justices of the peace, a commission which Holland said was not of peace but of war. The dispute continued into 1443 when the freemen of the city, including a large crowd of lesser citizens, deposed the chamberlain who had served since 1434 and elected a new man. The mayor had this meeting dispersed and then held another election by those 'lawfully' summoned for the purpose which, not surprisingly, re-elected the previous chamberlain. The defeated candidate was then accused of saying that the mayor was not the mayor of those who had not elected him, although he denied the charge when presented with it.

Such conflicts were not merely about political principle but also involved wider social issues. In 1442, a preacher at St. Paul's claimed that the best mayor that London had ever had was its first mayor, one (mythical) Walsh, who was a cordwainer, a craftsman, rather than a merchant. In the following year a tailor claimed that the city's craftsmen, not its merchants, were the basis of its prosperity. These troubles died down after Holland's exclusion from the court of aldermen in 1444, the same year in which the city obtained a new charter making the mayor and aldermen into justices of the peace, a move already denounced by Holland and which a carpenter had described in the previous year as a treacherous means of enserfing the Londoners. Whilst they lasted, such conflicts raised, in practice, if not in terms of abstract political theory, issues such as the popular basis of authority, the nature of the city's government, the extent of the civic franchise, popular participation in government, the social value of the artisan and equality before the law.[32] They present a rather different conception of the city's rulers from the one presented in official sources such as the *Liber Custumarum* which Reynolds relies upon. The principles of rule by the 'better sort' and ascending authority from the community thus had a potentially uneasy co-existence. Urban political life had an inherent potential for conflict over the degree of popular involvement in town government, a struggle which implicitly raised issues of principle, rather than just the virtue of individual officers.

That medieval townsmen viewed their rulers with an uneasy mixture of suspicion and deference and that they could, on occasion, perceive their rulers as oligarchs is important in explaining political conflict, but this does not mean that historians need share their opinions. When *historians* refer to town rulers as 'oligarchic' they are not offering an assessment of the rulers' moral worth. 'Oligarchy' in this context is not the opposite of worthiness but of 'democracy', the latter being, as Tait long ago pointed out, a useful shorthand expression for movements to open up town government, a matter of degree not an absolute.[33] Total democracy was not envisaged. At Leicester in 1489 the commonalty still chose one of the ruling twenty-four as its mayoral candidate, whilst in London Ralph Holland was a draper and an alderman rather than a poor craftsman. Women were, of course, excluded from participation in urban politics; the electors of Grimsby's members of parliament were all male even though women were liable for the local tax which paid the members' expenses.[34] The poor were similarly excluded. At Grimsby the freedom of the borough could only be obtained by a substantial fine (forty shillings before 1498, twenty shillings afterwards), by a seven year apprenticeship or by inheritance, provided that the would-be burgess owned land worth at least two shillings a year within the franchise over and above any charges on it.[35] Urban government thus involved both rule by the rich *and* authority drawn from the 'community'. The key question is did the late medieval period see a shift in the balance between these principles and a decline in the possibility of at least some degree of popular supervision of town rulers? Did government become more, or less, open? Was there a shift from an ascending to a descending concept of authority within the towns?

III

One school of thought argues that England's towns in the later middle ages became more open and flexible in response to the economic changes of the period: weavers and fullers, once excluded from the civic franchise, were now admitted as burgesses; the proportion of freemen within the urban population rose as the number of freemen's admissions was maintained or even grew despite the fall in total population; finally, councils were enlarged, allowing greater popular participation in town government.[36] What was the significance of these changes?

The issue of the admission of weavers and fullers to the civic franchise is of minor importance for our purposes, since this seems to have been a pre-plague development rather than a flexible urban response to make towns more attractive in the late medieval age of labour shortage. At Norwich weavers were admitted to the franchise from 1317, at York from 1319, at Colchester by 1327 and at Leicester by 1334.[37] But what of wider trends in freeman admissions? Do freemen's rolls reveal a growing proportion of the urban population enjoying burgess status? The interpretation of such records is far from straightforward. Firstly, there is the technical problem that the freemen's lists of individual towns may be more comprehensive at some periods than others, making it difficult to chart accurately numbers of freemen or trends in admissions.[38] Secondly, as Bridbury has warned, even if such lists are accurate they may not reveal a growing proportion of freemen in those towns where the second half of the fourteenth century was a period of population growth.[39] Thirdly, it is only possible to assess the number of freemen, and hence the proportion of freemen in the total population, if we take into account the outflow as well as the inflow into the freedom. Thus at York in 1350, following the Black Death, 212 freemen were admitted, almost four times the annual average of 1345–9. Increased admissions may, more than anything else, be an indication of high mortality, making it difficult to use them as indicators either of total population or of the number of freemen.[40] Finally, even if the numbers of freemen were maintained in a period of declining total population this may not necessarily have been a flexible response to demand from below. At Grimsby in 1383, for instance, it was said that a great number of outsiders had come to the town to ply their trades and crafts as if they were burgesses whilst refusing to bear their share of the costs and burdens of town government: 'it is not lawful and reasonable that foreigners should be free to traffic unless they take up the freedom of the town and bear charges of the burgesses.' In 1389 Peter Gotson and William Bray who traded in the town as if they were burgesses claimed that they would not become burgesses whatever the mayor might do. Fines for admission to the borough freedom could be an important source of civic revenue: in 1421–2 almost a third of the chamberlains' income at Grimsby came from instalments of such fines.[41] As at Hull, where financial difficulties tended to lead to a drive to recruit new burgesses, trends in freemen's admissions could be the result of pressure from above rather than the result of lesser townsmen wishing to obtain this 'attractive' status.[42]

What is the meaning of the creation and enlargement of town councils, the most significant change in town government in the later middle ages? To what extent did such councils make town government more representa‑ tive and open? We need to distinguish two types of council. The first arose in response to pressure from below for some formal representation in town affairs, the second appeared not as a means of broadening, but of restricting, popular involvement. An example of the former type is Norwich where, in 1415, conflict between the commonalty and the ruling twenty‑four over the mayoral election led to the creation of an additional council of sixty. The introduction of a council at Lynn in 1420–1 was a similar response to popular pressure. But perhaps the most famous example comes not from the fifteenth but the fourteenth century: the reforms restricting the power of the London aldermen and the creation of a common council based on guild representation in 1376. Elsewhere pressure from below led not to the creation of a new council, but to the enlargement of the existing council. At Exeter, from 1435 to 1437 and again from 1450 to 1455, membership of the town council was doubled with the introduction of twelve councillors 'for the commonalty' drawn from outside the ranks of the self‑selecting electoral panel of thirty‑six which had previously chosen the council.[43]

Such reforms were, however, often shortlived. At Exeter the democratic experiment came to an end in 1455. Although a town council of twenty‑four was retained, it was elected, once more, by the electoral panel of thirty‑six and, as before 1450, was dominated by members of the thirty‑six. At London the reforms of John of Northampton and the guilds were reversed from 1384 with the return to election of the common council by wards, the revocation of the ban on aldermen serving for two consecutive years and restrictions on the common council's role in the election of the mayor, on the wards' role in electing aldermen and on the men who could be candidates for the mayoralty; a trend which was confirmed in 1394 when it was ordained that henceforth aldermen should hold office for life.[44] Similarly, the reforms introduced at Southampton in 1491 by Thomas Overy, the mayor, which were intended to ensure that the twelve jurors who nominated the borough officers should themselves be chosen by the common assembly of burgesses and which created four 'conservators' drawn from the elite and the commons to help enforce the new ordinances, were soon disregarded. 'In a neat reversal of Overy's intentions, vitiating immediately much that he had tried to achieve, another hand, almost contemporary in style, corrected the town's copy of the ordinances. At every point in the text where the word "conservator" had been used, "alderman" was substituted in its place. It was an amendment clearly very much to the taste of the establishment.'[45]

Why did such reforming movements have so little long-term success? One reason is the fact that although popular movements raised issues of principle by implication, these issues were rarely raised in any explicit theoretical form. The occasion for such movements tended to be some particular grievance: an 'unjust' tax, a mayoral election, the violation of what was perceived as custom. If their occasion was short term then so too were the methods of action of such movements, the 'crowd' with its disturbances and unruliness, complained of at Leicester and Northampton in 1489, rather than political parties. Such actions could have only a limited impact. The very fact that the rich dominated town government meant that protest tended to take the form of disorder which could easily be dismissed as unlawful, as in the case of the election of the London chamberlain in 1443. Furthermore, the town rulers had their own sanctions against those who threatened them. A day in the borough gaol was enough to end the rebellion of John Astyn of Grimsby who in 1389 refused to pay his bustage assessment and claimed that he would not be ruled by the mayor but only by his fellows and equals.[46] If local powers were insufficient then the authority of the Crown could be called in on the side of the 'lawful' government, as at Lynn in 1416. In such cases the Crown was often more concerned with the threat to public order than with the grievances which had created it.[47]

Even where democratic reforms were achieved they were often undermined by long periods of popular apathy. At Lincoln, in 1422, it was ordained that forty commoners should be present to ratify the use of the common seal, but this was later reduced to twenty because of the difficulties of obtaining a quorum. Similarly, at Lynn, the reforms of the early fifteenth century were followed by long bouts of political indifference.[48] Urban political conflict could, by implication, raise the issue of the role of the commonalty in town government and call for structural change, but it offered no long-term alternative to the personal rule of the rich. Town government was, despite the growing importance of salaried officials such as the town clerk,[49] largely the work of amateurs. It conferred power and status on those involved but it could also be expensive and time consuming. In 1468, for instance, four ex-mayors of Grimsby pardoned the borough of £58 13s 4d of debts on account of 'the poverty of the commonalty' whilst in 1491 William Vicars, despite his burgess oath to 'bear all the charges of office from the highest to the lowest that belong to the borough of Grimsby, at any time that I, by due action, be chosen to them', was allowed to name one man as a burgess of Grimsby (and so, presumably, to collect that man's burgess fine) in order to compensate him for the 'great charges' involved in taking on the mayoralty. Grimsby men were similarly unwilling to serve as bailiffs and were increasingly drawn from the ranks of new burgesses who took on the office instead of paying a burgess fine. When Peter Thompson had attempted to appoint Peter Smyth as his deputy as bailiff in 1508 he did so because he considered it to be 'a great labour' for him to occupy the office.[50]

Given that town government was often little more than an executive committee for managing the common affairs of the richer townsmen it is not surprising that when political conflicts occurred they were often *within*, rather than against, the urban elite, a pattern which medieval England shared with other pre-industrial societies.[51] Richard Aby of Grimsby, whom we have already noted refusing to pay his bustage assessment in 1389, was himself an ex-bailiff of the borough, a juror at the sessions of the peace and a royal commissioner.[52] Geoffrey de Askeby, against whom Aby complained in 1389, was himself imprisoned by the mayor of Grimsby in 1392–3 (and was only released through the intervention of the sheriff of Lincoln) even though he himself had twice been mayor.[53] In 1398–9 it was William Wele, four times mayor of Grimsby, who complained to the Chancellor that the mayor of Grimsby had wrongly farmed out the borough ferry.[54] Such complaints typically resulted in individual redress rather than the institutional change which could result from popular movements. The lack of stable merchant dynasties meant that there was rarely a faction of rich 'outs' trying to join the 'ins' and willing to ally with the lesser townsmen. Disputes within the elite which spilled over into wider social and political conflicts, as at York in 1381 and 1482, were very much the exception.[55] Doubtless most townsmen were more concerned with the dull economic compulsion of obtaining their daily living, rather than with urban politics. Their interventions in political life were intermittent and, given their reliance on the 'crowd' and the lack of political parties to safeguard their gains, their victories were often short-lived. Thus, whilst movements for democratic reform did exist in the late medieval town and could obtain an increased popular participation in town government, their achievements were not great.

IV

Not all late medieval town councils were the result of such popular movements. On the contrary, the development of town councils could be used to restrict, as well as to extend, urban democracy. The classic examples are Leicester and Northampton where, in 1489, the election of the mayor of the assembly of burgesses was replaced at Leicester by the mayor and twenty-four, and at Northampton by the mayor and his brethren (i.e. former mayors), choosing forty-eight burgesses and together forming an electoral panel. In both cases the creation of the forty-eight was an explicit attempt to replace popular election with election by a 'packed' council.[56]

The appearance of a town council at Grimsby may have had a similarly restrictive effect on the burgesses' participation in town government, although the example of Grimsby may show that as historians we are often too eager to look for signs of change. At Grimsby, where the borough's liberties were completed by the charter of 1318 and the town's administrative structure was virtually complete by 1400, the keynote in civic government was continuity rather than change. The only major change which did occur in the fifteenth century was the evolution of a mayor's council. Unlike larger towns, Grimsby had not developed a council in the thirteenth or fourteenth centuries.[57] However, in 1403 twenty councillors are mentioned for the first time and by 1422 the council had evolved into its final form of twelve of the 'more lawful and discreet men of the town' to advise the mayor, bailiffs and coroners 'for the good government of the commonalty of the town'. Outsiders could refer to the twelve as the town's 'common council' but within the borough they were referred to as the 'mayor's secret (i.e. confidential) council', a council of the type found elsewhere as early as the thirteenth century, rather than an outer or common council as developed at late medieval Norwich and Lynn.[58] The council could give its assent to the mayor's decisions and could itself ordain by-laws but, in practice, the appearance of the council made little practical difference to the running of the town. Other ways of carrying out the same tasks had existed before the council's emergence (notably by jury in the borough court or by assembly in the common hall) and such methods continued to be used afterwards.[59] In so far as the development of a council did lead to change in Grimsby's government it may have restricted popular involvement rather than opening it up. The council elected in 1475, for instance, included at least five past mayors, the council of 1481 (six of whom had been serving in 1475) at least six.[60] This was a rather more closed means of carrying out borough business than the use of juries of burgesses in the town court. In 1389–90, for instance, four such juries had elected officers, enquired who had taken documents from the borough chest, decided that the common clerk should go to London on the borough's business and reviewed the town's ordinances at the request of the mayor. Only five men served on all four juries.[61] Grimsby's government became even more oligarchic as the council began to expand its role. By the late fifteenth century the council nominated two of its members as candidates for the mayoralty from whom the commonalty (in practice an electoral panel) made its choice. Such changes were, however, hardly dramatic. A small number of richer and administratively experienced townsmen had always controlled the town through their domination of the borough court, which was not merely seen in judicial terms but was also the deliberative, legislative and executive focus of the borough's government.[62]

The shift from informal plutocracy towards a more formal oligarchy can be seen in a number of late medieval towns and typically involved restrictions on who could stand as mayor, the replacement of burgess assemblies with councils, the appointment of officers from above rather than by election, and the introduction of office for life.[63] It can also be seen in the growing distinction between the upper officers and the rest of the community as at Grimsby where, by 1498, ex-mayors had the title of 'aldermen' and were empowered to keep the peace in the absence of the mayor, and at Colchester, where the borough 'auditors' evolved into aldermen, distinguished from the rest of the town's councillors by their liveried robes. At York there was an increasing emphasis on the dignity of office with the emergence of the title of 'my lord mayor' and by the mayor processing, preceded by his sergeant carrying the civic sword and mace.[64] Hull was typical of this trend from plutocracy towards a more formally organized oligarchy. The town had always chosen its mayor from a small group of leading merchants but from 1440 he was to be drawn from the newly instituted liveried aldermen who held office for life, itself a contrast with the council of eight which had been annually elected in the late fourteenth century. In 1443 the aldermen's powers were further enhanced with the requirement that the commonalty should henceforth elect the mayor from one of two candidates put forward by the aldermen. Vacancies amongst the aldermen were to be filled through election by the burgesses but their choice was restricted to two candidates nominated by the aldermen.[65]

All of these tendencies combined, of course, in those towns which developed close corporations such as Bristol (1499), Exeter (1504) and Lynn (1524), the examples made famous by Tait's classic work. The Lynn charter of 1524, for example, made it the 'closest of close corporations' and totally swept away the popular element introduced into the town government in the early fifteenth century. The town was in future to be ruled by the mayor, twelve aldermen and eighteen common councillors. The eighteen were chosen by the mayor and twelve and could be removed at will; the twelve were to serve for life. The first twelve aldermen were nominated by the Crown, but in future they were to be selected by the eighteen who were also to elect a mayor annually from the ranks of the aldermen.[66]

However, the fact that towns became more oligarchic in the later middle ages does not mean that their government had once been 'popular' in form.[67] It is impossible to identify some primitive golden age of urban democracy. Urban 'patriciates' had emerged from the landowners, rentiers and officials of feudal society. They were then transformed into plutocracies of the richer merchants and traders which by the late fifteenth century were beginning to change their form, if not their essential content, through 'a deliberate policy of oligarchy.'[68]

V

'The growth of oligarchic magistracy' was thus not only 'the most obvious theme in English urban history from 1500 to 1700';[69] it was a trend which had its origins in the late fourteenth and fifteenth centuries. But why did this tendency emerge victorious? Oligarchy could result from a fear of social disorder associated with popular government. As the Recorder of Nottingham said in 1512: 'if you suffer the commons to rule and follow their appetite and desire, farewell all good order.'[70] Certainly, the role of the commonalty was reduced in mayoral elections at York, Leicester and Northampton in 1489 because of the fears of disorder which accompanied the election.[71] More oligarchic forms of government could also be introduced in response to the failure of democratic reforms. At London the defeat of John of Northampton and the guilds saw a return not to the situation before 1376, but the introduction of new measures which enhanced the power of the aldermanic elite.[72] Restrictions on the Colchester electorate introduced in the early 1430s were also a response to 'many troublez, parlous discordes and inconuencientes' arising from the multitude of people who attended elections 'presumyng and usurpying entresse in the seid eleccions wher in dede they owe noon to have.'[73]

The growth of the activities of town government in the early modern period may have been a factor encouraging the emergence of a more oligarchic, standing committee system of town government, but this is less likely to have been a factor in the later middle ages when there was little significant change in the type of activities carried out by the borough administration. More important, as Clark and Slack argued, may have been the growing economic and financial difficulties of certain towns.[74] With the decline in urban population there were fewer rich merchants to share the burden of town government, hence the statute of 1512 which legally opened up town office to bakers, brewers, vintners, fishmongers and other victuallers who had been excluded by an enactment of two centuries earlier.[75] At Grimsby this trend can be seen in the decline in the number of men eligible or willing to stand as mayor. In the twenty-two years of Richard II's reign seventeen individuals served as mayor, of whom only three served more than once; in the twenty four years of Henry VII's reign only twelve men served as mayor and by this date it was unusual for mayors to serve only once.[76] At Colchester too, the development of more oligarchic forms of government may have been a response to hard times, a conscious attempt to attract and commit the richer townsmen to participation in town government.[77] Yet, ironically, the prosperity of the urban economy could also lead to increased oligarchy, as in late fifteenth and early sixteenth-century Exeter, where the polarisation of wealth resulting from the expansion of the cloth trade saw town government becoming increasingly closed and subject to the control of the wealthy.[78]

It has been argued that the most important cause of urban oligarchy originated outside the towns, in the Crown's obsession with the need for small knots of reliable men in every town, a policy promoted by charters of incorporation and conciliar intervention.[79] How significant was such royal intervention? Was incorporation, for instance, no more than 'a piece of lawyer's nonsense, skilfully contrived to appeal to the trumpery pretensions of the burgess class'?[80] Certainly, the five classic points of incorporation (power to have a common seal, the right to make by-laws, perpetual succession, power of suing and being sued as a corporation, the right to hold lands) made little difference to a town's liberties.[81] Boroughs had long used common seals without any chartered right. Grimsby had possessed its own 'sigillum communitatis Grimebye' since the early thirteenth century and from the early fourteenth century the borough's mayor had also used an official seal. Oxford had owned a common seal as early as 1191.[82] Neither was the right to make by-laws an innovation. Some towns, such as London and Norwich, had, as we have seen, already been given this right by charter, but elsewhere it was simply taken for granted that borough courts would regulate the detailed aspects of town life which could hardly be included in a royal charter. Even manorial courts were obliged to make ordinances for local communities in this way.[83] Perpetual succession had always been implicit in grants of charters to burgesses and their heirs, and in any case towns still felt the need to obtain confirmation of their liberties even after they were legally incorporated.[84] Fictitious personality was the essence of incorporation yet, in practice, individual townsmen remained liable for distraint for debts of the community despite the corporation's ability to sue and be sued in its own name.[85]

The main practical benefit of incorporation was thus the ability to hold land. Towns had, of course, held land long before the age of incorporation. At Grimsby the borough had received a grant of the town wastes in 1341 in return for an annual rent of three shillings to the Exchequer. The community administered the land through the borough chamberlains who collected rents and paid them into the common chest.[86] The extension of the mortmain legislation to the boroughs in 1391 had, however, made it more difficult for towns to acquire land, an important issue in an age of declining municipal incomes. Indeed, the concept of incorporation had itself emerged in response to the Crown's mortmain legislation which claimed that 'mayors, bailiffs and commons of cities, boroughs and other towns which have a perpetual community . . .be as perpetual as people of religion.' Nevertheless, even after incorporation, towns such as Hull could continue to buy licences to acquire land in mortmain despite having already formally acquired this right.[87]

That chartered incorporation made little difference to a borough's status and liberties can be seen from the judgement of 1467–8 whereby all towns which already held at fee farm were henceforth to be regarded as incorporate.[88] But this does not mean that medieval townsmen themselves saw incorporation as insignificant, since towns often sought a 'political' answer to what we would regard as an 'economic' problem. Thus the Hull charter of incorporation was explicitly granted in consideration of the burgesses' charges and expenses in the service of the Crown and 'for the relief and increase of the town.'[89] Even in the late sixteenth century the author of 'A *Discourse of Corporations*' still had to argue that 'it is the site and place where every town or city is builded which is the chief cause of the flourishing of the same, or else some special trade or traffic appropriate to the same, and not the incorporation thereof.'[90]

If incorporation was of little practical significance to the towns, why were townsmen willing to pay for charters of incorporation? The answer (apart from incorporation's supposed economic benefits) lies in the other grants contained in such charters. Indeed, given the impact which these grants had on borough government it may be wrong to see the charters which contained them as essentially 'charters of incorporation'. Such charters could also be the final stage in the separation of borough and shire, with their grants of county status and the exclusion of sheriffs, escheators and coroners from borough affairs. They could prevent the interference of the stewards and marshals of the king's household and the clerk of the market. Most importantly, they adapted town government to the emergence of the justice of the peace, the main change in English local government in the later middle ages, by excluding county justices and allowing mayors and aldermen to sit as justices of the peace and of labourers within the borough.[91]

Early royal charters had largely been concerned with the relations between borough and royal administration; they had usually ignored the question of how the towns themselves were to be administered. Late medieval charters were much more concerned with the organization of borough administration, in particular with the methods to be used in the election of mayors and aldermen, a concern which led to a growing uniformity in town government.[92] The provisions of such charters could certainly enhance the trend to oligarchy. They imposed restrictions on who could stand as mayor, replaced election with co-option and emphasised the dignity of town officers with their enhanced powers as sheriffs, escheators and coroners. Above all, they made town officers into justices of the peace and of labourers, an extension of their policing and economic powers which, in London at least, was seen as a means of undermining the customary good rule of the city to the detriment of its artisans.[93] Such charters did not only enhance the power and status of town rulers through their *specific* provisions. In more general terms they mark a shift in the source of authority exercised by the borough officers away from the community and towards central government, i.e. towards a descending rather than an ascending concept of authority and legitimacy. This shift of emphasis can be most clearly seen in the case of Lynn in 1524 where the twelve aldermen created by royal charter were themselves chosen by the Crown, rather than through election by the burgesses.[94] Similarly, the reorganization of mayoral elections at Leicester and Northampton in 1489 meant a move away from election by the assembly of burgesses to one involving a council of forty-eight nominated from above, an innovation which was itself the result of an act of parliament rather than the outcome of agreement within the borough or of borough custom.[95]

The intervention of the Crown was thus certainly a force favouring 'oligarchy' in late medieval towns, but was this the main factor which encouraged the growth of more closed forms of urban government as Clark and Slack suggest? It is, after all, doubtful whether the Crown had a coherent policy towards the towns in the late medieval period, although there may have been a general concern about the type of men now liable to be borough J.Ps. Royal intervention in the boroughs tended to be a *response* to some local disorder or petition rather than the mainspring of change, although it was a response based on assumptions about the dangers of popular interference in government similar to those held by the town rulers.[96] Royal charters were usually the result of some local initiative or problem and often bear the marks of the petitions which produced them.[97]

In so far as the impetus for change in borough government came from outside individual towns, then the influence of other towns as models may have been as important as that of the Crown. An example of town rulers emulating each other in this way is found in the grants of county status made in the later middle ages. Bristol was the first town to acquire the status of a separate county (in 1373), when the grant was made in order to resolve the specific problems caused by the city's division between the counties of Somerset and Gloucestershire.[98] But once Bristol had acquired this status other leading towns followed suit: York (1396); Newcastle (1400); Norwich (1404) and Lincoln (1409). By the mid-fifteenth century even towns such as Hull and Southampton were being made into separate counties.[99] There seems to have been a similar process of diffusion at work in the tendency for towns to adopt the idea of appointing aldermen for life and of restricting candidature for mayor to aldermen (as at Nottingham (1448), Stamford (1462) and Grantham (1463)) or at least to those nominated by the aldermen (as at Hull (1443)).[100] The influence of London, where aldermen were elected for life from 1394 and where (from 1385) the new mayor was chosen by the existing mayor and aldermen from the two candidates chosen by an electoral assembly, was particularly important here, since many towns consciously looked to London as a model, although the royal chancery *was* also a force for the diffusion of methods of government which had been originally devised for specific, local reasons.[101] The growing pomp and ceremonial of late medieval town government were also spread through a similar mixture of urban competition for status and a royal willingness to sell charters of liberties.

Medieval town government was thus based on the potentially uneasy co-existence of the principle of rule by the 'better sort' on the one hand with that of community's right to consultation and representation on the other. The late medieval period saw a shift in the balance of these principles which resulted in more institutionalised and closed forms of rule by the rich ('oligarchy') and an emphasis on a descending concept of the rulers' authority. However, other areas of town government still remain to be discussed. In particular, we need to examine the policies actually adopted by town rulers. What policies were adopted? Whom were they intended to benefit? How successful were they? Did they reflect a protectionist response to an age of economic saturation?[102] Another area of research is the relationship between the towns and 'bastard feudalism', for if the ideal of urban political theory was one of harmony and unity, then this unity could be threatened by divisions between rival affiliations and by loyalties which crossed town boundaries.[103] Our concern here, however, has been with the more familiar conflicts of rich and poor, ruler against ruled. To understand *these* conflicts we need to understand the ideals and principles which underlay medieval political activity. But in order to do this we need to take account not only of the explicit theory propagated by the town rulers but also of the views implicit in the actions of those who have not left sources of their own behind them, views which often give a rather different assessment of medieval town rulers from that expressed in our official sources.

Notes

I would like to thank Dr R.G. Davies and Mr R.B. Dinn for suggesting improvements to an earlier draft of this paper.

1 A.R. Bridbury, *Economic Growth: England in the Later Middle Ages* (London, 1962); R.B. Dobson, 'Urban decline in late medieval England', *TRHS*, Fifth series, vol. 27

(1977), pp. 1–22; C. Phythian-Adams, 'Urban decay in late medieval England' in P. Abrams and E.A. Wrigley, eds., *Towns in Societies* (Cambridge, 1978), pp. 159–85; A.R. Bridbury, 'English provincial towns in the later middle ages', *EcHR* second series, vol. 34 (1981), pp. 1–24; S.H. Rigby, "Sore decay" and "fair dwellings": Boston and urban decline in the later middle ages', *Midland History*, vol. 10 (1985), pp. 47–61.

2   S.H. Rigby, 'Urban decline in the later middle ages: some problems in interpreting the statistical data', *Urban History Yearbook 1979*, pp. 46–59; S. Reynolds, 'Decline and decay in late medieval towns: a look at some of the arguments and concepts', *Urban History Yearbook*, 1980, pp. 76–8; S.H. Rigby, 'Urban decline in the later middle ages: the reliability of the non-statistical evidence', *Urban History Yearbook 1984*, pp. 45–60; S.H. Rigby, 'Late medieval urban prosperity: the evidence of the lay subsidies', *EcHR* Second series, vol. 39 (1986), pp. 411–16, with replies by A.R. Bridbury (pp. 417–22) and J.F. Hadwin (pp. 423–26).

3   R. Flenley, 'Introduction' to *Six Town Chronicles of England* (Oxford, 1911).

4   L. Toulmin Smith, ed., *The Maire of Bristowe is Kalendar*, Camden Society, New Series, vol. 5 (1872).

5   H.T. Riley, ed., *Munimenta Gildhallae Londoniensis*, vol. I: *Liber Albus* (Rolls Series, vol. XII, 1859); *Historical Manuscripts Commission, Fourteenth Report, Appendix, part VIII* (London, 1895), 1895), p. 22; The *Liber Custumarum* is printed in C.A. Markham, ed., *The Records of the Borough of Northampton*, vol. I (Northampton, 1898), pp. 198–430 and in C.A. Markham, ed., *The Liber Custumarum* (Northampton, 1895).

6   A.S. Green, *Town Life in the Fifteenth Century*, II (London, 1894),pp. 269–70, 440–42; J.C. Cox, ed., *The Records of the Borough of Northampton*, vol. II (Northampton, 1898), pp. 14–17; C.W. Colby, 'The growth of oligarchy in English towns', *EHR*, vol. 5 (1890), pp. 633–53; Bridbury, *Economic Growth*, pp. 58–64.

7   See, for instance, H.M. Jewell, *English Local Administration in the Middle Ages* (Newton Abbot, 1972), p. 56; E. Miller, 'Medieval York', in P.M. Tillott, ed., *VCH A History of the County of York: the City of York* (London, 1961), p. 79; J.L. Bolten, *The Medieval English Economy, 1150–1500* (London, 1980), pp. 260–1.

8   Z. Razi, 'The Toronto school's re-constitution of medieval peasant society: a critical view', *Past and Present* No. 85 (1979), pp. 152–7; Z. Razi, 'The struggles between the abbots of Halesowen and their tenants in the thirteenth and fourteenth centuries' in T.H. Aston *et al.*, eds, *Social Relations and Ideas*, (Cambridge, 1983) pp. 151–3; P.S. Cohen, *Modern Social Theory* (London, 1978), ch. 5; N. Abercrombie, S. Hill and B.S. Turner, *The Dominant Ideology Thesis* (London, 1980), ch. 2; S.H. Rigby, *Marxism and History* (Manchester, 1987), pp. 136, 281, 284–8.

9   S. Reynolds, 'Medieval urban history and the history of political thought', *Urban History Yearbook 1982*, pp. 14–23; S. Reynolds, *An Introduction to the History of English Medieval Towns* (Oxford, 1977), pp. 135–6, 171. The analysis offered here follows much of Reynolds' work whilst emphasising rather different conclusions. See also S. Reynolds, '1483: Gloucester and town government in the middle ages' in N.M. Herbert *et al.*, *The 1483 Gloucester Charter in History* (Gloucester, 1983), pp. 43–50.

10   Reynolds, 'Medieval urban history and the history of political thought', pp. 22–3; H.T. Riley, ed., *Munimenta Gildhallea Londoniensis*, vol. II, part I: *Liber Custumarum* (Rolls Series, vol. XII, 1860), pp. 16–25.

11   J.W.F. Hill, *Medieval Lincoln* (Cambridge, 1948), p. 279.

12   J.I. Kermode, 'Urban decline? The flight from office in late medieval York', *EcHR* Second series, vol. 35 (1982), pp. 191, 195.

13   South Humberside Area Record Office (SHARO.) 1/102/1 Mayor's Court Book (cited as MCB below), f. 124; Toulmin Smith, *The Maire of Bristowe is Kalendar*, pp. 72–3; Reynolds, 'Medieval urban history and the history of political thought', p. 23.

14   Markham, *The Liber Custumarum*, p. 6; CCR 1392–6, p. 162. See also W. Hudson and

J.C. Tingey, *The Records of the City of Norwich* vol. I (Norwich, 1906), p. 94; M.D. Harris, ed., *The Coventry Leet Book*, part II, (EETS vol. 135, 1908), pp. 555–6.

15 W. Ullman, *A History of Political Thought: The Middle Ages* (Harmondsworth, 1965), pp. 12–13, 159–61; S. Reynolds, *Kingdoms and Communities in Western Europe* (Oxford, 1984), *passim*.

16 A. Ballard, 'The English boroughs in the reign of John', *EHR*. 14 (1899), p. 99.

17 B. Wilkinson, *The Medieval Council of Exeter* (Manchester, 1931), p. 44.

18 Riley, *Liber Albus*, p.3; *CPR 1391–6*, pp. 355–6.

19 MCB ff. 29, 125v; SHARO 1/100 Grimsby Court Rolls (cited below as GCR), 8th December, Tuesday after St Lucy, Tuesday after Epiphany, Tuesday after St Hilary, 15th February, 1st March, 8th March, 13 Richard II (dates as in original roll for ease of reference); Hudson and Tingey, *The Records of the City of Norwich* vol. I, pp. 30, 64–70.

20 M. Sellers, ed., *York Memorandum Book* part II, 1388-1493 (Surtees Society vol. 125 (1915) p. 246.

21 Abercrombie *et al.*, *The Dominant Ideology Thesis*, ch. 3.

22 C. Phythian-Adams, *Desolation of a City*, (Cambridge, 1979), chapter 11.

23 SHARO 1/600 Chamberlains' accounts 3 Henry IV, 10 Henry IV, 5 Edward IV; MCB f. 35; SHARO 1/50 1498 Ordinances; K.J. Allison, 'Medieval Hull', in K.J. Allison, ed., *VCH A History of the County of York: East Riding* vol. 1 (Oxford, 1969), p. 30; Phythian-Adams, *Desolation of a City*, pp. 137–9; Toulmin Smith, *The Maire of Bristowe is Kalendar*, pp. 74–80.

24 M.K. James, 'Ritual drama and social body in the late medieval English town', *Past and Present* No. 98 (1983), pp. 1–29; L. Mumford, *The City in History* (Harmondsworth, 1979), p. 320; C. Phythian-Adams, 'Ceremony and the citizen: the communal year at Coventry' in P. Clark and P. Clark and P. Slack, eds., *Crisis and Order in English Towns 1500–1700* (London, 1972), pp. 57–85.

25 Reynolds, *An Introduction to the History of English Medieval Towns*, p. 170; Reynolds, 'Medieval urban history and the history of political thought', pp. 20–22.

26 *Ibid.*, pp. 15, 18–19.

27 *Rotuli Parliamentorum* vol. VI. p. 432; M. Bateson, ed., *Records of the Borough of Leicester* vol. II 1327–1509 (London, 1901), pp. 319, 324–7.

28 *Rotuli Parliamentorum* vol. VI., p. 432.

29 B. Moore, *Injustice* (London, 1979), pp. 23, 27, 46, 510; Bateson, *Records of the Borough of Leicester*, pp. 326–7; Hudson and Tingey, *Records of the City of Norwich* vol. I, p. 71.

30 J. Tait, *The Medieval English Borough* (Manchester, 1936), pp. 319–20; *Historical Manuscripts Commission, Eleventh Report, Appendix Part III* (HMC, Lynn) pp. 191–203, 245–6.

31 Q. Skinner, *The Foundations of Modern Political Thought* volume I, (Cambridge, 1978), pp. 47–8, 60; Reynolds, 'Medieval urban history and the history of political thought', p. 20.

32 The section on Ralph Holland is entirely based on C.M. Barron, 'Ralph Holland and the London radicals 1438–44' in *A History of the North London Branch of the Historical Association together with Essays in Honour of its Golden Jubilee* (London, 1970), perhaps the best study of urban political conflict in late medieval England.

33 Tait, *Medieval English Borough*, p. 338.

34 MCB ff. 27, 28v, 30, 49, 49v, 54; SHARO 1/800/1 and 1/800/2, Assessments for parliamentary expenses.

35 MCB *passim.*; SHARO, 1/50 1498 Ordinances.

36 Bridbury *Economic Growth*, pp. 58–64.

37 *Ibid.*, pp. 58–9.

38 A.F. Butcher, 'Canterbury's earliest rolls of freemen admissions 1297–1363: a

reconsideration' in F. Hull, ed., *A Kentish Miscellany* (Kent Records vol. 21 (1979)), pp. 1–26.

39 Bridbury, *Economy Growth*, p. 62.

40 R.B. Dobson, 'Admissions to the freedom of the city of York in the later middle ages', *EcHR*, Second series vol. 26 (1973), pp. 17–18.

41 *Ibid.*, pp. 16, 20; *CCR 1381–5*, pp. 338–9; GCR Tuesday after St Hilary 13 Richard II; SHARO Chamberlains' account 9 Henry V.

42 Allison, 'Medieval Hull', p. 37.

43 Tait, *The Medieval English Borough*, pp. 310–11, 317–8; *Records of the City of Norwich* vol. 1, pp. 36, 93–108; *HMC Lynn*, pp. 245-6; R.R. Sharpe, ed., *Calendar of the Letter Books of the City of London: Letter Book 'H'* (London, 1907), pp. 35–44, 59–60; Wilkinson, *The Medieval Council of Exeter*, pp. 6–8, 24–6.

44 *Ibid.*, pp. 26–7; Sharpe, *Letter Book 'H'*, pp. 227–8, 277, 408–10, 436; R. Bird, *The Turbulent London of Richard II* (London, 1949), chapter 3.

45 C. Platt, *Medieval Southampton* (London, 1973), pp. 176–7.

46 GCR Tuesday after St. Lucy 13 Richard II.

47 *HMC Lynn*, pp. 195–203; A.P.M. Wright, 'The Relations between the King's Government and the English Cities and Boroughs in the Fifteenth Century' (Unpublished D.Phil. thesis, Oxford, 1965), chapter 2.

48 Hill, *Medieval Lincoln*, pp. 276–9; Tait, *The Medieval English Borough*, pp. 320–1.

49 See, for instance, R.H. Britnell, 'The oath-book of Colchester and the borough constitution 1372–1404', *Essex Archaeology and History* vol. 14 (1982), pp. 94–101; S.H. Rigby, 'Boston and Grimsby in the Middle Ages' (Unpublished PhD thesis, London, 1983), pp. 69–72.

50 MCB ff. 39v, 43v, 44, 125v.

51 G. Sjoberg, *The Pre-Industrial City* (New York, 1965), p. 223.

52 See GCR References in note 19 above and Rigby, 'Boston and Grimsby in the Middle Ages', p. 99.

53 PRO C1/7/265.

54 PRO SC8/299/14937.

55 Miller, 'Medieval York', p. 82; R.B. Dobson, 'The risings in York, Beverley and Scarborough, 1380–1381' in R.H. Hilton and T.H. Aston, *The English Rising of 1381* (Cambridge, 1984), pp. 119–24.

56 *Rotuli Parliamentorum* vol. VI, pp. 432–3; Bateson, *Records of the Borough of Leicester* pp. 324–5.

57 S.H. Rigby, 'Boston and Grimsby in the Middle Ages: an administrative contrast', *JMH* vol. 10 (1984), pp. 51–7; E. Searle, *Lordship and Community* (Toronto, 1974), p. 432.

58 GCR 16th October 5 Henry IV; 6th October 1 Henry VI; *HMC, Fourteenth Report, Appendix, part VIII*, pp. 246, 248; MCB ff. 46, 55.

59 MCB ff. 10v, 44, Rigby, 'Boston and Grimsby in the Middle Ages', pp. 86–7.

60 MCB ff. 24v, 40.

61 GCR 19th October, Tuesday after Epiphany, Tuesday after St Hilary, Tuesday after St Ambrose 13 Richard II.

62 *HMC, Fourteenth Report, Appendix, part VIII*, pp. 246, 248. SHARO 1/310, Record of election of mayor and bailiffs; SHARO. 1/50 1498 Ordinances. See also Searle, *Lordship and Community* p. 432.

63 *HMC, Fourteenth Report, Appendix, part VIII*, pp. 246, 248; *Rotuli Parliamentorum* vol. VI, pp. 432–3; R.H. Britnell, *Growth and Decline in Colchester, 1300–1525* (Cambridge, 1986), p. 233; G.H. Martin, *The Royal Charters of Grantham 1463–1688* (Leicester, 1963), p. 31.

64 SHARO 1/50 1498 Ordinances; Britnell, *Growth and Decline in Colchester*, pp. 223–5; Miller, 'Medieval York', p. 70.

65 CChR 1427–1516, p. 10; CPR 1441–6, p. 181; Allison, 'Medieval Hull', pp. 30–6.
66 Tait, The Medieval English Borough pp. 321, 330–3; HMC Lynn, pp. 206–7.
67 C. Gross, The Gild Merchant volume I (Oxford, 1890), p. 108.
68 A.B. Hibbert, 'The origins of the medieval town patriciate', Past and Present No. 3 (1953), pp. 15–27; Miller, 'Medieval York', pp. 71–9; Reynolds, An Introduction to the History of English Medieval Towns, p. 176; Bridbury, Economic Growth, p. 58.
69 P. Clark and P. Slack, 'Introduction' to Crisis and Order in English Towns, p. 25.
70 W.H. Stevenson, ed., Records of the Borough of Nottingham vol. III, (London, 1885), p. 341.
71 Miller, 'Medieval York', p. 83; Rotuli Parliamentorum vol. VI., p. 432.
72 Bird, The Turbulent London of Richard II, passim.
73 Britnell, Growth and Decline in Colchester, p. 220.
74 Clark and Slack, 'Introduction', p. 21.
75 Statutes of the Realm vol.III (Record Commissioners, 1818), p. 30.
76 Lists of mayors based on PRO E368 LTR Memoranda Rolls and Grimsby Court Rolls.
77 Britnell, Growth and Decline in Colchester, pp. 234–5.
78 M. Kowaleski, 'The commercial dominance of a medieval provincial oligarchy: Exeter in the late fourteenth century', Medieval Studies vol. 46 (1984), p. 384.
79 Clark and Slack, 'Introduction', pp. 22, 46, n.69.
80 Bridbury, 'English provincial towns in the later middle ages', pp. 11–12; A.R. Bridbury, 'Late medieval urban prosperity: a rejoinder', EcHR Second series, vol. 37 (1984), p. 555.
81 M. Weinbaum, The Incorporation of Boroughs (Manchester, 1937); M. Weinbaum, ed., British Borough Charters 1307-1660 (Cambridge, 1943), pp. xxiii–xvi.
82 SHARO Grimsby seal matrices, C. Platt, The English Medieval Town (London, 1976), p. 129.
83 Tait, The Medieval English Borough, p. 317; M.M. Postan, The Medieval Economy and Society (London, 1972), pp. 117–9.
84 See, for instance, CChR 1300–26, p. 410; HMC, Fourteenth Report, Appendix, Part VIII, pp. 238–9.
85 Bridbury, 'English provincial towns in the later middle ages', pp. 5, 11, n.3; T. Madox, Firma Burgi (London, 1726), pp. 180, 217–8, 232.
86 CFR 1337-47, p. 220; SHARO, 1/600 Chamberlains' accounts 3 Henry IV.
87 Statutes of the Realm vol. 2 (Record Commissioners, 1816), p. 80; S. Reynolds, 'The idea of corporation in western Christendom before 1300' in J.A. Guy and H.G. Beale, ed., Law and Social Change in British History (London, 1984), pp. 27–33. CChR 1427–1516, p. 9; CPR 1441–46, p. 180.
88 Weinbaum, The Incorporation of Boroughs, p. 88; Gross, The Gild Merchant, volume I, p. 104.
89 CChR 1427–1516, p. 8; R. Tittler, 'Late medieval urban prosperity',EcHR Second series vol. 37 (1984), pp. 552–3.
90 R.H. Tawney and E. Power, eds., Tudor Economic Documents vol. 3 (London, 1924), pp. 273–4.
91 Weinbaum, The Incorporation of Boroughs chapters 4, 5; CChR 1427–1516, pp. 8–11; Martin, The Royal Charters of Grantham, pp. 29–47.
92 Weinbaum, British Borough Charters, p. xxiii.
93 R.H. Hilton, 'Towns in English feudal society', Review vol. 3 (1979), p. 16; CChR 1427–1516, pp. 10–11. Martin, The Royal Charters of Grantham, pp. 33–43; Barron, 'Ralph Holland and the London radicals', p. 69.
94 HMC Lynn, p. 206.
95 Rotuli Parliamentorum vol. VI, p. 432.
96 See, for instance, Statutes of the Realm vol. II, p. 243.
97 See, for instance, F.B. Bickley, ed., The Little Red Book of Bristol vol. 1 (Bristol, 1900),

pp. 115–26; Weinbaum, *The Incorporation of Boroughs*, pp. 71, 81. For the early modern period see R. Tittler, 'The incorporation of boroughs', *History* vol. 62 (1977), pp. 25–6; S. Bond and N. Evans, 'The process of granting charters to English boroughs 1547–1649', *EHR*, 91 (1976), p. 108.

98 N.P. Harding, ed., *Bristol Charters 1155–1373* (Bristol Record Society, 1930), pp. 119–23.

99 Weinbaum, *The Incorporation of Boroughs*, pp. 54–9, 67, 71.

100 W.H. Stevenson, *Royal Charters Granted to the Burgesses of Nottingham AD 1155–1712* (London, 1890), pp. 63–7; CChR 1427–1516, p. 165; Martin, *The Royal Charters of Grantham*, p. 31; *CPR 1441-6*, p. 181.

101 Bird, *The Turbulent London of Richard II*, pp. 35, 42–3; Tait, *The Medieval English Borough*, pp. 317–8; *HMC Lynn*, p. 197.

102 A.B. Hibbert, 'The economic policies of towns' in M.M. Postan, E.E. Rich and E. Miller, eds., *Cambridge Economic History of Europe* vol. III (Cambridge, 1963), especially pp. 206–229.

103 See, for instance, Wright, 'The Relations between the King's Government and the English Cities and Boroughs in the Fifteenth Century', pp. 38–44; I. Rowney, 'Government and patronage in the fifteenth century: Staffordshire 1439–59', *Midland History* vol. 8 (1983), pp. 56–7; E. Gillett, *A History of Grimsby* (Oxford, 1970), pp. 61–2; R. Horrox, 'Urban patronage and patrons in the fifteenth century', R.A. Griffiths ed., *Patronage, the Crown and the Provinces in later Medieval England* (Gloucester, 1981), pp. 145–66.

5

Obvious Observations on the Formation of Oligarchies in Late Medieval English Towns

Jennifer I. Kermode
University of Liverpool

Susan Reynolds reminded us in 1982, that oligarchies were not automatically assumed to be corrupt nor out of line with contemporary notions of natural justice in the middle ages, and they were a common form of government in medieval boroughs.[1] As with many aspects of medieval urban history, the debate has long antecedents, and historians have tried to establish whether or not these governments were becoming more exclusive and less accountable in the fifteenth century.[2]

The oligarchies of York, Beverley and Hull, are focussed upon here. I propose to explore some of the factors which directly determined the size and degree of openness of their oligarchic councils; external influences; election systems; population size; the significance of ability, wealth, occupation and age in the selection of officers; and finally the growing political sophistication of townsmen in general and their reaction to oligarchy.

Structural oligarchies can readily be identified in many medieval boroughs and further qualifications can be added. Many oligarchies were plutocratic, some mercantile and the majority were probably self-perpetuating. The majority of English boroughs were governed by one of two systems: either an hierarchy of elected officials of which the most important were the mayor, or equivalent, sheriff/bailiff, and chamberlain/treasurer, plus one or more councils; or a council of twelve keepers/wardens who collectively fulfilled the functions of the elected officials plus outer councils.[3] In fifteenth-century Hull and York, both royal boroughs, government was by hierarchy plus councils: in York a mayor, two sheriffs and three chamberlains plus three councils; the twelve aldermen, the twenty four, and the forty eight. In Hull there was a mayor, one sheriff and two chamberlains, plus one council of twelve aldermen. Beverley was a seignorial borough, governed by twelve keepers or governors.[4]

There is no positive correlation between economic success and the charter rights of towns, as Steve Rigby demonstrated in his study of Boston and Grimsby.[5] Seignorial boroughs could prosper as much as their free rivals, although many failed. The form of a town's charter did not necessarily affect the degree of open or closeness of its government either, but it did influence the structure of government so that royal boroughs usually had a standard hierarchy of mayor, sheriffs or bailiffs, chamberlains and lesser officials. Seignorial boroughs were more varied, and might have variations such as twelve wardens or keepers; or the lord's steward or bailiff plus some burgesses.[6] Royal boroughs were not as open to direct manipulation by intermediate lords such as abbots, bishops and laymen but they were not beyond royal authority however large and powerful they might become. London and York both had their liberties suspended in the late fourteenth and early fifteenth centuries respectively, and in 1495, the York council was threatened with replacement by Henry VII if it could not govern the city.[7]

More commonly, royal recognition was sought by towns changing the structure of their governments, in some cases no doubt long after these had been put into effect, and similarly changes in election procedures were referred to the Crown or another seigneur for approval. However, sad, discreet, wise, or positively bursting with worship the members of town councils might have been, suitability to govern was only part of their means of legitimising their claim to authority. The approval of a higher authority at some point was as important.

One might expect to find outsiders directly manipulating urban politics to get their supporters elected to office, but such interference is difficult to establish. Patricia Jalland demonstrated the independence of northern boroughs in choosing their own MPs and few occasions of external meddling were recorded.[8] In 1481 Edward IV had a *contretemps* with the York council over the dismissal of John Eaglesfield as swordbearer and finally accepted its decision. Henry VII tried to get his man Richard Green appointed recorder of York in 1485 and 1486, during the illness and after the death of Miles Metcalfe who had been a supporter of Richard III. The council successfully parried that attempt to erode its autonomy, but accepted Henry's advice in the 1490s on law and order measures.

In 1471 Edward IV chose the mayor in a disputed election but apart from hints in 1483 that one mayoral candidate in York was partisan to Richard of Gloucester, and the sycophantic behaviour of the York council towards Richard during the preceding years,[9] there is little to suggest that external influences played much part in shaping the membership of the councils of any of the three towns. Maybe their loyalty was never doubted and anxiety was aroused only during national conflicts.

Hierarchic systems of government ensure oligarchy, but the bureaucracy of the modern pluralist state and a democratic electoral system, bolstered by public accountability, ought to provide checks on the autocratic tendency of oligarchies. In medieval towns such checks were generally absent. Concentric rings of councils were rarely summoned: the York forty eight and the Beverley thirty six and forty eight, (there was no outer council in Hull), appear fleetingly in the records as spectators to the inner councils' actions. In the late 15th century, as we shall see, the ruling groups in Beverley and York, began to involve more people in the process of elections of officials but not the outer councils *per se*. The role of the commonalty, i.e. the non-office-holding burgesses, was to approve the oligarchs' decisions.

The test of how open or closed an oligarchy was, is not simply to count how many mayors or keepers were members of particular families or occupations, but is to describe the degree of control exercised over the procedure for electing those men. If this discussion implies that there was usually pressure from an excess of ambitious individuals to get elected to higher offices, that is because most regulations were concerned to prevent repeated service. If they were self-perpetuating oligarchs, at least they all wanted a turn at the top.

As briefly as possible then, what do we know about the process of elections in these three towns. Hull and York will be discussed together because both were governed by a standard hierarchy, and Beverley will be discussed separately. The mayor of York was elected, at least from 1343, to serve from 3 February and his actual election was on 15 January. From 1392 and possibly earlier, the retiring mayor nominated two or three aldermen, from whom the commonalty, that is all the burgesses, elected one to serve as mayor, and he took his oath in the presence of the commonalty. In 1372 it was decided that no-one was to be elected who had held office within the last eight years, but the regulation was not kept, and after 1392 no-one was to be re-elected until all of the aldermen had served.[10]

As a consequence of riots in 1464 Edward IV ordered that the procedure should be changed. The retiring mayor was to summon the searchers of each craft on 14 January to order them to ensure that all their members should come to the Guildhall on election day, 15 January. The craftsmen were to nominate two aldermen, neither of whom had been mayor twice, nor had been mayor during the five preceding years. The nominations were then to be handed to the mayor and the council, which included the recorder and common clerk. The mayor and council were to vote secretly and their votes were to be counted by the non-voting officials. In 1516 the mayor claimed two votes, but whether this was or had been customary, was not recorded. The aldermen with the highest number of votes would be declared on 3 February.[11]

Further unrest led to another change in procedure in 1473 whereby the crafts chose one alderman directly, who was to serve as mayor.[12] In 1489, perhaps as a consequence of a rising by the commons of the rural areas which evoked a response in York and led to the occupation of the city by the country rebels, the council petitioned the king to have the 1464 procedure restored. Henry VII agreed in January 1490 in time for that year's election, and confirmed the procedure in 1492.[13] Further election riots occurred in 1504 but there was no change in the election procedure until 1517, ironically as a consequence of jealousies amongst the aldermen. Thereafter an election committee, composed of craft representatives and twenty-eight senior searchers, was to nominate the mayoral candidates.[14]

The mayor was assisted by three bailiffs up to 1396. The bailiffs were elected for 29 September, to coincide with the Exchequer's financial year, and at least from 1357 the bailiffs chose their own successors. The men chosen had to have two pledges each as security and once elected were presented to the mayor and commonalty for approval. The bailiffs chose their subordinate officials themselves.[15] After 1396 the three bailiffs were replaced by two sheriffs, who became solely responsible for two new courts, a court in Ainsty and a monthly county court. They were responsible for accounting for the farm of the city and for collecting the city's revenues; tolls, rents and court issues. The sheriffs were elected on 21 September and took office on 29 September. They were elected by those 'to whom the election pertained', members of the council who deliberated in the inner chamber of the Guildhall while the mayor and commonalty waited outside to be told of the choice.[16] At least from 1418 the sheriffs were members of the twenty four and remained as members after their year in office was ended. Their election was the key to the mayoralty since new aldermen were chosen exclusively from the twenty four, and in 1504 some members of the commonalty asked to be allowed to nominate candidates but were refused by the mayor and council. In 1499, the mayor had to be reminded not to select new aldermen on his own.[17]

The last important annually filled office was that of chamberlain. There were three chamberlains, increased to four in 1483, six in 1487, and reduced to three again in 1509.[18] In 1376 the chamberlains' election was moved from 29 September to 3 February to coincide with the mayoral election. They were chosen by the new mayor and council on that day and after 1475 election to the office was restricted to those men who had previously served as bridgemaster.[19]

The mayor and council were assisted by a number of non-elected officials, appointed by the council. The council comprised the twelve aldermen and the twenty four. In the 15th century two aldermen were associated with each of the six wards in the city. Aldermen served until they died or were too old or ill to attend meetings, and vacancies were filled by the remaining aldermen choosing a replacement from the twenty four within four days. The twenty four were, of course, excluded from these deliberations. After 1418 membership was limited to ex-sheriffs. It seems unlikely that the twenty four often had twenty-four members, as new members were recruited only from the office of sheriff, and numbers fluctuated above and below twenty-four depending on the supply of ex-sheriffs, willing to attend.[20]

The structure of Hull's government was similar to that of York. The mayor was the central figure in government and he was elected annually at least from 1434, by a secret ballot on 30 September. The full procedure was recorded for the first time in 1443. The aldermen nominated two of their number, one of whom was chosen by the burgesses as mayor. It was ordered in 1440 that no-one should serve for two successive years. The mayor was assisted by two bailiffs, elected annually on the same day as the mayor, at least from 1434. In 1440, when Hull achieved county status, the bailiffs were replaced by one sheriff. According to the charter of 1440, those who had previously served as a bailiff were excluded from the shrievalty, but one of the bailiffs in 1439–40, William Spencer, was elected the first sheriff. The sheriff was to be elected by the burgesses from among themselves but by 1443 the nomination of two candidates was in the hands of the aldermen, and one candidate was chosen by the burgesses. The town's financial affairs were the responsibility of two chamberlains, elected annually after 1443 from four nominees of the aldermen.[22]

The mayor was advised by a council which had existed informally since 1339. In 1351, for example, the mayor and bailiffs were assisted by the *probi homines* in approving craft legislation, and in 1356 the chamberlains were ordered not to make any payments or gifts without the assent of the mayor and six of the best burgesses. In 1379 it was decided that eight burgesses should be elected annually 'd'asser ove le maier' and bailiffs, and of the eight elected in that year, three had served previously as mayor, one as bailiff, one later served as mayor, and one, Thomas Swynefleet, was married to the niece of a former mayor, Geoffrey Hanby. Thereafter no official was to be re-elected within three years.[23]

In 1440 the council was given formal status as a council of twelve aldermen, whose function was to advise the mayor, expressing only their own opinions, and giving honest advice as they would expect to receive as mayor in turn. If the mayor ignored their advice he could be fined. Aldermen served for life and from 1443 vacancies were to be filled by the burgesses choosing one of the two candidates nominated by the remaining aldermen.[24] The aldermen were associated in pairs with the six wards of the city.[25] There was no formal outer council as in York and Beverley, from which aldermanic candidates were drawn, but from time to time an informal group was summoned, composed of those who had served as sheriff and as chamberlains, and those who were 'likely to serve' as chamberlains.[26] Craft guilds were slow to emerge in Hull and apparently played no formal role in elections but 'worthy' burgesses, chosen by their fellows, assisted the common clerk in taking votes at civic elections. In 1458/9, the candidates themselves chose the men to go 'with the book' amongst the voters. The ballot was secret in Hull, and in 1456 burgesses had to be reminded to vote once only.[27]

There are several points to emphasise. First the supremacy of the aldermen in both towns as the pool of candidates for the mayoralty; in controlling the nomination of candidates to the major offices (the mayoralty and shrievalty in Hull and shrievalty only in York) and in directly appointing their own successors. Second, the greater degree of participation allowed to the burgesses of Hull in choosing between candidates for vacancies on the aldermen's bench and in electing one of the shrieval candidates by 1443, compared to the lateness, 1504, of the York burgesses in asking for a role in the nomination of their sheriffs. Third, the changes introduced in York were the result of continuous, targetted pressure from the burgesses whereas no equivalent unrest was recorded in Hull.[28]

Further comparisons between York and Hull can usefully be made before turning to Beverley. Self-perpetuation was clearly integral to the election processes in York and Hull, even though greater participation was possible in Hull, but how widely did the offices circulate? Between 1300 and 1364, there had been only fourteen mayors in York, some serving for several years at a time; the most persistent being Nicholas de Langton, jnr., who was mayor from 1322–33 and again from 1338–41. His father had been mayor previously and his son John was mayor from 1352–63. The Langtons derived most of their wealth from their rural estates and could be described as the remnants of the *viri hereditarii*, more common in York's government in the thirteenth century. Compared to the repeated mayoralties of the fourteenth century and possibilities of family dominance, the office circulated widely in the fifteenth century when eighty-five different mayors served.[29] They were increasingly more experienced in government and all but three of the mayors serving between 1400 and 1509 had enjoyed previous service; seventy as both chamberlain and sheriff (87 per cent). Similarly 81 per cent of sheriffs serving between 1397 and 1509 had already served as chamberlain.

The situation in Hull was noticeably different to that in York, in that repeated mayoralties were common in both the fourteenth and fifteenth centuries. Up to 1399, 31 per cent of mayors had had two terms in office and between 1400 and 1509, 31 per cent of the mayors served twice. Of the fourteenth century mayors, 14 per cent served three or more times, and 16 per cent of the fifteenth-century mayors did so.[30] An ordinance was passed in 1460, forbidding a man from serving two successive terms as mayor, but otherwise there were no objections to repeated mayoralties.[31]

A high proportion of Hull mayors had also had previous experience in office. Of sixty seven fifteenth-century mayors, 88 per cent had served as bailiff or sheriff, and 52 per cent as both chamberlain and bailiff or sheriff. After 1440, when the information is fuller, the proportion is higher; 91 per cent served as bailiff or sheriff, and 60 per cent as both chamberlain and bailiff or sheriff.

Not only was repeated office-holding common in Hull, so was the willingness of individuals to serve in other minor offices, such as one of the four bailiffs of the Tripett, as coroner, and as one of the four auditors after their terms as chamberlain and sheriff.[32] Given the slightly greater participation of the Hull burgesses, the opposite situation might have been expected, but no objections to the oligarchy were recorded and elections apparently proceeded in Hull with none of the periodic outbursts experienced in York and Beverley. Recession affected Hull later than York and Beverley: not signifying in the town's records until the 1440s, whereas Beverley's economy was already slowing down by 1400 and York's by the 1410s.[33] Hull also had its accounts regularly scrutinised by four auditors,[34] which must have gone some way towards allaying suspicions of fraud and incompetence even though the auditors were generally former or future aldermen.

The dramatic difference between York and Hull might have been due to the more advanced political ambitions of the York burgesses and the legislation introduced to limit repeated office-holding. The push for wider circulation of offices began in York in the 1350s when the dynastic grip of John de Langton was challenged by the growing number of burgesses new, wealthy merchants spawned especially by the expanding cloth trade.[35] The tension between the new entrepreneurs and the old guard continued into the 1381 revolt, but legislation passed in 1372 had opened up the mayoralty.[36] By the fifteenth century ambition or at least criticism of the oligarchy, had passed on to others and it was popular pressure in 1464, 1473, 1489, 1504 and 1517, which brought about change in the procedure for electing the mayor.

A simpler explanation seems more likely. Civic office was restricted to burgesses, maybe as few as 50 or even 22 per cent of the adult males.[37] Hull with a population of maybe, 2,500 by the end of the fifteenth century compared with York's possible 8,000, simply had a smaller pool of eligible candidates to draw from.[38] Government could only continue in Hull if men served as mayor, sheriff, auditor, but rarely chamberlain, more than once or twice. The major constraint then was demographic, and not simply a difference in ambitions.

What of Beverley, with its population of 4,000 or so in 1377?[39] Fortunately the case of Beverley introduces further elements. The town was governed by twelve keepers, later known as governors, under the bailiff appointed by the town's seigneur, the archbishop of York. Four attempts were made in the fourteenth century to introduce a triumvirate of an alderman and two chamberlains.[40] At least from 1345 the keepers were elected annually on 25 April by the burgesses with the assent of the retiring keepers and with the archbishop's representative present. Those elected were to be 'the most honest and wealthy men' and the burgesses could elect whomsoever they wished within that qualification.[41] In 1359 the keepers changed the procedure in the so-called Magna Carta which they issued, perhaps as a result of the election riots of 1356.[42] They severely limited the role of the burgesses by giving the retiring keepers the right to nominate eighteen of the 'more sufficient men' of Beverley, excluding those who had served as keepers within the preceding three years, and the burgesses elected twelve as the keepers. Burgesses who absented themselves on election day were liable to a fine of 6d. and those who refused to hold office were liable to a fine of 40s.[43]

Hints that the system was being abused appeared in 1457, when members of the commons demanded that the elections should be conducted according to the customs of the borough as set out in the Magna Carta and on the traditional 25 April. Maybe the abuse continued, in spite of the keepers' approval of the demands in 1457, since the keepers sensed trouble and issued several law and order regulations in 1461, prohibiting unauthorised meetings in the Guildhall or the friaries.[44] In the same year, the keepers decided to be called 'aldermen' or 'governors'. Rioting erupted during the 1465 election, but no reforms were introduced. By 1498, a new council, the thirty six, was mentioned for the first time, and the new keepers were being elected from twelve of its members, twelve others nominated by the retiring keepers and certain burgesses 'assisting in the Guildhall'. None of these twenty-four nominees were to have served in the preceeding two years. A further six worshipful men who had not previously held office completed the list of thirty candidates and the burgesses had to choose the twelve new keepers. Because 'the whole town' felt that the number of candidates was too large, the number was reduced to eighteen in 1498 by excluding the twelve candidates with previous experience who were not members of the thirty six.[45]

The keepers were collectively responsible for the town's financial administration and shared out most of the other responsibilities between them, assisted by minor, paid officials.

An outer council had emerged by the mid fifteenth century and lists of some of its members have survived for 1465 and 1467. It was composed of former keepers and the aldermen of fourteen craft guilds and was known as the forty eight. In 1465 there were forty-five members present with the twelve keepers and only seventeen in 1467. The names were simply listed and were not a record of attendance at any particular meeting in 1465 or in 1467. The forty eight had to attend the Guildhall when summoned by the keepers and in 1467 the penalty for non-attendance was 6d.[46]

Another outer council had emerged in Beverley by 1498 and by 1536 it comprised the twelve keepers and twenty-four 'assistants'. It may have replaced the forty eight or, from 1498, there were three councils in all; the twelve keepers alone, the thirty six incorporating the keepers, and the forty eight. If a member of the thirty six fell ill, died, or had to resign, the burgesses chose a replacement.[47] Although repeated office holding was therefore common, it did not prevent the keepership from circulating widely. The relatively large number of men required each year, compared with the six or so required in York and Hull, meant that repeated office holding was inevitable in a town with a small population and a man could be fined £2 for refusing office.[48] Of the 347 keepers identified between 1300 and 1502,[49] just over one half, 197, served once only, and just under half, 150, served as keeper several times. Eighty-eight served three or more times, the majority of them serving three to five times. In the thirty-five years between 1436 and 1470, when the names of keepers have survived for consecutive years, there were only a few occasions when the three-year restriction was abused.

One of the consequences of the restriction which is apparent between 1436 and 1470 was that groups of men regularly served together. For example, Thomas Wilton, William Cockerell, Roger Cockerham, Guy Bridekirk, John Ulceby, Ralph Ward and John Redesham served together as keepers in 1439 and again in 1443. That meant that in those two years over half the keepers were the same. William Northrop, Stephen Tilson and William Morethwayte served together as keepers three times in 1445, 1449 and 1453. Ralph Ward served with John Ulceby snr. in 1439 and 1443, and with John Ulceby jnr. in 1455. This continuity can be demonstrated several times during the 1436–1470 period, and reveals a continuity of government comparable with that of the aldermanic benches of York and Hull. It is remarkable how often the same individuals occur within associated groups and suggests that effective coalitions within Beverley's ruling elite were possible.[50]

It would appear that although access to the oligarchy was reasonably open to all burgesses, there was a recognised elite which constituted a core of experienced men within the twelve, three or four of whom were keepers in any given year. An examination of the involvement of families, and not just of individuals, confirms this conclusion. Just as the names of certain men occur several times, so members of the same family appear regularly among the keepers. Forty-eight families produced more than one keeper between 1300 and 1502, and the involvement of some of these families lasted for a considerable period. The outstanding example is the Coppendale family,[51] which was active in Beverley government for at least 150 years. Nine members of the family served as keeper between 1345 and 1465, six of them once only. The other three, Stephen, Thomas and John, served respectively four times between 1388 and 1408, five times between 1402 and 1422, and seven times between 1437 and 1469. There were Holmes active in government for nearly 150 years between 1306 and 1433, but it was a common name and they were not necessarily all from the same family. Twelve families were active for over forty years, some continuously such as the Tirwhits, four of whom served between 1344 and 1421, or the Slefords, two of whom served between 1399 and 1467. Some families were active sporadically, such as the Atkinsons, three of whom served between 1366 and 1502.

In addition to the long careers of some individuals like William Spencer, active for thirty-three years, or Thomas Swanland, active for thirty years, the persistence of an elite within the twelve, and the continuing dynastic tradition of certain families, meant that the burgesses of Beverley saw the same names elected keeper time and time again.[52]

Dynasties were not unusual in English towns and the persistence of family names was not always due to direct succession. Late-fifteenth early-sixteenth century Totnes, in Devon, was invigorated by the recruitment of the country cousins of established families into the town.[53] In early-sixteenth century Chester, there was a similar pattern of 'dynastic' office-holding, maintained by new arrivals from country branches of city families. Indeed several Chester mayors retained firm links with the county, deriving as much income from family estates as they probably did from trade.[54] Perhaps the existence of long-term dynasties in late-medieval towns has more to tell us about the nature of their economies than about their politics.

If the circulation of offices depended as much on the size of the population of a town as it did upon legislation, what determined the choice of one individual rather than another? Occupation, and therefore wealth, was clearly a factor, most particularly for members of the council and for men serving as sheriff and mayor. Quite apart from considerations of the expenditure expected on hospitality and generally maintaining oneself as befitted a senior civic official, they had to be men who could afford to absent themselves frequently from their employment regularly throughout the year, and in the case of the mayor and sheriff, during each week to run the borough courts. Chamberlains attended council meetings rarely, and by invitation. But sheriffs, mayor and aldermen could be summoned in York as little as fourteen times as in 1493–4, or as often as fifty-four times, as in 1493–4.[55] The mayor and aldermen, as in Hull, also served as ex officio justices of the peace. Craftsmen with day-to-day commitments were clearly less able to devote so much time to council business and it is no surprise to find many medieval town councils dominated by merchants. To judge by the number of times regulations were repeated in York, imposing fines for absence and late arrival, not even the successful always displayed a proper sense of duty![56]

So merchants, the more successful traders, and a handful of wealthy craftsmen were obvious choices for the higher offices; apparently anyone could become a chamberlain, although in the late fifteenth century some towns did try to ensure some competence, by insisting on previous service in a lesser office such as bridgemaster in York, from 1475, and levelooker in Chester, from 1541.[57] Just as today, the solution to economic decline was sought in improving the quality of management.

Apart from previous experience, wealth, suitability of occupation (never any butchers in York, but generally innkeepers became acceptable),[58] were there other considerations which influenced a man's progress up the *cursus honorum*? Reasonably full records in York after 1476[59] make it possible to focus more sharply on individual political careers. Not all sheriffs chose to take their automatic place in the twenty-four after their term of office, but for those who did and became aldermen, their promotion usually came within ten years and for 50 per cent, within six years. Selection seems to have had little to do with ability or reliability since there were men whose attendance at council meetings was exemplary but they never became aldermen. William Tate, a tailor and sheriff in 1478, attended almost every meeting of council until 1503 but was not favoured with a seat on the aldermannic bench. Likewise Thomas Allen, a baker and sheriff in 1470 attended regularly until he was too ill in 1500. What impact one wonders, did the presence of a core of stalwarts have upon the city's politics, or were they mere committee fodder?

Whatever they were, they witnessed many contemporaries promoted to the aldermen's bench after very desultory attendance as members of the twenty four. Few aldermen had to wait for more than four years to be elected mayor; the average was two years. A notable exception was John Hagg, a merchant, who waited eighteen years after serving as a sheriff to become an alderman, and he never served as mayor. Most merchants wishing to journey up the *cursus honorum* could expect to serve as a chamberlain when they were between twenty-six and thirty-six years old, as a sheriff two or three years later, and as mayor six to eleven years after that; on average twenty-two years after becoming a freeman of York.

The absence of reliable records of freeman entry into Hull and Beverley makes such a close analysis difficult, but the impression is that in Hull men were elected chamberlain within ten years of becoming free, but election as bailiff or sheriff did not follow as quickly as in York; the majority waiting a further ten years but 40 per cent of the merchants traced became sheriff within five years. The mayoralty was achieved on average within ten years, but there was no pattern to their subsequent terms as mayor, which could occur between one and twenty years later.[60]

The names of the Beverley keepers survive for consecutive years between 1436 and 1470.[61] Those who served several times could expect to hold office every four years or so until they died. Very few men were re-elected within three years of their preceeding term, and given the collective nature of Beverley's government, long-service with accumulated experience and consequent respect was the only goal. Since Beverley did not return MPs, there was not even the carrot of jaunting up to London, as there was for successful York and Hull men. 75 per cent of York MPs had served as mayor, and 66 per cent of the Hull MPs. Men from all three towns were liable to be put on royal commissions of array, oyer and terminer, dykes and ditches throughout Yorkshire.

The hierarchies of York and Hull tempted some ambitious men to get to the top rapidly, and they stand out easily amongst the majority. Nicholas Lancaster, for example, served as mayor without previous experience of civic office, within thirteen years of becoming a freeman in 1472. The rise of Nicholas Blackburn jnr. was even more rapid and he was elected mayor only seven years after becoming free in 1422. He had served as a chamberlain and a sheriff. Both Lancaster and Blackburn were sons of established York merchants, and may have owed their success to their fathers' reputations. Blackburn's father had served as mayor and died a very wealthy man leaving at least £600 in 1432. Lancaster's father was engaged in overseas trade but did not hold office. Sons who survived and followed their fathers into local government were uncommon but John Gyllyot jnr. was another who had an exceptional political career, perhaps as a consequence of his parentage, and of his own financial success. He became a chamberlain in 1482, within one year of his entry, sheriff two years later, and mayor for the first time within six years. In 1509 he left at least £700 and a large urban estate.[62] His son Peter looked as though he might follow an unusual family tradition when he became a chamberlain in 1522, one year after he had become a freeman, but he died three years later without holding another office.

Many careers progressed in fits and starts but the high flyers moved rapidly from office to office. In Hull, Edmund Coppendale, free in 1450, was elected chamberlain one year later, sheriff two years after that in 1453, and mayor six years later in 1459. However, he was elected mayor for a second time in 1477, eighteen years after his first mayoralty. William Goodknapp was another high flyer. He was free in 1488, elected a chamberlain in 1490, sheriff in 1493, and mayor for the first time in 1497. He was elected mayor for a second term in 1503, but was in Calais at the time and Robert Garner was elected in his place seven weeks later.[63]

It will be apparent that to get close to the heights of civic power in York and Hull, a man usually had to wait until he was fairly old, by contemporary standards, and indeed, merchants as a group had a longer life-expectancy than the average (two thirds for whom entry dates and dates of death are known, lived over thirty years after becoming free, that is to an age of fifty-two, and one-fifth for over forty years).[64] Death most commonly occurred between the ages of fifty and sixty. What is not so obvious is whether or not there was a particular regard for age, since those rapidly promoted were not hindered by their youth. The aldermanic bench was undoubtedly a repository of wisdom and clear thinking, and in Beverley there was a group of *venerabiles*,[65] who were consulted from time to time like the Delphic oracle. Probably, the twenty to twenty-five year wait to become mayor was necessary, while a man worked up his business to the state where he could maintain it through cursory supervision or had accumulated sufficient wealth to be able to spend much of his time governing. So much for experience and financial independence. Which brings me to my last consideration; the reaction of those being governed to their oligarchies. We must conclude that in Hull no-one profoundly resented their rulers, since no co-ordinated opposition was recorded,[66] even though insulting the mayor was punishable with a fine or imprisonment, as in York, and equivalent punishments were imposed on people insulting the Beverley keepers.[67] There is evidence in York that individual resentments against the oligarchs were probably common, and ranged from feelings of helplessness by ordinary townsmen in legal cases involving aldermen to the actual murder of an ex-mayor, William Wells, in 1487.[68] The sort of group action which flared up periodically in York in the second half of the fifteenth century, implies something more. The revolts usually occurred on the mayor's election day, when the crowd felt they had some leverage by not rubber-stamping the proceedings. There were many other aspects which cannot be considered here, but a constant theme was disatisfaction with the running of York's corporate finances, the protection of common land, and the extravagance of the mayor and council.

The only way the commons could make specific criticism and suggestions known, was by petitioning the council and they did so on at least four recorded occasions, 1475, 1484, 1490 and 1504. The content of the 1504 petition is not known.[69] In 1475 they suggested that only experienced men, ex-bridgemasters should be elected chamberlain, and that only men able in goods and discretion should be elected bridgemasters. In 1484, the commons' demands suggest a general dissatisfaction with the quality of the government and the conduct of its officials. The common seal was only to be delivered with the commons' assent; aldermen were no longer to act as captain of the city troops because of the cost; officers of the mace and sword were not to sell their offices, and successors had to be chosen by the council with the commons' assent; the mayor's officials were to make sure the streets were properly cleaned weekly or be sacked; and finally forestalling by hucksters and innkeepers, and the sale of poultry by countryfolk door-to-door was to be stopped and all goods to be sold by them only in the Thursday market.[70] In 1490 they asked for the mayor's fee to be reduced from £50 to £20; for the recorder to be paid no more than 20d; for no legal counsel to be retained by the city; for the mayoral accounts since 1469 to be audited; and for those responsible for excessive expenses to be made to repay them. The first demand is hardly surprising since the mayor at the time, John Gyllyot, jnr., became an extremely wealthy man and in 1509 left over £400 to endow a chantry, a sum which could easily have cleared the city's debts overnight.[71]

Parallel to these complaints, was a suspicion that the grazing rights of the burgesses on common pasture around the city were being lost, either through the incompetence of the council, or through its over-willingness to compromise or give in to gentry pressure. Similar suspicions surfaced in other late medieval towns.[72] In York the frustrations of the commons rose to such a peak during a dispute with the Vicars Choral over grazing, that a full-scale riot broke out in 1494, headed interestingly by the weavers, and the mayor and council were threatened by Henry VII with replacement.[73]

Similar unrest broke out in Beverley in 1423, 1457 and 1465, and according to the burgesses' petition of 1457, in that year at least, disatisfaction centred on their demands that elections should be conducted according to custom.[74] There is no doubt that the economic recession in both Beverley and York fuelled political unrest, but what exactly did the commons want? Did they simply want better government or 'ballot-box' control over their rulers? Or did they want a formal role in decision- making, or indeed an end to oligarchy?

It has been suggested that generally 'most subjects demanded only the traditional and accepted right of consultation and objected only to the traditional evils of peculation and misgovernment'.[75] Such a judgement was probably appropriate of the commons of Beverley and Hull, although the former shared in community ambition to be free of the archbishop as seigneur. But events in York imply more radical objectives. Since a consequence of one of the early election day confrontations in York in 1464 was a change to a more representative procedure, we must infer that greater participation in elections was an issue. As we have seen subsequent unrest lead to further changes, all focussing on the mayoralty, and it was not until 1504, that the commons of York (whoever they were exactly), targetted the key office of sheriff,[76] going so far as to send a deputation, led by a merchant Robert Whetley, to the archbishop of York on 16 August, asking if they could have a share in the election of the sheriffs. The council stoutly defended the *status quo*, but must have been feeling a little shaken, since the commons had hired a lawyer to present their bill of complaints in April that year. Following the abortive meeting with the archbishop, Robert Whetley kept up the pressure, this time appearing before the mayor on 26 August as the council was making arrangements to collect two royal aids, to ask how individuals had been assessed for the levy.[77]

The growing sophistication of the York commons, or one or two of them, prevailed. In the end, the role of the craft guild as representatives of the wider body of burgesses was formally recognised. Throughout the commonalty's struggle for greater participation, the searchers of all the crafts had been increasingly used as a representative body to liaise with the council. From 1464 a committee of searchers chose two aldermen as mayoral candidates, and one as mayor from 1473. In 1489 the council relied on them to encourage a peaceful election. It is probable that the searchers in their turn constituted an establishment within the commonalty, since their nomination was often in the hands of the retiring searchers or of the alderman of the guild. Nonetheless they did constitute a recognisable group and there is evience to suggest that although the council was not prepared to concede a more significant constitutional role to the commonalty, it was prepared to be more co-operative with the searchers. On election day 1505 the searchers were allowed to present several bills of complaint to the council, one of which was concerned with the trading rights of aliens within the city. Further bills were allowed to be presented in 1509 and on those occasions at least the searchers were being allowed to offer advice on the commonalty's behalf, instead of waiting on the wishes of the council.[78] After a disputed election provoked by rival aldermen in 1517, Henry VIII decided that in future a newly constituted common council, with a stronger craft representation, should act as a check on the inner council of aldermen and the twenty four. The new common council was to replace the former outer council of the forty eight and was to consist of two representatives from each of the thirteen major crafts and one representative from each of the fifteen minor crafts. This body was to be augmented by the twenty-eight senior searchers of the crafts at election time, when the nomination of candidates for the offices of mayor and sheriff and for vacancies on the aldermanic bench, was in its control.[79]

The commonalty had achieved a constitutional victory. Although it was still represented by the craft guilds, membership of the common council was technically open to any craftsman and was not confined to the craft establishment, i.e. the searchers. The membership of the nominating committee established in 1464 had not been specified but after 1517 all craft guilds, including the minor ones, had to be represented. Membership of the forty eight had similarly never been defined but after 1517 most of the craft guilds had to be represented on the common council. However, its role was no greater than that of the old forty-eight, and was still summoned only when the mayor and the inner council decided.

It was not simply a matter of the political determination of an ambitious occupational group which dictated the nature of oligarchy in late medieval towns.[80] Fluid societies tend to be more aware of complex social and occupational distinctions, and 'arrivistes' to be defensive. Was an oligarchy which allowed a wide circulation of offices, more likely to maintain a 'class' cohesion to provide stability beyond the lifetimes of individuals? Oligarchies varied even when structurally similar due to a variety of factors; some functional, others contrived. York and Hull provide salutory examples of oligarchies similar in structure, yet dramatically different in respect to the circulation of their major offices. Disatisfaction became more sophisticated in York during the course of the fifteenth century, as the commons tempered their mass protests with detailed petitions suggesting solutions as well as identifying problems. But why was the myth of the able governing ably questioned in York and Beverley and not in Hull? It could have been because the economic recession bit more deeply in York and Beverley and perhaps the more advanced craft organisation[81] there developed political skills amongst the commons. It may have been simply that in small towns such as Hull expectations were lower, that demographic constraints made repeated office-holding unavoidable, and their oligarchs conceded a degree of access to political participation denied the commons in York. Slight though they were, such concessions may well have been sufficient to convince the burgesses of Hull that their rulers also believed that they 'ben all one bodye corporate . . . and ben all inlike prevaliged of the commonalte which has borne non office in the cite.'[82]

Notes

1   S. Reynolds, 'Medieval urban history and the history of political though', *Urban History Yearbook* (1982), pp. 14–23; and *An Introduction to the History of English Medieval Towns* (1977), pp. 176–7. See also S.L. Thrupp, *The Merchant Class of Medieval London*, paperback edition (1962), pp. 14–27.
2   E.F. Jacob, *The Fifteenth Century* (Oxford, 1961), p. 385; C.J. Hammer, 'Anatomy of an Oligarchy; the Oxford Town Council in the Fifteenth and Sixteenth Centuries', *JBS*, xviii (1979), pp. 1–27; C. Platt, *The English Medieval Town* (1976), pp. 119–24, 190; P. Clark and P. Slack, *English Towns in Transition, 1500–1700* (Oxford, 1976), pp. 128–9, S.H. Rigby, above, pp. 64ff.
3   A.S. Green, *Town Life in the Fifteenth Century* (1894), vol. II, chapters 8–16; Platt, *English Medieval Town*, pp. 119–122; Reynolds, *An Introduction*, p. 173. For single town studies see A. Rogers, 'Late Medieval Stamford: A Study of the Town Council, 1465–92', in A. Everitt, ed., *Perspectives in English Urban History* (1973); B. Wilkinson, *The Medieval Council of Exeter*, History of Exeter Research Group, Monograph no. 4 (Manchester, n.d.).
4   K.J. Allison, 'Medieval Hull', in K.J. Allison, ed. *The Victoria History of the Counties of England. Yorkshire East Riding*, I (1969), pp. 29–37. [Hereafter *VCH Hull*] E. Miller,

'Medieval York', in P. M. Tillott, ed., *Ibid. The City of York* (1961), pp. 70–2, 74, 77–8. [Hereafter *VCH York*]. A.F. Leach, *Beverley Town Documents*, Selden Society, XIV (1900), pp. xxi, xxiii. [Hereafter *Bev. Town Docs.*]

5   S.H. Rigby, 'Boston and Grimsby in the Middle Ages: an administrative contrast,' *JMH*, 10 (1984), p. 51.

6   A. Ballard and J. Tait, *British Borough Charters, 1216–1307* (1939), pp. xvii–cii; Reynolds, *An Introduction*, pp. 115–6.

7   M. McKisack, *The Fourteenth Century* (Oxford, 1959), pp. 467–8; A. Raine, ed., *Y[ork] C[ivic] R[ecords]*, II, Yorks. Arch. Soc. Rec. ser., ciii (1941), pp. 115–6.

8   P. Jalland, 'Revolution in Northern Borough Representation', *Northern History*, 11 (1976).

9   *VCH York*, pp. 61, 63; *YCR* I, YAS Rec. ser. xcviii (1939), pp. 48–9, 68–9. In 1476, a dismissed common clerk appealed to Percy for support, but the York council successfully enlisted Richard of Gloucester's aid, in maintaining its right to freely elect its own officials. *YCR*, I, pp. 8–11, 15–16.

10   York City RO C/Y f. 49v.; M. Sellars, ed. *York M[emorandum] B[ook]*, vol. I, Surtees Soc., cxx (1912), p. 116; vol. II, Surtees Soc. cxxv (1915), p. 255.

11   *CPR 1461–7*, p. 366; *YCR*, III, YAS Rec. ser. cvi (1942), p. 52.

12   *CPR 1476–7*, p. 416.

13   *YCR*, I pp. 50, 54–5; York City RO House Book 7 f. 22v.

14   *VCH York*, p. 137; *YCR* III, pp. 51–60.

15   York City R.O. C/Y f. 313; *VCH York*, pp. 71–2; *York MB II*, p. 259.

16   *York MB II*, pp. 52, 74–5, 259; House Book 9, f. 50.; *VCH York*, p. 72.

17   *York MB II*, p. 75: House Book 9, f. 19v.; *YCR II*, p. 141; III, p. 8.

18   F. Collins, ed., *Register of the Freemen of the City of York*, I, Surtees Soc. xcvi (1897), p. 207 *et seq.*: *YCR*, I, p. 87.

19   *York MB I*, pp. 33–4; York City RO House Book 7, f. 109.

20   *Ibid.*, pp. 75, 258, 261; House Books 8, f. 37v., 9, f. 27v.

21   Hull City RO BRE 1: p. 164; *CPR 1441–1516*, pp. 180–1.

22   *VCH Hull*, pp. 31–3; *CChR 1427–1516*, pp. 8–11; *CPR 1441–6*, pp. 180–1.

23   Hull City RO BRE 1: pp. 90, 170, 173, 210, 271.

24   *CPR 1441–6*, pp. 170–1; BRE 1: p. 13, BRG 1: f. 13v.

25   E.g. BRB 1: ff. 10, 69–70.

26   E.g. BRB 1: ff. 67, 77v., 81.

27   *VCH Hull*, p. 36; BRE 1: p. 164; BRE 2: ff. 93 (i), (ii); BRB 1: f. 55v.

28   The Hull records are curiously silent when it comes to popular protest. The changes introduced in 1379, were undoubtedly due to pressure to widen participation. Continued frustration may partly explain the involvement of Hull men in the troubles of 1381, but as the record notes only a few names in passing, it is not clear how far the town witnessed any violence, nor that the individuals were protesting about anything more than the government's tax demands. R.B. Dobson, 'The Risings in York, Beverley and Scarborough, 1380–1381', in R.H. Hilton and T.H. Aston, eds. *The English Rising of 1381* (1984), p. 117. However, at least £400 were demanded from Hull by the Crown between 1397 and 1400, twice the city's annual expenditure, but no disturbances were recorded. E. Gillett and K.A. MacMahon, *A History of Hull* (1980), p. 63; *CPR 1396–9*, p. 181, *1399–1401*, pp. 209, 353.

29   *VCH York*, pp. 71–2.

30   These calculations have been made from lists based on the York *Freemen's Rolls*, the returns of sheriffs in PRO *Lists and Indexes*, IX, and the Hull Bench Books, and corporation deeds.

31   Hull City RO BRE 1 p. 21.

32   For these offices, see *VCH Hull*, pp. 33–4; BRB: 1 f. 32. Edmund Coppendale was an auditor at least ten times, and first served one year after his term as sheriff. Thomas

Etton was another willing auditor and served at least eleven times. BRB 1 ff. 46, 49, 65v., 72v., 80, 95v., 107, 110v., 113, 116, 120v., 127v., 129v., 132, 142.

33 J. Kermode, 'Merchants, Overseas Trade, and Urban Decline: York, Beverley and Hull c. 1380–1500', *Northern History*, xxxiii (1987), p. 55.

34 Hull City RO BRB 1 f. 23.

35 For the figures see *VCH York, pp. 114–6.*

36 *York City RO C/Y f. 313v.; CPR 1364–7*, p. 208. In 1372 it was agreed that no-one should be re-elected mayor until eight years had elapsed since he had last served. *York MB I*, p. 16.

37 J.N. Bartlett, 'The Expansion and Decline of York in the Later Middle Ages', *EcHR*. 2nd ser. xii (1952–3), p. 22; J. Leggett, 'The 1377 Lay Poll Tax Return for the City of York', *YAJ* xliii (1971), p. 170.

38 In 1442 there were about 356 burgesses in Hull, BRG 1 ff. 16–19; comprising maybe 29 per cent of an adult male population of 1,250. The population was about 2,500 in 1377 and in the mid 16th century. *VCH Hull*, p. 157; J.C. Russell, *British Medieval Population* (Albuquerque, 1948), p. 141.

39 Russell, *British Medieval Population*, p. 141.

40 In 1382, royal orders confirming the re-institution of the government by twelve keepers, after the imposition of a triumvirate during the 1380–81 unrest, referred to two previous occasions when triumvirates had ruled. North Humberside R.O. Beverley Cartulary f. 18. An alderman and two chamberlains governed the town in 1385 and 1386, Account Roll 1386.

41 Beverley Cartulary f. 16; G. Poulson, *Beverlac: or the Antiquities and History of the Town of Beverley, in the County of York* (Beverley, 1829), pp. 126–8.

42 Beverley Cartulary, f. 31.

43 Beverley Cartulary ff. 6, 16.

44 Great Guild Book ff. 7v., 21.

45 *Ibid.* ff. 7v., 21, 26.

46 Beverley Governors' Minute Book ff. 76, 191v., 206.

47 Great Guild Book ff. 26, 27v.

48 *Bev. Town Docs.*, p. 11. William Morethwayte's career was typical of the active Beverley politician. Between 1441 and 1454 he was keeper four times, in 1441, 1445, 1449 and 1453, and each time he was elected over three years since his previous term in office. Roger Rolleston held office eight times in all, five times between 1436 and 1470, and his elections did not break the three year restriction either.

49 All the following analysis is based on a list derived from the Beverley Cartulary, Great Guild Book, Governors' Minute Book, and Account Rolls in the North Humberside RO, Beverley.

50 Richard Halitreholm, Nicholas Brompton, Robert Jackson and William Penycoke served together in 1438, 1441 and 1446. In 1450, Nicholas Brompton and Robert Jackson again served together, with William Mayn, Henry Tasker, Simon Sprotlay, Thomas White, Thomas Darlington, John Copy, John Graybarn and Edmund Portington. Four years later in 1458, all the 1450 keepers served again, with the exception of Robert Jackson, and four years after that, in 1462, the last four men in the group and Nicholas Brompton again served together. Hammer came to the opposite conclusion about the government of Oxford. 'Anatomy of an Oligarchy..', *JBS*, xviii (1979), p. 25.

51 Although there is no direct evidence to link the fourteenth-century Coppendales with the fifteenth-century family of that name, it was not a common name. The fourteenth-century family was extensive, with several branches, and it seems likely the fifteenth-century Coppendales were their descendants, as both had members active in overseas trade and local government.

52 Several of the men who served repeatedly were overseas traders. Nicholas Brompton,

Roger Cockerham, Robert Jackson, William Penycoke, John Redesham, Simon Sprotlay and Thomas Wilton were all active exporters at a time when few Beverley merchants were surviving the mid-century recession. A handful of gentlemen served as keepers from time to time, and several came from families which had been or were to become active overseas traders. Roger Rolleston, for example, was the son of a merchant William Rolleston, and served as a keeper eight times. William Cockerell, whose son became a merchant, served four times.

53 L.M. Nicholls, The Trading Communities of Totnes and Dartmouth in the late Fifteenth and early Sixteenth Centuries. M.A. thesis, Exeter, 1960, pp. 134–5.
54 E.g. the Alderseys, Duttons, Mainwearings, Savages.
55 York City RO House Books *passim*.
56 YCR I, pp. 8, 88, 142.
57 *York MB*, II, p. 246; Chester City RO, Assembly Book 1, f. 79v.
58 Cf. Norwich, where an alderman-elect had to renounce his butcher's trade in 1508. W. Hudson & J Tingay, eds. *The Records of the City of Norwich* (Norwich, 1906–1910), vol. 2, p. 107. A similar condition was imposed in 1504 on a York inn-keeper, John Petty, YCR III, p. 10; House Book 9, f. 20v. The same suspicions were evident in regulations passed in other towns, for example in Norwich and Winchester. F. Blomefield, *An Essay Towards a Topographical History of the County of Norfolk*, vol. III (1806), p. 129, T. Atkinson, *Elizabeth Winchester* (1963), p. 63. The prejudice against inn-keepers had faded in York by the mid-sixteenth century. D. Palliser, *Tudor York* (1979), p. 107. Butchers did serve as keepers in Beverley though. E.g. Account Roll 1416; Great Guild Book f. 60.
59 This analysis is based on the attendance lists in the House Books.
60 Robert Chapman's was typical. Free in 1464, he was a chamberlain in 1474, sheriff in 1478, and mayor in 1487 and again in 1493. Hull City RO, BRG: 1 ff. 24, 26v., 27 (a); BRB: 1 f. 118v.
61 In the Account Rolls and Governors' Minute Book.
62 BIHR, Probate Register II f. 605; IX f. 324.
63 Hull City RO BRG: 1 ff. 18v., 21, 23, 25v., 27, 28, 29v.: BRB: 1 f. 146; M479/2/27.
64 Based on the assumption that men became freemen at 21–22. See Hammer, The Oxford Town Council, *op. cit.*, pp. 24–5 where he concludes that the biologically successful won the final prize; the alderman's scarlet.
65 Beverley Cartulary, f. 7v.
66 There were sporadic outbursts of violence (E. Gillett & K.A. McMahon, *A History of Hull* (1980), p. 63; VCH Hull, p. 30), but none of a large scale specifically associated with the election period were recorded. However, the 1443 reforms which curtailed the direct choice of the mayor by the burgess, were made 'for the quietness of the town'. CPR 1441–6, pp. 180–1.
67 VCH Hull, p. 30; BRB: 1 ff. 105–6; VCH York, p. 70; YCR I, p. 32, II, p. 148, III, pp. 14, 36; Beverley Cartulary, ff. 7–7v.
68 Two late fifteenth-century incidents serve to illustrate this feeling. Richard Wayte, a vintner of York, complained in Chancery that he was unlikely to have a fair hearing in York, in a case of recovery of debt, because the other party, Thomas Neleson, was rich and 'of standing in the city.' A similar resentment was expressed against the powerful position of aldermen by a York merchant, William Scauceby, who served as chamberlain only. He petitioned Chancery over a case of debt involving William Wells, and claimed Wells would be believed in York because he was an alderman. PRO C1/64/485; 67/53; YCR II, pp. 14, 15, 17.
69 YCR II, p. 3, II, p. 191.
70 VCH York, p. 80; MB York, II, pp. 246–7; YCR I, pp. 104–6, 112.
71 *Ibid.* I, pp. 55–6; Borthwick Institute, Probate Register VIII ff. 32–4.
72 As in 1483 when the council conceded Lord Lovel's claim to pasturage in Knavesmire.

He was Richard III's chamberlain at the time and had been pushing his claim unsuccessfully since 1479, *Y.C.R.* I, pp. 30, 81. See also Reynolds, *An Introduction*, pp. 176, 178.

73 *Y.C.R.* II, pp. 105–7, 109–116. 'Enclosure' riots had occurred earlier in 1484 and 1492. *Ibid.* pp. 100, 103–5.

74 Beverley Account Roll, 1423; Great Guild Book, ff. 7v., 21, 21v., 26.

75 Reynolds, *An Introduction*, p. 186.

76 On one earlier occasion, September 1493, one of the sheriffs had been chosen from four candidates selected by the *assistantes*, possibly representatives of the community. House Book 7, f. 85.

77 YCR III, pp. 6, 8, 9; House Book 11, f. 19v.

78 CPR 1467–77, pp. 328, 329, 416; YCR II, pp. 40, 43; III, p. 17; House Book 11, ff. 29v., 44v.

79 *VCH York*, p. 137; YCR III, pp. 51–9.

80 Maryanne Kowaleski cited various factors which ensured that 'the oligarchic pool remained small but not stagnant' in late fourteeenth century Exeter. 'The Commercial Dominance of a Medieval Provincial Oligarchy: Exeter in the Late Fourteenth Century', *Medieval Studies*, 46 (1984), pp. 379–80.

81 There is no doubt that the economic recession in York had encouraged political splintering within some craft guilds in the 1420s, when the apprentice cordwainers were forbidden to form confederations or conventicles, or to usurp the authority of the guild mistery by making their own ordinances, *York MB* I, p. 193. In September 1486, Henry VII was confident that the most influential malcontents in the city were guildsmen and that they had lead the riots in October 1484. He promised a 'sharp remedy' to any who proved stubborn, and ordered penalties for any 'incorporats' or guildsmen who assaulted civic officials. YCR I, pp. 124, 168–9, 176.

82 A principle ennunciated by the York commons in 1475. *York MB* II, p. 246.

6

Women in Fifteenth-Century Town Life

P.J.P. Goldberg

Clare College, Cambridge

A visitor walking through the streets of York in the fifteenth century might have been struck by the number of churches and of clergy, by the bustle of activity in the markets, on the river or in the principal thoroughfares, but also by the contrasts. In the suburbs of mean cottages, in the cheap tenements crowded before the walls, or in the narrow side alleys Poverty lurked. Here women earned a meagre living spinning wool or sewing garments for piece rates. Here the upholder sold her second-hand clothes and here also the huckster plied her trade, her baskets full of tallow candles, cheese, salt and butter, pieces of cloth and lengths of yarn. These also were the haunts of pimps and prostitutes. In the central parishes of St Crux and St Martin le Grand, along Petergate and Stonegate, however, were the substantial houses of merchants, mercers, drapers and goldsmiths. Numbers of servants augmented these households, and women servants would be conspicuous amongst those serving in the shop, sewing, preparing food, fetching water. At the market place women would again be prominent – countrywomen selling poultry and dairy produce, women selling fish and fruit, butchers' wives selling black puddings.[1] Women would thus be seen to be an integral part of everyday life. Yet they would not be found in the council chamber and in the fifteenth century women rarely held guild office or indeed any of the offices regulating urban society. When John of Ely was presented by a London jury in 1422 for farming his office of keeper of the assay of the oysters to unqualified women it was stated that it was contrary to the worship of the City 'that women should have such things in governance'.[2] In law the married woman's husband was responsible for all debts she might incur, and she required his permission to make a will.[3] Few women were admitted to the franchise.[4] It is against this ambivalent backdrop of everyday activity and legal incapacity that any exploration of the fifteenth century urban society as experienced by women must begin.

The purpose of this present paper is not so much to look at the position of women in the urban labour market and economic activity, or how this may have eroded over the course of the century, but to focus instead on some less well documented aspects of urban society and social life.[5] At this stage it would be rash to project any comprehensive overview. Instead an attempt is made to illustrate several facets for which the surviving sources appear most promising. The sources chiefly comprise wills drawn from the Exchequer and Dean and Chapter courts for York and the depositions from matrimonial and other litigation in the consistory court of York.[6] A number of other urban sources together with some literary material has been added to this nucleus. The first part of the paper is concerned with women's social contacts and the possible feminine contribution to society through lay piety and charity. This is followed by a discussion of the social networks that operated to bring female servants into particular households and young people together in marriage. Consideration is given finally to two related areas of female economic activity that have wider social implications, viz. brewing and prostitution.

Women appear regularly to have associated together as a social group, but unlike men, only occasionally on a formal basis. Outside Norwich there is no evidence for communities of pious lay women living after the manner of the beguines of the Low Countries and the Rhineland.[7] Little evidence can be found for female craft guilds. There is a reference to a 'Brewstergild' in Beverley in 1364, and women only are referred to in the 1503 ordinances of the Southampton wool packers.[8] The London silk-women certainly enjoyed a degree of group solidarity if no formal guild association.[9] The clearest evidence, albeit the most enigmatic, for a formal association is provided by the existence of groups of 'wives' at various towns. In 1430 Agnes Stanssal, a widow, left 6s 8d to 'the wives' of Doncaster where she lived.[10] In practice the term 'wife' is ambiguous and this bequest could refer to an association of widows.[11] The 1437 record of the order of procession for the feast of Corpus Christi at Winchester includes the wives [uxores] bearing a single torch following the various crafts and the guilds of St Thomas and St Anne.[12] At Chester 'the wurshipfull Wyffys' were responsible for the pageant of the Assumption of the Virgin within the annual Corpus Christi Play.[13] In view of the traditional devotional relationship between the mercers and the Assumption it may be that the pageant was in fact performed by the wives of the mercers, hence the appropriateness of the epithet 'worshipful'. Much the same social group may lie behind references to the mayoress 'and her sisters' in both Coventry and York sources.[14] Most associations between females were, however, of a less formal nature. Women came together to assist and give support during childbirth. Women were much more likely than men to share a house.[15] A York cause of 1410 suggests that it was common for women to sleep in the same bed, and it is apparent from a cause dated 1382 that Isabella, daughter of Alan de Belyngham, then aged twenty-one 'or more', shared both roof and bed in Aldwark with Elena de Leyrmouth for she testified that on one occasion she was obliged to share it with Elena's lover as well.[16] Rental evidence further demonstrates a propensity for women without spouses to live in close proximity to one another. Derek Keene has described a concentration of women in Colebrook Street, Winchester around St Mary's nunnery.[17] Economic necessity rather than spiritual solidarity underlies similar concentrations of women in Aldwark and the suburbs of Barker Hill and Layerthorpe in York. In 1399, eighteen of the twenty-five tenants of one group of properties owned by the Vicars Choral were female.[18] Similar groups of women associated with cottage accommodation in Micklegate, Hamerton Lane and Rotten Row are conspicuous in the city's Ouse Bridge rentals, and in 1425 Joan Heseham bequeathed clothing to a group of eight women said to be living in the thistles ['in thystels'] next the suburb of Bootham.[19]

There is much evidence to show that women regularly built up their own friendship networks. This is reflected in the wills of female testators which are characterised by large numbers of small bequests to females, both kin and non-kin.[20] Thus when Margaret de Knaresburgh, sempster, died unmarried in 1398 she bequeathed items from her wardrobe to, among others, Isabella Barneby of Coppergate, Agnes Dowson of her own parish of All Saints, Pavement and one Agnes Covyntre living in the churchyard there.[21] This last can probably be identified with the 'poor old woman' remembered in the will of Avice de Pontefract a few years after.[22] Such gifts were tokens by which a woman's friends would be reminded of her after death and pray for her soul. The importance in life of women friends is parodied in the Chester Corpus Christi pageant of Noah's Flood where Noah's wife refuses to join the Ark unless her gossips are also saved from drowning.[23] The natural inclination of women for the company of their friends was indeed often a matter of dispute between married couples.[24] Christine de Pisan, addressing the wives of urban artisans, warns them against leaving their homes to visit friends and catch up on the latest gossip.[25] Similar advice is given by the Goodwife to her daughter:

> Go thou not into the town as it were a gase
> From oon hous to another for to seke the mase:. . . .[26]

One of the places women might go to enjoy their own society was the tavern. The early sixteenth century poem *Elynour Rummynge* describes the exclusively female clientele of an alehouse where barter prevailed.[27] A later fifteenth century verse comments sarcastically of women that:

To the tavern they will not go,
Nor to the alehouse never the mo,
For, God wot, there hartes wold be wo
To spende ther husboundes money so. [28]

Even the Goodwife warns her daughter '. . . thei that tavernes haunten/ Her thrifte thei adaunten'. [29]

On another level women were often active in the life of the parish church and of the religious guilds. Margery Kempe was not alone in following the liturgy in a service book. [30] Isabella Persay of York left a primer and psalters in both English and French at her death, and Agnes Bedford, d. 1459, the widow of one of Hull's leading merchants, bequeathed 'my primer which I use daily' in addition to a book of prayers to one Agnes Swan, probably her daughter. [31] Bequests of service books along the female line or alternatively to the parish church are not uncommon. Isabella Haucelyn of York, for example, left her primer to her sister Katherine, whereas Joan Louth left her missal to the altar of St James in her parish church of St Andrew. [32] A devotional interest in various images housed in the parish church is likewise demonstrated by testamentary bequests. Thus Alice Carre of St Stephen's parish, Norwich left her best coral beads for the use of the images on the feast days of the various saints represented and asked that her small coral beads be 'daily about the image of St Anne'. [33] Others made gifts of images to their places of worship. In York Alice Grymmesby left an alabaster head of St. John the Baptist, and Janet Holme gave images of the Trinity and St. Helen to the church of St. Maurice. [34] Bequests to improve or beautify the parish church are likewise found. Joan Bedale left 13s. 4d towards a candelabrum for her church of St John at Ouse Bridge end, York and Joan Litster left a like sum for making stalls in Rotherham parish church. [35] A York widow, Alice Croule bequeathed her blue bed hangings to serve as an altar cloth, and Margaret Gateshed apparently directed that her bed be used for an Easter sepulchre in her church of All Saints, North Street. [36] Sometimes women specified their place of burial within the parish church. Thus Mary Letheley, d. 1427, asked to be interred by her usual stall in St. Andrew's, York. [37] Bequests of possessions and monies indicate a similar attachment to the various religious guilds, themselves often associated with individual parish churches. Isabella de Langwath, in a will that describes her 'sinner's soul' ['animam meam peccatricem'] and 'wretched body' ['corpus meum miserum'], asked specifically for the prayers of the brothers and sisters of the York Paternoster guild at their meetings. [38] It may be noted that the ordinances of the guild of St Mary at Beverley allowed its elder sisters to have a voice in the election of their alderman, and there is no evidence that women were generally excluded from any of the welfare benefits or social activities of these associations.[39] A number of women enjoyed membership of several such guilds. Thus the York skinner's widow, Alice Poumfreyt, made small money bequests to the guilds of the Paternoster, St Christopher and the Franciscan guild of St Francis respectively.[40] It is possible that guilds associated with the friaries were especially popular with women and this must reflect the appeal of the mendicant orders to women and widows in particular.[41] A number, like Alice Poumfreyt, preferred to be buried in a friary rather than in their own parish.[42] Lady Marjory Salvayn asked to be buried in the Franciscan friary in York at her death in 1496 and left a relic of St Ninian to the friars there.[43] Another York woman, Margaret Otryngton, not only requested burial within the church of the Dominicans, but named friar John Orr as her executor and left her bed of Norfolk work and quilt to one William Kirkeby, S.T.D.[44]

Another aspect of lay piety that has wider social implications was the provision of alms for the sick and the needy. Though charity was not a female prerogative as the regular deathbed bequests to the poor and to the various *maisonsdieu* of the will-making classes testify, it was certainly the concern of many better off women. This may have been a response to the social convention that saw woman as the nurturers, the carers in society.[45] At a lower social level, for example, women frequently found employment as sick nurses, and lay women were attached to hospitals.[46] One of the precepts of the Goodwife to her daughter was to remember the poor and bedridden.[47] This was a theme widely propagated during the late medieval era through the canon of the Seven Corporal Acts of Mercy. This is the message pictured in the early fifteenth century glass of All Saints, North Street in York and it was proclaimed each year in the mercers' pageant of Domesday.[48] Thus when Roger Marshall testified to the good character of a York widow, Agnes Grantham, he drew attention both to her care for her *familia* and her charity to the poor in the form of bringing them wood, fuel and other necessaries.[49] Turning again to testamentary data it is possible to find numerous other examples of charitable provision by women. Prof. Jordan in his study of philanthropy in London observed that female testators 'were particularly concerned with the plight of the poor'.[50] A Bristol woman, Katherine Calfe, provided for thirteen poor women to eat at her table on the day of her burial in 1408. She also asked that two cloths be divided among impoverished bedridden women.[51] Joan Spenser of York left one mark to be distributed among the widows and other tenants of her property in St. Andrewgate.[52] On a grander scale, Joan Gregg was the founder of a maisondieu for thirteen poor people in Hull, and Agnes Broune of Scarborough built a maisondieu at the end of her garden. This she endowed by her will with six quarters of sea coal yearly.[53] In Leeds, Alice Nevile provided houses and an annuity specifically for two poor women.[54] How far such post-mortem bequests reflect the pattern of everyday almsgiving, and how far this charitable provision materially affected the poor and destitute must, however, remain open questions. It is worth remarking here that charity seems often to have focussed on the benefactor's parish or neighbourhood rather than the wider community. Provision may thus have been more effectively concentrated, but at the same time the gulf between rich and poor parishes may only have been increased.

The social polarity between parishes is well illustrated by the concentration of servant-keeping households in prosperous central parishes. In many larger towns some third or more of all households employed servants, and it was in service that many young people must have passed the period between childhood and adulthood.[55] Deposition evidence suggests that girls often left home at around twelve years or a little older. Unlike their male counterparts and outside of London, few enjoyed formal apprenticeships, but it would be wrong to suppose that their function was of a purely housekeeping variety and it appears that their skill with the needle was especially valued.[56] Female servants do not appear very often to have stayed in one household until they married. Instead they frequently moved from one household to another, staying in each perhaps only a year or two.[57] It is the means by which young women found themselves positions that are explored here.

The annual hiring fairs of rural England are well documented from the early modern period, but there is evidence that their roots lie in the medieval era.[58] In Coventry a fair held on Good Friday 'be which people were lette for service' is noted in 1452.[59] In York Martinmas and Pentecost are frequently given as the dates for entering or leaving service. Thus William Nevile, esquire left provision in his will dated 1469 for his servant girl to remain until the following Pentecost, and in 1410 Agnes Kyrkeby testified to having left the service of the mercer, William Pountfret, the previous Martinmas when he was joined, according to her own deposition, by Isabella Nesswyk.[60] Elsewhere in midland and southern England Michaelmas appears to have been the customary hiring date.[61] But though servant hiring fairs may be of greater antiquity than hitherto supposed, they were certainly not the only means by which servants and employers were brought together. More informal networks operated alongside the marketplace. Using York records it is frequently noticed that servants were related by blood or marriage to their employers, either because this is explicitly stated or because they have surnames in common. Thus one Joan Yarm was described in her deposition in a matrimonial cause of 1439 as both servant and *consanguinea* in the fourth degree to her master, William Wright.[61] Since the surnames are only sometimes recorded and relatives by marriage would in any case bear different surnames, the true proportion of kin relationships between servant and employer is necessarily understated. Ties of kinship sometimes existed also between servants. A York brewer, for example, remembered his servants Joan and Margaret Dewe at his death in 1465.[62] Similarly Joan Amgill, the servant of John Smith, pewterer was probably the sister of his apprentice John Amgill.[63] Vivien Brodsky, describing migrants to Jacobean London, has suggested that brothers in apprenticeships may often have helped secure positions for their sisters and the same may have applied here.[64] Likewise it is possible that Margaret Hall followed her sister Elena into her first recorded position with one John Close, goldsmith.[65]

Margaret Hall well illustrates another possible contact network centered on the parish or neighbourhood. In 1442 she was in service with the goldsmith just named of the parish of St John at Ouse Bridge end in York. In 1460 she was employed by Richard Hebson, a chandler living in the same parish and remained there with his widow until the latter's death in 1468.[66] Joan Howson can likewise be associated with the parish of St Mary, Bishophill Senior first as servant to a fuller and three years later in 1431 to a widow.[67] A third point of contact, which overlaps with this last, was that of trade. It is likely that Margaret Acclom, servant to a fishmonger of St Denys' parish, was a migrant from the important fishing town of Scarborough.[68] John Usburn's servant, Joan was herself the daughter of his trade associate in the dyers' craft, John Kyrkby.[69] The daughters of the mercantile elite similarly appear to have gone into service in like households. Joan Bedale, for example, who died whilst still in service to Agnes Cliff, a merchant's widow, was herself the niece of a merchant and alderman.[70] It is only by chance that such relationships can be reconstructed from the surviving records, but they do provide yet another insight into the multiplicity of informal contacts that operated in the late medieval town.

Being a servant was in many ways a stage in growing up and adapting to adult life. The attitude of employers to their servants was indeed somewhat paternalistic. Servants and even former servants are regularly remembered in the testaments of their employers, and bequests of clothing, beds and bedding, household and kitchen utensils, money and occasionally property are to be found in the case of female servants.[71] It is implicit in such provision that employers saw their unmarried servants as future householders. There is certainly much evidence that servants found marriage partners whilst in service and married on completion of their contracts.[72] A small number of women may, however, have remained in service for much of their working lives. The Margaret Hall noted earlier was a servant over a period of at least 26 years. Others may have left service in order to set up in trade in their own right. Thus Marjory Kyrkeby, formerly servant to the merchant Thomas Bracebrigg, was described as a pinner in his will dated 1436.[73] An analysis of deponents involved in ecclesiastical causes in the consistory court of York indicates that single women in their early twenties are regularly to be found outside service and this is especially true of the earlier part of the fifteenth century. [74] It is probable that such oportunities were to diminish over the course of the century and that the nature of service also responded to wider economic and demographic pressures. [75] The evidence from York testamentary sources suggests that whereas a wide variety of artisans employed female alongside male servants during the earlier decades of the fifteenth century, by the end of the century they employed only male servants. In the generally wealthier mercantile households, however, servant groups became increasingly feminised. [76] This again must be seen in the context of the erosion of female work opportunities in a period, for York at least, of growing recession and unemployment. [77] Female servants may thus have become increasingly associated with non-productive functions and the advertisement of wealth. The status of female servants would consequently have declined to the point that the daughters of the well-to-do remained at home. Writing of London one century later, Brodsky found that a high proportion of her sample of generally high status city-born women were living with their parents at the time of their marriage. She contrasts this with the pattern of downward social mobility associated with migrant females entering service out of economic necessity. [78]

In finding and choosing marriage partners women outside the landed classes do seem to have enjoyed a considerable degree of freedom. The advice of the Goodwife to her daughter was merely that she should always consult her friends about any proposal of marriage she might receive. [79] There is no hint here that marriages were arranged. The evidence of matrimonial litigation in the ecclesiastical courts tends to support this view. [80] In the first half of the century especially women seem to have engaged in courtship quite freely and to have broken off unsatisfactory courtship relationships by mutual consent. [81] This degree of individualism in marriage formation was sustained by the early independence from parental authority afforded to children by the institution of service, and by the relative economic independence enjoyed by women in service or within the wider labour market.

Marriage itself was a ceremony of simple formality. The couple, holding hands, exchanged words of present consent [per verba de presenti] before a small group of relatives, friends or fellow servants. The woman made no promise of obedience to her spouse. The contract was invariably sealed by the couple kissing and sharing a drink from a single cup. Advantage seems to have been taken of holidays and festival days. Thus Margaret Thweng contracted to John Kirkeby in the parish of St Lawrence in York on the feast of the dedication. Present were her brother and his wife, another brother and one further witness. [82] On another occasion Agnes Louth was milking a cow outside Beverley Gate in Hull when John Astlott approached with his parents and asked her to marry him. The couple then went inside the town to buy a pennyworth of ale. [83] By the later fifteenth century, however, the daughters of the urban élite were perhaps more likely to remain at home and recession was undermining women's economic independence generally. The choice of marriage partner was thus increasingly constrained by parental influence and economic necessity. Thus William Shirwod, a York merchant, in a matrimonial cause dated 1467 tried to impede the marriage of his daughter then living at home with him, since he had not given his consent.[84] By the next century this view would be supported by numbers of Protestant divines.[85]

Moving from the question of marriage formation to experience of married life one enters yet deeper waters. On one level marriage was an economic partnership. Wives were expected to learn their husbands' trades, to assist where necessary and to direct servants in their husbands' absence.[85] Most married women supplemented the familial income by carding or spinning. The wives of butchers and skinners made tallow candles, and, in some more substantial artisan households, women engaged in brewing.[87] On another level, marriage must have been punctuated by the burden of childrearing and repeated pregnancy.[88] One York couple had twelve children in 26 years of marriage, a rate consistent with natural fertility combined with breastfeeding. Indeed the most effective form of contraception was perhaps the practice of prolonged breastfeeding, although an unmarried woman observed in a York cause of 1486 was advised 'thow berist stuff must or theyr uppon the to thentent thow shalnot be gotten with child when thow japys or lyeth with men'.[89] The level of infant or child mortality must have reduced family sizes in a more traumatic manner, but this need not have undermined the bond between parent and child.[90] Iconography of the later fifteenth century reflects a growing identification with the family unit into which the identity of the married woman is merged. Children are frequently represented on monumental brasses dating from this period, and the east window of Holy Trinity Church, Goodramgate in York made sometime after 1470 shows the families of St Anne, St Mary Cleophas and St Mary Salome.[91] This trend coincides with a probable increase in family size due to a likely decline in the mean age at marriage for women.[92] At the same time women increasingly appear in written records solely with reference to their husband, living or deceased, and not, as in the earlier fifteenth century, in their own name. It also appears significant, since in law a husband's permission was required, that very few married women were having testaments registered by the latter part of the century. Only two of the 89 wills of York women testators registered in the Exchequer court in the period 1470–1500 related to married women as opposed to 68 or half the 136 such wills for the period 1398–1408.[93] Terms of marital affection are occasionaly found in wills. Thus Thomas Tate of York referred to his wife Marion as *dilectissima* and *carissima*, and Joan Relleston appointed her husband John to supervise her will '*ex corde mea quatinus ex benigna affectione maritali dignetur*'.[94] Conversely, wives were invariably named as executors to their husbands' testaments. Wills were, however, formal documents and the general absence of phraseology beyond the mundane and necessary is unsurprising. Records of divorce proceedings, technically actions for legal separation *a mensa et a thoro* allowed in circumstances of excessive cruelty or adultery, are a similarly negative source, though the apparent absence of such litigation in the York consistory court after 1450 may suggest a greater willingness on the part of wives to put up with unsatisfactory husbands in times of economic retrenchment.[95]

The brewing of ale by married women has already been noticed. In the absence of a safe water supply, ale was drunk in quantity. Its barley content lent it an additional nutritional value. The regular supply of ale was thus essential to any community. As in the countryside it was women who were prominent in both the manufacture and distribution of ale.[96] Fines, nominally for breach of the Assize of Ale, but apparently levied by way of a license dependent on the scale of brewing activity were imposed on some 238 individuals listed in the Norwich leet roll of 1390–1 and on similar numbers in equivalent York records of the mid fifteenth century.[97] It is probable that most individuals whose activities incurred the fines were married women, though it is their husbands' names that are regularly recorded. Only widows and a few unmarried women traders are noted by name, although in the York material many widows are misleadingly described as 'wives'.[98] It was only the wives of better off artisans that could have had access to the capital required to purchase expensive lead brewing equipment in addition to fuel and malt. It may be remembered that 'on of the grettest brewers' of Lynn for a while was Margery Kempe, the daughter of a mayor and herself married to a merchant of good family.[99] Beatrix Sleford of Hull still owed a York merchant 50s. for brewing vessels at his death in 1406, a debt he forgave her in his will.[100] Other women may have inherited equipment, and bequests of brewing utensils are regularly found in the wills of female testators. Agnes Lyndley of Scarborough, for example, at her death in 1478 bequeathed the equipment in her brewhouse to her married daughter Katherine.[101] Few women appear to have been actually dependent upon brewing for a livelihood, but rather added to the familial income by their activity. It may be that married brewsters had direct control over the profits of their enterprise; Margery Kempe claimed that it was in order to satisfy her taste for expensive clothes that she turned to brewing.[102] For some, however brewing was more than just a profitable part-time activity. A York widow, Agnes Grantham, apparently supported herself and maintained servants through this trade, supplying *inter alia* the master of St Leonard's hospital and his household.[103] Agnes Barbour of Goodramgate in York traded as both a barber and a brewster. Her unmarried status is confirmed by her unsuccessful attempt of 1439 to enforce a contract of marriage with a Whitby man who was already contracted to a woman of the same town.[104] Margaret Calton had earlier been employed in service when she was admitted to the franchise of York as a brewster in 1449. It is possible that she married shortly after as she is recorded paying brewing fines only between 1449 and 1451.[105]

Very few male brewers were admitted to the franchise at York before the fifteenth century and Maryanne Kowaleski had found only one male brewer in Exeter in the period 1373–93.[106] Beer had been imported from the Low Countries from the later fourteenth century, and in Hull leave was granted as early as 1428 to one William Beerbrewer to settle and trade.[107] It is possible that urban female brewsters only lost ground to professional male brewers as the fifteenth century progressed. The introduction of beer brewed with hops favoured the larger scale producer as the product did not deteriorate so quickly. The use of hops was, nevertheless, only slowly accepted. The brewster portrayed in Hell in the Chester pageant of the Cooks and Innkeepers laments:

> With hops I made my ale strong;
> Ashes and herbs I blent among,
> And marred so good malt.[108]

Women, however, probably retained their hold over the retail of ale. A Nottingham brewster was said to have supplied only inferior ale under a contract to a man trading at Lenton Fair, but to have reserved her best ale for sale at home.[109] Alison Clark, a York widow, desired that ' a holl brewing of ale yeiven to my customers' at her death in 1509.[110] Some brewsters employed tapsters to assist them. Agnes Grantham's servant Alice Rayner was described as her public ale taverner.[111] Many women, known as tipplers, earned a living solely through the sale of ale and were thus drawn from lower down the social spectrum than those actually engaged in brewing. Such traders are found among the women *intrantes* at Canterbury and similarly among the women licensed to trade at Nottingham. No less than four of the eleven women licensed there in 1478–9 are designated 'tippler', one of whom, Alice Chadwyk, is first noticed so engaged in 1459–60.[112] These retailers sold ale not by the gallon, but in smaller, often unauthorised measures, a matter of grave concern to civic authorities wanting to curb prices as an aspect of wage regulation. The Chester brewster further confesses that:

> Of cans I kept no true measure:
> My cups I sold at my pleasure.[113]

Of twenty-six persons presented by a Queenshythe jury for selling ale in their houses by the hanap or mug in 1422, twenty-one were female, fourteen of whom were married.[114] The previous year an ordinance had been made in Coventry forbidding brewsters to sell ale other than by official sealed measures, and a London ordinance of 1411 had demanded that persons 'selling ale in their houses provide themselves with pewter pots . . . sealed with the seal of the Chamber'.[115] Similar regulations are to be found elsewhere with sufficient regularity to suggest that they were frequently flouted.

A more serious civic concern is reflected in measures designed to regulate the hours of taverns. In 1405 it was ordered that there was to be an annual proclamation in the town of Beverley forbidding tavern keepers to open their doors to other than trusted guests after nine at night.[116] Taverners at Nottingham in 1463 were likewise ordered not to admit suspect persons and to close at nine. Leticia Dodsworth and Elizabeth Fox were presented for violating this ordinance and Leticia was actually ordered to leave town.[117] Taverns and tavern society, though an integral part of the social life of the medieval city, posed a threat to order and good government and needed strict regulation. Taverns were often associated with prostitution and a sub-economy of petty crime. It may be remembered that among the patrons of Beton the brewster's tavern were Clarice of Cokkeslane and Peronelle of Flaundres.[118] With the economic recession of the latter part of the century, these were matters of increasing civic anxiety. The Nottingham ordinance of 1463 can be seen as part of a general drive against prostitution.[119] The same concern lies behind a series of ordinances passed in Coventry in 1492 which virtually equate the tapster with the prostitute: no person of the city is to receive any tapster; no tapster is to receive any man's servant or apprentice.[120] By the mid sixteenth century in the depths of depression, the city authorities saw in the numbers of brewers and tipplers able to make a living out of excessive charges the cause of the decline of more substantial industries:

. . . Wherby almyghtie God is highlie displeased, the comen-Welthe of this Citie greatlie decayed, and vice, Idlenes, & other innumerable myscheves norisshed and encreased. . .[121]

The attitude of civic and ecclesiastical authorities to prostitution seems ambivalent. In some towns prostitutes and brothels were regulated. There is evidence for this at Southampton by the late fifteenth century, but it is most fully documented in the case of the stews of Southwark within the liberty of the bishops of Winchester.[122] In Hull the corporation leased an area of land by the Humber just outside the town walls and three arches of the walls themselves to prostitutes at an annual rent of £3 6s 8d.[123] Such policies made attempts to keep prostitues outside the walled area of towns at least credible. In Winchester, however, an earlier policy of expelling prostitues was replaced in the fifteenth century by one of levying fines.[124] The civic authorities in Exeter appear to have profitted likewise from regular fines imposed on prostitutes.[125] Ecclesiastical bodies gained both from their position as urban landlords and from their spiritual jurisdiction in matters of morality. Derek Keene has observed that the major landlords of Winchester prostitutes were the abbot of Hyde and the wardens of the Trinity Chapel and St John's hospital respectively.[126] In York the Vicars Choral rented cheap tenements to known prostitutes whose clients were often themselves vicars choral.[127] The consistory court there additionally employed professional prostitutes to act as jurors in cases where annulment of marriage was sought on grounds of impotence.[128]

The prostitutes themselves are generally obscure. Their poverty is evident from their concentration in cheap cottage and tenemental properties often in marginal inner urban areas or alternatively in the suburbs.[129] In York large numbers of prostitutes can be associated with a group of cottages owned by the Vicars Choral on the corner of Aldwark and St Andrewgate where rents were only four to six shillings *per annum*.[130] They seem to have moved around frequently, rarely staying in one place more than a few years at a time. Thus one Matilda del Wodde was presented for fornication in St Andrewgate in 1423 and in suburban Bootham in 1424 and 1425 before moving out of the jurisdiction of the Dean and Chapter, if not the city.[131] Joan Cryspyn was similarly presented whilst resident in Goodramgate in 1440, Aldwark in 1442 and again in 1448 and finally in Swinegayle from 1452.[132] Few women, however, were presented as regularly as Joan Cryspyn and, even allowing for the relative ease with which York prostitutes at least might move from one jurisdiction to another, it is evident that many of the women observed turned to prostitution only occasionally, when trade was slack and legitimate forms of employment scarce. This is demonstrated, as Derek Keene found at Winchester, by the frequency with which women with bynames of spinner, shepster and kempster are noticed.[133] In York the bynames of cook and sempster are especially common. A number of women there bore the surname Scott and this may indicate that local prejudices effectively denied these northern migrants access to employment. That migrants generally were especially well represented among women involved in prostitution is suggested by both Keene and Kowaleski in their studies of Winchester and Exeter respectively.[134]

As has been suggested previously, religious were frequently, but by no means exclusively, the clients of prostitutes. Maryanne Kowaleski, in her study of late fourteenth century Exeter, has been able to show that one professional prostitute, Emma Northercote, actually pursued her clients, who included priests, through the borough courts to recover debts owed for her services.[135] In York in 1424 Elizabeth Frowe was presented as a procuress for the Austin friars and Joan Scryvener as such for friars and priests generally.[136] In 1500 William Bell, the warden of the Franciscans of Nottingham was presented as a common pimp.[137] This pattern is also reflected in sexual slander. Joan Pokellyngton was ordered in 1422 to stop calling her neighbours in Grape Lane, a notorious centre for prostitution otherwise known as Grapecunt Lane, 'false thieves and priests' whores'.[138] Marion Burton was publicly defamed by Margaret Sawer, living in a lane opposite the Bedern, as an 'oldefrerhure' and 'prestehure'. Margaret herself admitted to being pregnant by her former employer, Master William Heryng.[139] Single women were especially vulnerable to this kind of slander, but it would be unwise to conclude that this represents an active prejudice against the unmarried woman. The evidence suggests that areas where prostitutes were concentrated were relatively well defined and well known. Within these areas it is possible to identify actual brothels, some of which were managed by women. Joan Plumer is thus observed operating in Goodramgate, York in the early fifteenth century and Margaret Clay likewise during the 1450s.[140] Much soliciting seems, however, to have been done through procuresses. Agnes Hudson of Swinegayle was presented in 1447 for leading a woman to spend the night with one Thomas Peny at his own house.[141] In London, where prostitution within the city was outlawed, one Margery and a Joan Wakelyn appear to have worked in partnership. On one specified occasion Margery procured Joan to go to a Lombard's house and Margery received 4d of the 12d Joan earned from this transaction.[142] Professional pimps and procuresses may have been responsible for first involving girls, with or without their consent, in prostitution. Their are several instances of York prostitutes procuring their own daughters, and in London in 1439 it was found that a girl, Isabel Lane, was procured against her will by Margaret Hathewyk acting for Lombard clients.[143] The histories of most prostitutes are, however, obscure. Joan Lawrence of York was said to be thirty-six when she acted as a juror in an impotence case. If she can be identified with the person indicted for fornication in Bishophill in 1412, she would then have been only sixteen. She was presented again for fornication between 1431 and 1432 at which time she was living in one of the Aldwark cottages of the Vicars Choral. When she left that property she moved out of the Dean and Chapter's jurisdiction and is thus lost from record.[144] Isabella Wakefield is first noticed as an apprentice to Christiana de Knarisburgh, sempster. In 1402 she unsuccessfully attempted to enforce a contract of marriage in the Church court with one Thomas Fox, with whom she had had a sexual relationship. From 1403 to 1432 she was regularly presented as a prostitute, procuress and brothel keeper. From at least 1409 she was living in St Andrewgate and was several times a tenant of the Vicars Choral. In 1414 she was described as living with a priest named Peter Bryde. Sometime after

1432 she must have died for her name disappears from the rentals of the Vicars Choral and the surviving capitular court book. She would then have been aged about fifty.[145]

By the later fifteenth century more women may have been forced into prostitution as they were increasingly denied access to other forms of employment. The exclusion of women from the weavers' craft at Coventry, Bristol, Hull and Norwich is but the best known example of a more widespread trend.[146] The York evidence may be compatible with both a growth in prostitution and the areas where prostitutes congregated. Certainly it is possible to detect a note of increasing alarm in the attitudes of civic authorities. The Nottingham ordinances of 1463 have already been cited, and numbers of people were subsequently presented there for running brothels, receiving servants with their masters' goods and allowing servants to play at dice.[147] An ordinance proscribing brothels in Leicester was issued in 1467.[148] The most far reaching civic legislation was, however, that attempted at Coventry in 1492. This included the ordinance:

> that no senglewoman, beyng in good hale and myghty in body to labour within the age of l yeres, take nor kepe frohensfurth housez nor chambres to them-self. . . but that they go to service til they be married.[149]

The success of such social engineering designed to eradicate prostitution in a city experiencing severe economic dislocation must be doubted, and this particular clause was much modified only three years later.[150] But the implication of this legislation, namely that women were not presumed to have any independent livelihood, but were expected instead to accept the submergence of their identity within the family either as servants or as wives, cannot go unnoticed. To provide for the daughters of the poor and dowryless that they might marry, and to protect marriage and family from the pernicious influence of poverty became, in York at least, by the latter decades of the century important works of charity. Thus John Carre, a former mayor of York in a will dated 1487 left 40s to each of 'xv pore madyns well disposed to mariage' and 'xx li. to pore men and pure women wedded kepyng housold togeder where most nede is w'in the Fraunches of York'.[151] Margaret Bramhowe likewise left her household utensils to be divided among recently espoused couples in need.[152] Charitable provision for the marriage of 'poor maidens' was to survive the Reformation and examples can even be found in the reign of Elizabeth.[153]

The beginning of this paper pointed, rather simplistically, to the contrasts within the material fabric of the urban community. It also pointed to a parallel contrast between the legal restraint, but comparative social freedom for women, and elsewhere I have argued that women enjoyed a remarkably high degree of economic independence particularly in the earlier decades of the fifteenth century.[154] I have attempted to explore something of the range and variety of social networks that were an essentially cohesive force within urban society, and I have argued that women could be an integral element in the operation of these social networks. At the same time I have found little evidence for a closed female society within urban society as a whole. Women did enjoy informal social activities often among women friends, but they were not sexually segregated.[155] Even within areas which normally appear male preserves it may be unwise to argue that women were actually excluded. It may be at least as significant, for example, that Marion Kent actually sat on the council of the York mercers' guild than that no other woman sat alongside her.[156] It may be equally as significant that women were admitted to the urban franchise than that most were not.[157] I want finally to suggest that the pattern of contrast was greater by the end of the fifteenth century than at the beginning, that society became more socially polarised, that women were more clearly subordinated to men, even that society became more patriarchal.[158]

Notes

1. For the topography of medieval York see A. Raine, *Mediaeval York* (London, 1955); the occupational topography is described from the 1381 poll tax returns printed as *The Lay Poll Tax Returns for the City of York in 1381* (Hull, 1953), ed. J.N. Bartlett; see also P.J.P. Goldberg, 'Women and Work in Two English Medieval Towns: A Study in Social Topography' in *Regional and Spatial Demographic Patterns in the Past*, ed. R.M. Smith (Oxford, forthcoming). For a discussion of trade and manufacture in late medieval York see H.C. Swanson, 'Craftsmen and Industry in Late Medieval York' (Unpublished D. Phil. thesis, University of York, 1980);P.J.P. Goldberg, 'Female Labour, Service and Marriage in the Late Medieval Urban North', *Northern History* xxii, pp. 18–38. For work on women in other urban economies see M. Kowaleski, 'Women's Work in a Market Town: Exeter in the late Fourteenth Century' in *Women and Work in Preindustrial Europe*, ed. B.A. Hanawalt (Bloomington,1986), pp. 145–64; essays by K.E. Lacey and D. Hutton in *Women and Work in Pre-Industrial England'*, ed. L. Charles and L. Duffin (London, 1985); E. Power, *Medieval Women* (Cambridge, 1975), pp. 53–69; D. Keene, *Survey of Medieval Winchester* (Oxford, 1985), pp. 387–92.
2. *Calendar of Plea and Memoranda Rolls of the City of London, 1413–37*, ed. A.H. Thomas (Cambridge, 1943), pp. 188–9.
3. F. Pollock and F.W. Maitland, *The History of English Law* (Cambridge, 2nd ed. 1898) ii pp. 429–30.
4. Only four women were admitted to the franchise of Norwich before the sixteenth century and even at York, where the franchise was more open, only about one per cent of all admissions were of females.
5. I have discussed the former in 'Female Labour'. See also P.J.P. Goldberg, 'Female Labour, Status and Marriage in Late Medieval York and Other English Towns' (Unpublished Ph.D. thesis, University of Cambridge, 1987).

6. BIHR, Prob. Reg.1–5 (Exchequer court probate registers); YML, D/C Reg. 1–2 (Dean and Chapter court probate registers); BIHR CP.E, F. (cause papers).

7. N.P. Tanner, *The Church in Late Medieval Norwich 1370–1532* (Toronto, 1984), pp. 65–6.

8. *Beverley Town Documents*, ed. A.F. Leach, Selden Society xiv (1900), p. 41; Power, *Medieval Women*, p. 61.

9. M.K. Dale, 'The London Silkwomen of the Fifteenth Century', *EcHR* iv (1933), pp. 324–35

10. BIHR Prob. Reg. 2 fo. 633v.

11. Goldberg, 'Female Labour', p. 30. See note 98 below.

12. *The Black Book of Winchester*, ed. W.H.B. Bird (Winchester, 1925), pp. 73–4.

13. The Pageant is now lost, but notice of it is given in the surviving banns.

14. *The Coventry Leet Book*, ed. M.D. Harris, EETS cxxxiv, cxxxv, cxxxviii and cxlvi (1907–13), pp. 405–6; C. Phythian-Adams, *Desolation of a City; Coventry and the Urban Crisis of the Late Middle Ages* (Cambridge, 1979), pp. 90–91; *Testamenta Eboracensia* v, p. 87.

15. Phythian-Adams, *Desolation of a City*, p. 90.

16. Agnes Kyrkeby testified that she 'cum ea (domina Christiana) transivit ipsam nudam in lecto pannis cooperendo prout consimili modo per vices alie mulieres et servientes eiusdem domus sepius fecerunt. . .' BIHR CP. F. 36; CP.E. 126.

17. Keene, *Medieval Winchester*, p. 388.

18. YML VC 6/2/38.

19. YCA, C 82–85; BIHR Prob. Reg. 2 fo. 501v.

20. This pattern is not confined to the medieval era, cf. R.T. Vann, 'Wills and the Family in an English Town: Banbury, 1550–1800', *Journal of Family History* iv (1979), pp. 336–7. An interesting discussion of female friendship networks and female common action in the early modern period is contained in R.A. Houlbrooke, 'Women's social life and common action in England from the fifteenth century to the eve of the civil war', *Continuity and Change* 1 (1986), pp. 171–89.

21. BIHR Prob. Reg. 2 fo. 14.

22. BIHR Prob. Reg. 3 fo. 111.

23. *Everyman and Medieval Miracle Plays*, ed. A.C. Cawley (London, 1955), Chester Pageant of the Waterleaders and Drawers in Dee, 11.200–8.

24. E.g. BIHR CP.E. 221.

25. Christine de Pisan, *The Treasure of the City of Ladies*, trans. S. Lawson (Harmondsworth, 1985), p. 168.

26. 'How the Good Wijf taughte Hir Doughtir' in *The Babees Book*, ed. F.J. Furnivall, EETS xxxii (1868), 11.67–8, p. 39.

27. John Skelton, *The Complete English Poems*, ed. J. Scattergood (Harmondsworth, 1983), pp. 214–30.

28. *Medieval English Lyrics*, ed. R.T. Davies (London, 1963), no. 123, 11. 26–30 p. 222.

29. 'How the Good Wijf', 11.71–2, p. 39.

30. *The Book of Margery Kempe*, ed. S.B. Meech and H.E. Allen, EETS cxii (1940), p. 20.

31. BIHR Prob. Reg. 3 fo 63; 'Meum primerum quo cotidie utor', Prob. Reg. 2 fo. 418. Agnes also bequeathed a 'cristenynge gyrdill'. An Italian acount of English society at the end of our period, based presumably on observation of well-to-do Londoners, describes the regular attendance at mass, 'the women carrying long rosaries in their hands, and any who can read taking the office of our Lady with them, and with some companion reciting it in the church verse by verse, in a low voice'. *A Relation. . . of the Island of England . . . About the Year 1500*, ed. C.A. Sneyd, Camden Society xxxvii (1847), p. 23.

32. BIHR Prob. Reg. 3 fos. 450, 479v.

33. Tanner, *The Church in Late Medieval Norwich*, p. 128.
34. BIHR Prob. Reg. 2 fo. 18; Prob. Reg. 5 fo. 335.
35. Reg. 3 fo. 556A; Prob. Reg. 2 fo. 287v.
36. The Latin can mean either bed or bed hanging and so the precise meaning is ambiguous. BIHR Prob. Reg. 3 fo. 296v; Prob. Reg. 2 fo. 52v.
37. BIHR Prob. Reg. 2 fo.505v.
38. BIHR Prob. Reg. 2 fo.604.
39. *English Gilds*, ed. J. Toulmin Smith, EETS xl (1870), pp. 149–50. Cf. Raine, *Mediaeval York*, pp. 91–2 on participation of women in the York guild of the Paternoster based on the now lost account roll for 1399.
40. BIHR Prob. Reg. 2 fo. 660v.
41. This observation is based on an analysis of the sexes of testators to various York religious gilds.
42. BIHR Prob. Reg. 2 fo. 660v.
43. BIHR Prob. Reg. 5 fo. 480.
44. BIHR Prob. Reg. 3 fo. 426v.
45. Cf. P.S. Gold, *The Lady and the Virgin* (Chicago, 1985), chapter 1.
46. As at St. Leonard's hospital in York: Goldberg, 'Female Labour', p. 32.
47. 'How the Good Wijf', 1.19 and pp. 167–72, 37, 44–5.
48. *Everyman*, ed. Cawley, York Pageant of the Mercers, 11.285–364.
49. BIHR CP. F. 36.
50. W.K. Jordan, *The Charities of London 1480–1660* (London, 1960), p. 30.
51. T.P. Wadley, *Notes or Abstracts of the Wills Contained in the Volume Entitled the Great Orphan Book and Book of Wills*, Bristol and Gloucestershire Archaeological Society (1886), p. 83.
52. BIHR Prob. Reg. 3 fo. 275v.
53. BIHR Prob. Reg. 3 fo. 555; Reg. 16 fo. 172v.
54. BIHR Prob. Reg. 5 fo. 106.
55. Goldberg, 'Female Labour', p. 21.
56. Ibid., pp. 24–5. I have discussed age at service in 'Marriage, migration, servanthood and life-cycle in Yorkshire towns of the later Middle Ages: Some York cause paper evidence', *Continuity and Change* 1 (1986), pp. 149–53.
57. Ibid. pp. 149–50; cf. James Ryther's remark that servants 'chaunge their maysters yearly': W.J. Craig, 'James Ryther of Harwood and His Letters to William Cecil, Lord Burghley', YAJ 56 (1984), p. 108.
58. A. Kussmaul, *Servants in Husbandry in Early Modern England* (Cambridge, 1981).
59. *Coventry Leet Book*, ed. Harris, p. 272.
60. BIHR Prob. Reg. 4 fo. 130v; CP. F. 36.
61. BIHR CP. F. 181.
62. BIHR Prob. Reg. 2 fo. 488v.
63. BIHR Prob. Reg. 2 fo. 599v.
64. V.B. Elliot, 'Single Women in the London Marriage Market: Age, Status and Mobility, 1598–1619' in *Marriage and Society: Studies in the Social History of Marriage*, ed. R.B. Outhwaite (London, 1981), p. 94.
65. BIHR Prob. Reg. 2 fo. 45v.
66. BIHR Prob. Reg. 2 fos. 143v, 401,441.
67. BIHR Prob. Reg. 2 fos. 543v, 658v.
68. Acclom appears to have been a common surname in Scarborough, though not in York, and the fishmongers associated with the Foss bridge traded in salt fish. BIHR Prob. Reg. 2 fos. 532, 533v.
69. BIHR Prob. Reg. 2 fos. 532, 533v.
70. BIHR Prob. Reg. 3 fos. 530, 556A.
71. Cf. the will of Alice Langwath, d.1467: BIHR Prob. Reg. 4 fo. 43.
72. Many matrimonial disputes arising in the consistory court at York concerned servants

or former servants: Goldberg, 'Marriage, migration', pp. 153, 155–8, n.b. the seduced servant's petition (158) was rejected by the court and not, as I there indicated, upheld; M.M. Sheehan, 'The Formation and Stability of Marriage in Fourteenth-Century England: Evidence of an Ely Register', *Medieval Studies* xxxiii (1971), p. 234 suggests the same was true at Ely.

73. BIHR Prob. Reg. 3 fo. 487v.
74. Goldberg, 'Marriage, migration', p. 152.
75. 'Female Labour', pp. 35–7.
76. Based on an analysis of sex ratios associated with servant groups noted in the wills of York artisans and traders c1380–1500: BIHR Prob. Reg. 1–5; YML D/C Reg. 1–2.
77. Economic decline at York has been much discussed and the picture painted by Neville Bartlett is unduly pessimistic, but there is some evidence that by the later fifteenth century a real contraction in the city's economy was experienced and that this was most acute within the city's export-weighted cloth trade: J.N. Bartlett, 'The Expansion and Decline of York in the Later Middle Ages', *EcHR* 2nd ser. xii (1959), pp. 17–33; D.M. Palliser, 'A Crisis in English Towns? The Case of York, 1460–1640', *Northern History* xiv (1978), pp. 108–25.
78. Elliot, 'Single Women', pp. 90–99.
79. 'How the Good Wijf', 11.32–5, p. 37.
80. This may be contrasted against the evidence from northern France discussed by Charles Donahue, Jr. in 'The Canon Law on the Formation of Marriage and Social Practice in the Later Middle Ages', *Journal of Family History* 8 (1983), pp. 144–58; cf. Goldberg, 'Marriage, migration', p. 160, and R.M. Smith, 'Marriage Processes in the Englsh Past: Some Continuities' in *The World We Have Gained: Histories of Population and Social Structure*, ed. L. Bonfield, R.M. Smith and K. Wrightson (Oxford, 1986), pp. 75–7.
81. Goldberg, 'Marriage, migration', pp. 155–60. I there wrongly implied that Prof. Helmholz saw the *causa matrimonialis et divorcii* as a common device to obtain divorce by fraud. Prof. Helmholz only notes this as a possibility and cites some examples. I very much regret that my text should have implied otherwise.
82. BIHR CP.F.182.
83. BIHR CP.F.46.
84. BIHR CP.F.244; Prob. Reg. 5 fo.84.
85. R.A. Houlbrooke, *The English Family 1450–1700* (London, 1984), p. 69.
86. Cf. 'How the Good Wijf', 1109 and pp. 116–7, 41; de Pisan, *Treasure of the City of Ladies*, p. 167.
87. Goldberg, 'Female Labour', pp. 29–30,33–4.
88. BIHR CP. F. 101. An appreciation of this burden may have helped persuade young women against the first offer of marriage in periods of economic prosperity. Delayed marriage would reduce the number of pregnancies they would have to experience since their reproductive life would be reduced and, being older, they would be less fertile. There is some evidence that breastfeeding was prolonged for some two years or more from a cause of 1365–6: BIHR CP. E. 89. There is little evidence that wet nurses were usually employed by other than the aristocracy. This again differs from, for example, the practice in Tuscany at the same period: cf. C. Klapisch-Zuber, 'Blood Parents and Milk Parents: Wet Nursing in Florence, 1300–1530' in Klapisch-Zuber, *Women, Family and Ritual in Renaissance Italy*, trans. L.G. Cochrane (Chicago, 1985), pp. 132–64. It may even be suggested, on the evidence of the cause just cited (CP.E.89), that women were disinclined to become paid wet nurses if it meant putting their own child's life at risk. Thus Elena, then servant to William de Huntyngton, refused to nurse the son of Elena and Gervase de Rouclif on the grounds that she loved her own (illegitimate) son as much as they loved theirs, and she would not put her child's life in risk for the sake of another. She did agree to nurse a daughter

subsequently born to Elena de Rouclif since her son, by then aged one and a half years, was still feeding. Another woman acted as a wet nurse since her own child had died soon after birth. It may finally be noticed that there is no English evidence for institutions designed to care for foundlings, and this again differs from the pattern in France or Italy.

89. BIHR CP.E.261. For a fuller discussion of contraception, but for the period before the Black Death, see P.P.A. Biller, 'Birth-Control in the West in the Thirteenth and Early Fourteenth Centuries', Past and Present 94 (1982), pp. 3–26. Birth control and abortion seem more logical responses to the need to control fertility than infanticide for which there is very little evidence, cf. B.A. Hanawalt, The Ties that Bound: Peasant Families in Medieval England (New York, 1986), pp. 101–2. It is difficult to detect within later medieval English society any rigid social stigma against the unmarried mother and thus of mothers desiring to rid themselves of unwanted babies either by destroying them or by abandoning them: see note 88 above.

90. This point is made by Barbara Hanawalt in her 'Childrearing among the Lower Classes in Late Medieval England', Journal of Interdisciplinary History 8 (1977), pp. 1–22, which contradicts the views of Lawrence Stone and Philippe Ariès.

91. M. Clayton, Catalogue of Rubbings of Brasses and Incised Slabs (London, 1929); P.E.S. Routh, 'A Gift and its Giver: John Walker and the East Window of Holy Trinity, Goodramgate, York', YAJ 58 (1986), pp. 109–21. On the fifteenth century cult of the Holy Kindred in Northern Europe see J. Bossy, Christianity in the West 1400-1700 (Oxford, 1985), pp. 9–10.

92. Goldberg, 'Women and Work'.

93. This trend is not confined to York and may even pre-date the Black Death. Certainly the right of married women to make their own testaments was openly debated in the early 1340s, but it would appear that by the mid fifteenth century the Church was increasingly disinclined to uphold this right. It is difficult to believe that this pattern was not in some way influenced by changes in social convention. I am most grateful to Prof. R.H. Helmholz from whose discussion of this issue I have benefitted greatly. See also the discussion in K.E. Lacey, 'Women and Work in Fourtenth Century London' in Women and Work, ed. Charles and Duffin, pp. 29–40.

94. BIHR Prob. Reg. 5 fo. 286: Prob. Reg. 2 fo. 43.

95. Goldberg, 'Marriage, migration', table 5, p. 157.

96. J.M. Bennett, 'The Village Ale-Wife: Women and Brewing in Fourteenth Century England' in Women and Work, ed. Hanawalt, pp. 20–36.

97. The Old Usages of Winchester demand that the unenfranchised advise the bailiffs of 'the quantite of here dedes': English Gilds, ed. Toulmin Smith, p. 355: Norfolk Record Office, N.C.R. Case 5, shelf b, leet roll 18; York City Archives, CC I, IA (Chamberlains' books of account, 1446–54).

98. The women noted in the lists of 'brewsters' fines' as uxores can invariably be associated from testamentary sources with men who had died prior to their appearance. Where the husband was still living into the period for which the record survives then his name, rather than that of his wife may be noticed. The concern of the civic authorities was to collect revenue and hence they recorded only the person responsible for paying the fine and not necessarily the person whose activities incurred the fine. In the case of married women this was the husband.

99. Book of Margery Kempe, ed. Meech and Allen, pp. 6,9.

100. BIHR Prob. Reg. 3 fo. 244.

101. BIHR Prob. Reg. 5 fo. 125.

102. Book of Margery Kempe, ed. Meech and Allen, p. 9.

103. BIHR CP. F. 36.

104. Five years later she was presented for fornication. She paid brewing fines over the period 1446–54 for which records survive: BIHR CP. F. 182; D/C AB. fo. 106; YCA

CC 1 pp. 17, 59, 120, 139; CC 1A fos. 22v, 35v, 39, 42v, 46v.
105. BIHR Prob. Reg. 3 fo. 23; YCA CC 1 p. 140; CC 1A fo.22v,35v; *Register of the Freemen of the City of York i: 1272–1558*, ed. F. Collins, Surtees Society xcvi (1896).
106. Kowaleski, 'Women's Work', p. 151.
107. *VCH, York: East Riding i: City of Kingston-Upon-Hull*, ed. K.J. Allison (Oxford, 1969), p. 52.
108. *Everyman*, ed. Cawley, 11.278–80, p. 168.
109. *Records of the Borough of Nottingham*, ed. W.H. Stevenson, (Nottingham, 1882–5), i pp. 346–8.
110. *Testamenta Eboracensia*, v 5.
111. BIHR CP. F. 36.
112. *Records of the Borough of Nottingham*, ed. W.H. Stevenson, ii pp. 242, 300.
113. *Everyman*, ed. Cawley, 11.273–4, 168. Cf. Langlang's Rose the Regrator who likewise sold her ale 'in cupmel': *The Vision of William concerning Piers the Plowman*, ed. W.W. Skeat (Oxford, 1886), passus V, 1.225.
114. *Calendar of Plea and Memoranda Rolls, 1413–37*, ed. Thomas, p. 140.
115. *Coventry Leet Book*, ed. Harris, 25; *Calendar of Letter- Books. . .of the City of London, Letter Book 'I'*, ed. R.R. Sharpe (London, 1909), pp. 97–8.
116. *Beverley Town Documents*, ed. Leach, 15. Cf. *The Making of King's Lynn*, ed. D.M. Owen (London, 1984), p. 422.
117. *Records of the Borough of Nottingham*, ed. Stevenson, ii pp. 277, 425.
118. Langland, *Piers the Plowman*, Passus V ll.304–26.
119. *Records of the Borough of Nottingham*, ed. Stevenson, ii p. 425.
120. *Coventry Leet Book*, ed. Harris, p. 544.
121. Ibid., p. 771; cf. ibid. pp. 786,801 and Statute of 11 Hen. VII c.2.
122. J.B. Post, 'A Fifteenth-Century Customary of the Southwark Stews', *Journal of the Society of Archivists* v (1977), pp. 418–28. The general lack of formal civic control of prostitution contrasts with evidence from a number of Southern European towns: L.L. Otis, *Prostitution in Medieval Society: The History of an Urban Institution in Languedoc* (Chicago, 1985); J. Rossiaud, 'Prostitution, Jeunesse et Société dans les Villes du Sud-Est au XVᵉ siècle', *Annales: E.S.C.* 31 (1976), pp. 289–325; M.E. Perry, '"Lost Women" in Early Modern Seville: The Politics of Prostitution', *Feminist Studies* 4 (1978), pp. 195–214.
123. *VCH Kingston-Upon-Hull*, ed. Allison, p. 75.
124. Keene, *Medieval Winchester*, pp. 390–1.
125. Kowaleski, 'Women's Work', p. 154.
126. Keene, *Medieval Winchester*, p. 390.
127. YML VC 6/2 various (rentals of the Vicars Choral): H2/1 fos. 4–14 (court of audience, spirituality of Bishophill); M2/1f (Capitular act book); BIHR D/C AB. 1 (Capitular act book).
128. For two such jurors, Joan Laurence and Isabella Eston, see BIHR CP.F. 111; D/C AB. 1 fos.83v, 85v; YML H2/1 fo. 4v (Laurence); CP.F.40; YML H2/1 fo. 6v (Eston,). See also R.H. Helmholz, *Marriage Litigation in Medieval England* (Cambridge, 1974), pp. 87–90.
129. Cf. Keene, *Medieval Winchester*, p. 392.
130. E.g. YML VC 6/2/44 (rental for Pentecost to Martinmas term of 1409) where seven of the 25 tenants can be identified with women presented for fornication in the Capitular act book, BIHR AB. 1.
131. Ibid. fos. 64v,67,69v.
132. Ibid. fos. 97v,98v,102,112,116v,122v,130,131v,135v,139,139v.
133. Keene, *Medieval Winchester*, p. 392.
134. Keene, Ibid.; Kowaleski, 'Women's Work, p. 154.
135. Kowaleski, Ibid.

136. BIHR D/C AB. 1 fo. 67.
137. *Records of the Borough of Nottingham*, ed. Stevenson, iii pp. 74.
138. BIHR D/C AB. 1 fo. 63. For Grapecunt Lane see ibid. fo.241v. This, together with Cock Lane and Love Lane, is a common name for a street associated with prostitution. In London's Cheapside there was a Popkirtle Lane.
139. BIHR D/C AB. 1 fo. 106v.
140. Ibid. fos. 27v, 44, 48v, 49; YML M2/1f fo. 49v (Plumer); BIHR D/C AB. 1 fos. 119v, 125v, 132v (Clay).
141. Ibid. fo. 110v.
142. *Calendar of Plea and Memoranda Rolls, 1437–57*, ed. Thomas, p. 13.
143. Margaret Cadde was prostituted by her mother Joan in 1453: BIHR AB. 1 fo.123; *Calendar of Plea and Memoranda Rolls, 1437–57*, ed. Thomas, p. 13.
144. YML VC 6/2/51,53; note 128 above.
145. BIHR CP.F.22; AB. 1 fo.27ff.; YML H2/1 fos. 8,8v; VC 6/2/44,48,51,53.
146. Phythian-Adams, *Desolation of a City*, pp. 87–8; Power, *Medieval Women*, p. 60; M.D. Lambert, *Two Thousand Years of Gild Life* (Hull, 1891), p. 206; *The Records of the City of Norwich*, ed. J.C. Tingey and W. Hudson (London, 1910), ii p. 378.
147. *Records of the Borough of Nottingham*, Stevenson, ii pp. 324–6,330, 346–8.
148. *Records of the Borough of Leicester ii: 1327–1509*, ed. M. Bateson (London, 1901), p. 291.
149. *Coventry Leet Book*, ed. Harris, p. 544.
150. Ibid., p. 568.
151. BIHR Prob. Reg. 5 fo. 327v.
152. '. . .*inter viros et mulieres nuper disponsatos necessitatem habentes*': BIHR Prob. Reg. 4 fo.34v (will dated 1471).
153. E.g. William Scarthe, shipmaster of Hull left 6s 8d for the marriage of four poor maids at his death in 1578: BIHR Prob. Reg. 21 pt. II fo.437. I am most grateful to Prof. M.C. Cross for this information.
154. Goldberg, 'Female Labour', pp. 35–6.
155. In this respect the culture of fifteenth century England was unlike that of Tuscany at the same date or of present day Islam.
156. *The York Mercers and Merchant Adventurers 1356–1917*, ed. M. Sellers, Surtees Society cxxix (1918), p. 64. Marion was a merchant's widow who continued to trade for several years following his death, perhaps during the minority of her son Henry. She died in 1500: BIHR Prob. Reg. 4 fo. 53v; Prob. Reg. 3 fo. 320; *The Customs Accounts of Hull, 1453–1490*, ed. W.R. Childs, Yorkshire Archeological Society Records Series cxliv (1986), pp. 128, 142, 148, 154, 158–61, 167, 170–2, 179.
157. See note 4 above.
158. Cf. the thesis argued by Martha Howell in *Women, Production and Patriarchy in Late Medieval Cities* (Chicago, 1986).

7

The Reformation and Regionalism: Further Reflections on the Church in Late Medieval Norwich

Norman P. Tanner
Campion Hall, University of Oxford

The starting point of this paper is my recent book on religion in late medieval Norwich.[1] In this work I tried to describe and analyse religion in Norwich, the provincial capital of East Anglia and one of the half dozen most important cities in England, during the late medieval period. This morning I am not going to provide any additional information. I have not done any further substantial research on the topic. What I would like to do is to stand back a little and to make a few reflections on Norwich in the wider context of the late medieval English Church and of Western Christendom in general. The two topics on which I should like to say a few words, using Norwich as a case-study, are these: first, the late medieval Church and the Reformation; secondly, and much more briefly, regionalism in the late medieval Church.

First, then, the late medieval Church and the Reformation. How did the late medieval Church prepare the way for the Reformation? What were the causal connections between the two? I must admit to a certain reluctance here since it has always seemed to me important to look at the late medieval Church in itself, without constantly thinking about the Reformation which followed. A nervous preoccupation with the Reformation, as if everything inevitably led to this, can distort our vision of the late medieval Church. Nevertheless the question remains an important one to ask from time to time, and so, hesitatingly and aware of the dangers, I shall attempt it. Norwich, moreover, is an especially interesting case-study because the contrast between the pre- and post-Reformation periods is apparently so sharp: seemingly a strong and healthy Church in the late Middle Ages, and yet a Puritan stronghold by the reign of Elizabeth and into the seventeenth century.[2] How did this change come about?

Well, I think that when considering the causal connections between the late medieval Church and the Reformation, it is essential to be aware of the various models of what was happening at the time of the Reformation which lurk at the back of our minds, because the model of the Reformation that we use, consciously or subconsciously, will strongly influence the way we see any causal connections between it and the late medieval Church. I think there have been five principal models as to what was happening at the time of the Reformation, and I would like to outline them briefly before applying them to our case-study of Norwich. So please excuse me if the next bit of this paper is condescendingly obvious to most of you.

First, the model of the Reformation as a natural reaction against the late medieval Church. That is to say, the Reformation as a reaction against a late medieval Church that was in such a decadent state that its collapse was more or less inevitable – an over-ripe apple that was bound to fall. This is the traditional interpretation of the Reformation. It survived so long as the Reformation was studied largely from a confessional stand-point, so long as, in other words, the overwhelming majority of Reformation historians were Christians, whether Protestant or Catholic, and who therefore wished to justify their churches, and therefore partly to justify their own beliefs, and often no doubt to justify themselves, in terms of what happened in the sixteenth century. For, this model of reaction was one that suited both Protestants and, somewhat paradoxically but at least to some extent, Roman Catholics. The only difference between the two parties was about whether the reaction was justified. Thus, Protestant historians argued that the Reformation was a justifiable reaction because of the decadent state of the late medieval Church. Roman Catholic historians, to oversimplify, agreed that the Reformation was a reaction against the late medieval Church, but argued that while the late medieval Church left much to be desired from a moral and disciplinary point of view – in terms of behaviour, practices and so on – nevertheless in doctrine the late medieval Church had not gone astray; and therefore the reaction initiated by the Reformation was understandable because of the moral laxity and so on, but was not justifiable from a doctrinal point of view. Roman Catholic historians didn't want to admit the need for changes or developments in doctrine, especially those which came from Luther and others outside the Roman Church. I think we can say that this was the prevalent interpretation of the Reformation down to the middle of the nineteenth century: that is, so long as the overwhelming majority of historians of the Reformation were themselves either Protestants or Catholics.

It is with the emergence, in the middle of the nineteenth century, of historians who were not themselves of any particular Christian persuasion that we see the emergence of a second model of the Reformation, a model of non-religious causes. To oversimplify, the Reformation was seen as not primarily a religious phenomenon at all; but as merely the result of other more basic underlying causes, be they economic or social or whatever. The religious changes of the Reformation were merely symptoms or results of these underlying economic or social forces, as it were like sparks flying off a catherine-wheel. Marx and Weber were surely the decisive influences here.

The third model is not easy to define but is perhaps best called socio-religious. In many respects it is the most recent interpretation. It is proposed by historians who want to preserve the best insights of the nineteenth and twentieth century economic and social historians, but who also wish to assert the fundamentally religious nature of the Reformation. Many of them have been influenced by the French *Annales* school; in some ways it is an application of *Annales* method to ecclesiastical history. Jean Delumeau is perhaps the best representative; Francis Rapp has applied it to the late medieval period; John Bossy is the best English representative.[3] These historians may differ as to their conclusions. But I think that at the heart of their interpretation, perhaps its most characteristic feature, is the distinction between what might be called content and form in religious change: the distinction between surface phenomena and the deeper movements underlying them. They would argue for example, that in the midst of all the apparent changes of the Reformation there were certain underlying continuities, such as the continuous trend towards a more personal and committed religion: and that there were basic similarities between the Reformation and the Counter-Reformation, despite their apparent contrariness.

Finally the fourth and fifth models, which in many ways go together. The fourth is of importation from outside. According to this model, the explanation of the Reformation in a particular locality is not to be sought primarily in the internal events of the locality but in what happened outside it. In England, for example, in the imposition of central government policies as well as in the influence of Luther, Calvin and other Continental figures. All historians would surely ascribe some importance to this model. However, there has been renewed emphasis upon its importance, particularly I think among historians who are unhappy with the first three models. Professor Scarisbrick, with his emphasis on the role of the English central government, is perhaps the best example;[4] Dr Whiting, in an article on iconoclasm, is another exponent.[5] This model often goes alongside the fifth and last one, that of the unpredictable decisions of a few great men. According to this model, the Reformation was not inevitable or determined in its outcome nor dependent upon impersonal forces, but resulted from the unpredictable decisions of a relatively few persons who happened to be positions of crucial importance. If Martin Luther had decided to stay within the Roman Church, or if Henry VIII had not fallen in love with Anne Boleyn, or Catherine of Aragon had borne him a son who lived, then things might have been very different, and so on. All except extreme determinists would ascribe some weight to this model. In its extreme form it may be outdated and associated with rather discredited historians such as Hilaire Belloc. But it, like the fourth model, is receiving renewed emphasis as historians find themselves increasingly unhappy with the first three models.

These, then, are what seem to me the five principal models that historians use when they speak about the late medieval Church as a cause of the Reformation. I would like now to return to Norwich and use it as a test-case. Taking each of the models in turn, I shall try to show how far Norwich did or did not support each of them. In this way I shall hope to make a small contribution to understanding how the late medieval Church shaped the Reformation.

The first model – that of the Reformation as a reaction against the late medieval Church – is the traditional and until recently the most widely accepted answer. Yet it is the model that the evidence from Norwich goes most against. The evidence from Norwich suggests a remarkably high level of support for Christianity in the city. Certainly nothing suggests a thoroughly decadent local church, leading to the Reformation as an inevitable reaction against this unsatisfactory state. Let me give some of the more striking evidence of this support for the local church. There is the sheer number of religious institutions and activities. Some of them were normal for a major English city, but many of them were on an exceptionally large scale. Remember, too, that all this was for a population of around 10,000.[6] Some fifty parish churches, almost all of them extensively rebuilt on a larger and grander scale between 1350 and 1530; most of them were well equipped with the books and liturgical items needed for church services, according to the inventory of church goods drawn up by the archdeacon of Norwich in 1368; and they had an average of almost two priests attached to each church, according to the visitation records of 1492; certainly they were very adequate for the religious needs of an average congregation of some 200 persons or fifty families.[7] In addition, there was a cathedral with a large Benedictine priory attached, four large friaries and three colleges of secular priests[8] (though only one nunnery[9]); Norwich contained the largest number of hermits and anchorites known to have lived in any English city after 1370, including London, namely forty or so;[10] and the only known communities in England closely resembling Continental beguinages, two or three of them flourishing in the mid-fifteenth century;[11] there were also almost 100 craft guilds, and some forty-five pious confraternities mostly attached to parish churches or religious houses.[12]

There is also the evidence of popular support for these institutions and activities. This argues against the local church being merely an empty shell, so to speak, without grass-roots backing. This support is of course not easy to measure. Some of it, however, is proved by the institutions and activities themselves: namely, those that were initiated and organised by the laity and so cannot be regarded as being imposed by the clergy against the laity's wishes. Such were craft guilds and pious confraternities; most of the hermits, anchorites and communities resembling beguinages; and many of the parish activities. Wills are also evidence here. I realise that the writing of wills was governed to some extent by conventions – by the scribes who drew them up and no doubt suggested bequests to the testators – but I don't think this should be exaggerated. After all, wills represent the highly personalised wishes of people at a solemn moment in their lives, and therefore they should be taken seriously. Moreover, the wide variety of bequests show that the testators did exercise considerable freedom of choice. The figures for Norwich are impressive, perhaps especially with regard to institutions and activities later attacked by the Reformers. The wills of 1,804 citizens written between 1370 and 1532 survive, and the following figures are based on a sample of 904 of them.[13] Over 90 per cent of them left bequests for parish churches.[14] Nearly two-thirds left specific bequests for masses and prayers for the dead, principally for their own souls; this was additional to the request for a (Christian) burial which was contained in almost every will, and additional to the more general requests for prayers contained in the residuary clauses; moreover the money left was often far too large to be merely conventional gestures, with a third giving at least £5 for masses and prayers, which was roughly the average annual wage of a building labourer in southern England at that time.[15] Half of them gave to one or more of the four friaries, most of these giving to all four.[16] The number giving to votive lights (mostly of saints) rose steadily throughout the fifteenth and early sixteenth century, reaching 48 per cent of the laity in the period 1518–32.[17]

Further evidence, against the view that the late medieval period inevitably culminated in the reaction of the Reformation, is provided by the resolution of several disputes between the citizens and various ecclesiastical bodies. Much the most serious was the dispute between the city government and the Benedictine cathedral priory. This complicated and longstanding dispute centred around the extensive privileges which the priory had acquired within the city and its suburbs at the time of, and shortly after, its foundation in the late eleventh century. Matters had come to a head in 1272, when the citizens had sacked and partly burned the priory and cathedral and had killed some thirteen tenants or employees of the priory. The dispute simmered throughout the rest of the medieval period, coming to a head again in 1453 with 'Gladman's

Insurrection', when the priory was again attacked, though this time nobody was killed. However, the dispute eased thereafter and was resolved largely in the city's favour by two royal charters of 1524 and 1525, which went in favour of the citizens on most points at issue.[18] The period after 1450 also saw the resolution in the city's favour of disputes with other religious houses, namely the abbeys of Wendling and St Benet of Hulme and the nunnery of Carrow.[19] In this sense the Henrician dissolution of monasteries was unnecessary from the point of view of the citizens of Norwich, not the inevitable culmination of conflicts. Moreover, with the exception of the dispute between the citizens and the cathedral priory, there is little evidence of anti-clericalism in the city.[20]

Indeed, positive evidence of support for the city's clergy is shown not only by the testamentary evidence shown above, but also by some interesting evidence about the number of sons of Norwich citizens who became priests or members of religious orders. We get some information about this from the episcopal registers when they mention the home towns of ordinands. They show that between 1413 and 1445, when the home towns were recorded regularly, almost three times as many ordinands for the secular priesthood were coming from Norwich as from the next most productive town, Lynn, and more than eight times as many as from any other town in the diocese.[21] The wills of Norwich citizens also provide interesting information about this. Of the sons mentioned in these wills (1,804 wills altogether), between 10 per cent and 11 per cent were mentioned as being priests or members of religious orders. This is a remarkably high figure, yet it must still be a considerable understatement since it does not include those sons who became priests or members of religious orders after their parents made their wills. The testators came predominantly from the upper ranks of urban society. The figures are therefore important in showing that the older and more institutional forms of religious life still had considerable appeal for a class of young men who might be expected to have been more than usually anti-clerical.[22] The proportion of daughters who were mentioned in the wills as being nuns was much lower at only 2 per cent,[23] reflecting the far smaller number of nuns than priests and male religious in medieval Christendom in general.

Finally, there is the apparent absence of Lollardy in Norwich. There is no evidence of early Lollardy in the city and none of its citizens is known to have taken part in Oldcastle's rising in 1414. There were only a handful of known cases of Lollardy in the city before 1510. The clearest evidence that the absence was real, not just apparent, resulting from lack of evidence, comes from the records of the trials of Lollards from Norwich diocese conducted by Bishop Alnwick between 1428 and 1431. The trials formed one of the largest drives against heresy ever undertaken in medieval England. They revealed that Lollardy was widespread in parts of

East Anglia, with several centres of some importance. This makes its lack of impact in the city of Norwich all the more remarkable. Moreover, the city might be expected to have yielded an unusually large number of suspects since it was the site of most of the trials and the bishop might be expected to have been especially vigilant in his own city. Yet only two of the approximately fifty men and women from the diocese who were convicted at the trials were from the city of Norwich, and there were only a few other indications that heresy had any influence in the city. This is, I think, one further indication that the religion provided by the local church was sufficiently rich and varied as to cater for the religious tastes of most citizens. There was no need to resort to Lollardy. No apparent need, too, to turn to the Reformation.[24]

You may begin to ask whether there was any evidence that Norwich was ripe for the Reformation. There were a few indications. There was a decline in testamentary bequests for masses and prayers for the dead in the 1520s;[25] the number of monks at the cathedral priory dropped gradually after 1460, and sharply in the early 1530s;[26] there was the case of Thomas Bilney, who was finally executed for heresy just outside the city gates in 1531, and there are some other indications of the growth of Lollardy in the city in the 1520s.[27] But these were for the most part very late developments, after Luther's appearance on the public scene. Moreover they represent, I think, a creeping insecurity about the value and future of the old religion, which was beginning to create a vacuum in the religious life of the city, rather than a vigorous reaction to the old ways. There is also some evidence from visitation records of immorality among the clergy, absenteeism from church on Sundays and feast-days, and abstention from the sacraments of the eucharist and penance at the prescribed times.[28] This evidence cannot be dismissed as trivial. Neverthless it seems well short of widespread dissent or a general collapse of standards. If we take the period 1450 to about 1520, with the resolution of the city's disputes with the cathedral priory and other religious houses,[29] with an ever increasing number of testamentary bequests of a religious nature,[30] and with the continuing vitality of both the older religious institutions and newer lay movements,[31] the church in Norwich appears in remarkably healthy shape on the eve of the Reformation. Few citizens would, I think, have considered the radical changes to come either imminent or necessary.

What then of the second model – that the causes of the Reformaion were essentially non-religious? Obviously I cannot enter this debate at all fully here since it involves, as you will be well aware, such basic presuppositions about the nature of historical causality, which would take far too long to discuss in this short paper. I would just like to make two brief remarks. First, there is the seriousness with which religion appears to have been taken by the citizens of late medieval Norwich. The sheer number and intensity of the religious institutions and activities mentioned above, all for a population of only about 10,000, is strong proof that religion was taken seriously in the city. It would be hard to reduce religion to other factors, be they economic or social or whatever. But secondly and on the other hand, there does appear an element of conformity in the citizens' religion. This is not easy to define. One suspects it from the ease with which the citizens accepted the changes of the Reformation, but there are also hints of it in the late medieval period. One has the impression of the majority of citizens following religious fashions. There is great support for the religious institutions and activities that come into being, but most of the citizens are supporters rather than initiators. In a sense there is a relative lack of personal commitment. The apparent weakness of Lollardy, or the paucity of citizens taking up religious standpoints which went against majority opinions, are perhaps expressions of this. Still, I wouldn't want to exaggerate this point and I am not sure where it leads to. I don't think it argues to superficiality in religion, nor that religion in the city can be reduced to non-religious factors. On the whole I think it argues that religion was communitarian rather than individualistic.

I should like now to turn to the third model, that of socio-religious causes, and to examine it in more detail. As I mentioned earlier, at the heart of this explanation lies the distinction between surface phenomena and underlying movements, between what might be called content and form in religion. In discussing the first model, that of the Reformation as a reaction against the late medieval Church, we saw the remarkable change of content in the city's religion before and after the Reformation. This change was apparently unprepared for. But can it be explained by a more underlying continuity? Yes, partly, I think, in at least three areas: religious education, religious development, and religiosity itself.

First, religious education. There is no doubt about the dramatic changes in the content of the citizens' religious knowledge before and after the Reformation. Doubtless the citizens of Norwich of around 1450, apparently devoted to a 'High Church' almost 'Baroque' religion, would have been amazed by the Puritan attitudes of so many of their fellow citizens of a century and a half later. But there is evidence of a continuing growth of religious education itself during those 150 years, and this is I think equally significant as the change in content, because if we understand education correctly we will expect it to lead to change. Our error is to think of religious education in purely static terms, namely, that improved religious education simply leads to the better expression and defence of old truths. But this is at least partly wrong. Religious education, like all education, is dynamic and involves growth, leading to deeper understanding which in turn naturally involves change and development. So we should expect some change with education, not just reinforcement of the status quo.

Certainly the evidence of a continuing rise in the level of religious education in Norwich during the fifteenth and early sixteenth century, or at least of a continuously high level, is impressive. It is most quantifiable for the clergy, especially the secular clergy with benefices (thanks to the surviving records of their appointments in the episcopal registers). Thus the number of the city's beneficed parish clergy who were university graduates rose from 8 per cent (12 out of 158) between 1370 and 1449, to 32 per cent (23 out of 71) between 1450 and 1499, and to 42 per cent (25 out of 60) between 1500 and 1532. Similarly with the beneficed clergy at the three colleges of secular priests in the city: 40 per cent (17 out of 42) were university graduates between 1370 and 1449, 81 per cent (38 out of 47) between 1450 and 1532.[32] For the religious orders, besides the university education which many received, there were schools for young monks and friars at the Benedictine cathedral priory and at each of the four friaries. Indeed, the school at the Franciscan friary attracted friars from abroad, including Peter de Candia the future pope Alexander V. The cathedral priory contained one of the finest libraries in the country, numbering at least 1,350 books at the priory's dissolution in 1539: Bale and Leland writing in the sixteenth century, showed that there were smaller libraries at the friaries. Moreover, of the 'famous writers' listed in Bale's *Scriptorum illustrium maioris Brytannie catalogus*, the remarkably high number of 28 of them were members of these five religious houses.[33] For the education of the laity it is more difficult to quantify. Hopefully they benefited from the apparently high standard of clerical education. They also showed an interest in education through scholarships. Thus between 1370 and 1532, fifty-eight of their surviving wills, all made in fact after 1450, contained bequests for young men, almost invariably priests or candidates for the priesthood, to study, usually at a university.[34] An alderman called Philip Curson, for example, stated in his will of 1502 that he would pay for his son, if he 'will be a priest', to 'be found to Cambridge schools to learn that faculty that his mind is most disposed on, till he is bachelor in the law or of art'; and Robert Elys wanted his wife to 'keep little Reynold to the school, if he will abide with her, to the time she knows whether he will be a man of the Church or not'.[35] There is also some evidence from the books left by both clergy and laity in their wills.[36] Unfortunately time does not permit a proper treatment of this here. Let me just take the case of Margaret Purdans, a widow who made her will in 1481. She bequeathed the following books: an 'English psalter' and a 'small psalter'; 'Le Doctrine of the Herte', which was presumably a translation of 'De Doctrina Cordis', the treatise addressed to a woman on how to lead a devout life which was usually ascribed to Bishop Grosseteste of Lincoln; an 'English book of Saint Bridget'; and 'a book called Hylton', which was presumably a work by Walter Hilton, the fourteenth century English mystic.[37] Her books seem to place her squarely in the line of devout and literate lay persons to which Dr Pantin drew attention.[38] The most famous case of all is of course Julian of Norwich, the anchoress and author of *Revelations of Divine Love*, if Walsh and Colledge are right about the high standard of her education.[39]

A second line of continuity is that of religious development. What I mean is this. It is usually assumed that the late medieval period was one of decline in religion, paralleling and accompanying the demographic, economic, social and political crises of the period. The thirteenth century is seen as the high point of the Middle Ages, and the fourteenth and fifteenth centuries as a period of decline from this. The model of the Reformation as a natural reaction against the late medieval Church is also influential. For if the reaction of the Reformation was justifiable, it must have been against a decadent church – a church that provoked a reaction. Or, on the wider scene, if the sixteenth century is to be seen as a century of light – the discovery of the New World, the Renaissance and the Reformation – then the earlier period must have been dark in contrast. The fault arises from looking at the late medieval period from the standpoint of either the thirteenth century or the sixteenth century, not in its own right. But since historians of the high Middle Ages and of the sixteenth century are more numerous than those of the late Middle Ages, so they are allowed to get their way! In fact the evidence from Norwich suggests the opposite, namely that the fourteenth and fifteenth centuries were a period of growth and development in religion, not of decline. Thus the period saw the continuing vitality in the city of the older religious institutions which had grown up in the early and high Middle Ages: the parishes, the secular clergy and religious orders. And it also saw the growth and development of newer religious movements which were specially characteristic of the late Middle Ages and more centred on the laity: anchorites, hermits and communities resembling beguinages; craft guilds and pious confraternities; chantries; the proliferaton of devotions to the saints. There was an apparently harmonious development of both the old and the new; development in the best sense. I have described this in more detail in my book.[40] My point is simply this: the period 1300 to 1530 as well as the Reformation period were times of development for religion in Norwich; the fact that there continued to be religious development is at least as significant as the content of this development, so that there was a certain underlying continuity even though the content of people's beliefs and attitudes changed markedly before and after the Reformation; after all one should expect development to lead to change, since development of its very nature involves an element of change.

The third line of continuity – at least of connection – between the late Middle Ages and the Reformation is that of religiosity, the level of religious awareness and practice. My point here is similar to what I have said before, and in a sense sums it up. I have argued that there seems to have been an unusually high level of religious awareness and practice in late medieval Norwich, that Norwich was an unusually religious city; and all the evidence suggests that this continued to be the case, namely that Norwich continued to be an unusually religious city, until at least the early seventeenth century. I think that this high level of religiosity, as it might be called, is just as significant as the ways – the practices and beliefs – in which it expressed itself; and that one has a continuity here despite all the surface changes. Indeed one should expect change from religious awareness since religion is something dynamic and moving, not something static; a journeying on, not just a confirmation in old attitudes and prejudices. Well, you may say this is a theological question and not really the concern of history. But I think the question – whether religion is changing or static – cannot be avoided by anyone who wishes to understand the connection between the late medieval Church and the Reformation. Because if you see religion as essentially static, you will see only disconnection at the Reformation, which is very hard to explain, at least in Norwich; but if you see religion as intrinsically involving development, you will be less surprised by the Reformation.

To conclude this third, socio-religious model of the Reformation. It has its strengths. It helps us to distinguish between various layers in religious change, and to see beyond or under external changes. Nevertheless it has its limitations. In particular, it would be wrong to draw the distinction between external phenomena and underlying movements too sharply. External beliefs and practices cannot be divorced from underlying attitudes; they are expressions of these attitudes. And while religion of its very nature may lead to change, this does not mean arbitrary change or change in any direction whatever. So while this model helps us to see elements of continuity in Norwich's religion before and after the Reformation, and indeed makes us expect change precisely because of the high levels of religious education, religious development and religiosity in the city, it nevertheless does not explain the actual changes that took place. Maybe the situation in late medieval Norwich leads us to expect some kind of change, but the actual changes that took place remain perplexing.

Finally, the fourth and fifth models – those of importation from outside and of the chance decisions of a few individuals. I shall only discuss them briefly. To some extent they, like the second one of non-religious causes, involve basic principles of historical causality, which cannot be adequately treated in this short paper. Moreover the correctness or not of the two models depends on events and actions that took place after the beginning of the Reformation, which is not the direct concern of this paper. I must content myself with making a few remarks about whether the late medieval period, in Norwich, does or does not support the two models as likely. I think it is important to remember that as I said earlier, these two models are proposed to a considerable extent out of frustration with the other three. Thus, historians are increasingly aware of a large measure of popular support for the religion offered by the late medieval Church, and this makes the model of reaction for the Reformation difficult to sustain; and many historians dislike what they see as the attempt to reduce the Reformation to non-religious or socio-religious causes. They are therefore attracted to the fourth and fifth models as possible explanations. Certainly the evidence from Norwich gives them considerable support for rejecting the model of the Reformation as a reaction against the late medieval Church, inasmuch as it provides impressive evidence of the citizens' support for their local church and the religion offered. On the other hand the evidence from Norwich, in giving some support to the third model of socio-religious causes, makes it less imperative to resort to the fourth and fifth models: we have at least some elements of an internal explanation. However, this third model, as I have argued, does not explain the actual changes that took place: it might lead us to expect change, but it does not explain the particular changes that took place. These latter remain perplexing if one looks at Norwich alone, so that the decisions of outsiders are a likely partial answer. This view is given some support by what I have described as the element of conformity in the citizens' religion; a willingness to be led by others.[41] Thus the Reformation in the city appears both as the result of a religious vacuum in the city and as a snowball which, once it begins to roll, follows its own unpredictable path down the slope, out of its own control, and therefore very subject to the pushes of outsiders. I should like finally to mention two very clear outside influences, the one well known and in the Reformation period, the other less well known and spanning both sides of the Reformation divide. The first is 'The Strangers' as they came to be called; some four thousand Protestant immigrants from the Low Countries who settled in Norwich in the reign of Elizabeth. They must surely be a major factor in explaining the Protestantism of Norwich. The second influence is less well known but perhaps no less important, namely the influence of Cambridge University. Dr Morgan demonstrated the university's influence on Norwich mainly for the Reformation period, but he also showed that it existed earlier;[42] my researches support his findings for the late medieval period.[43]

There is one final point that I would like to make by way of conclusion to this first section on the late medieval Church and the Reformation. It will be obvious from what I have said that Norwich emphasises the complexity of the causal connections between the late medieval and the

Reformation periods. This complexity is generally accepted by most historians today. But Norwich also emphasises the complexity of the late medieval Church itself. What I mean is this. Historians used to think of the late medieval Church and the Reformation as two neatly packaged parcels. There was debate about the causal connections between them, but there was not doubt about their nature; they were two clearly defined things. In recent decades historians have seen that the Reformation was a far more complex phenomenon than had earlier been realised. They have unwrapped the Reformation parcel, so to speak, and sorted out at least some of its component parts. But the late medieval Church also must be unpacked, and this process has been much slower. Indeed, this is for me a basic unease with most Reformation historians, that they tend to assume that the late medieval Church was a kind of monolithic whole. Of course they disagree about whether the late medieval Church was for or against the Reformation (for want of a better way of expressing it) – that is the point of their disagreement – but neverthless most of them tend to assume that the late medieval Church was a kind of monolithic whole, either wholly for or wholly against the Reformation. But when we unpack the late medieval Church we find that it is at least as complex as the Reformation, so that different pieces of it point in different directions as regards the Reformation; some for it, some against it. Certainly the evidence from Norwich supports this. For example, support for masses and prayers for the dead and for devotions to the saints seem to point against the Reformation; but on the other hand there is little evidence of enthusiasm for the papacy or of opposition to vernacular Bibles, which points in favour of the Reformation. Many other examples could be cited. Very complex contents are revealed in the late medieval box once the wrapping has been removed! It is not just a question of which of the five models a particular local church best fits into, but into which of the models do the individual pieces of that local church best fit. Moreover, we have complexity not only within a given town or locality, but also differences between town and countryside, between different regions of England, and so on.

This brings me to the second topic of this paper, regionalism in the English Church in the late Middle Ages. I shall be brief partly because of time and partly because the lack of research so far done on this subject makes adequate treatment impossible. In this latter respect the situation is different from the first topic. If anything, the connections between the late medieval Church and the Reformation have been discussed too much. My aim there was to shed a little new light on an old question. With regionalism in the late medieval English Church, however, I think the question has not been asked sufficiently. This is somewhat surprising since Reformation historians have made us familiar with the concept for the sixteenth century. Dickens, Elton, Haigh and others have made us familiar with, for example, the distinction between a more conservative and catholic North and West, a more radical and dissenting East and South. Regionalism is also a concept that has been applied to non-religious aspects of late medieval England. Thus we know that the English economy in the late Middle Ages was in many ways a collection of regional economies rather than a single national economy; political and social regionalism was highlighted by the Peasants' Revolt of 1381 and by the Wars of the Roses; there were regional dialects within the English language; and so on. Why not therefore apply the concept of regionalism to religious affairs? Should we not perhaps think of the late medieval English Church as a federation of regional churches more than as a single national church? I think that concentration on the question of whether the English Church was a national church or part of the international church, summed up in the Stubbs v Maitland controversy[44] and debates between Roman Catholic and Anglican historians, has obscured this third possibility of a federation of regional churches. Once again the preoc-cupations of earlier historians, largely following confessional lines, have been allowed to frame the question. The point has, of course, been made in some respects. We know, for example, that there was a certain regionalism in liturgical matters: the different rites of Sarum, York, Hereford, Lincoln, and so on. There were the great cycles of mystery plays with their regional centres: York, Chester, Coventry, Norwich and others. Dr Thomson has argued strongly for the regional nature of Lollardy.[45] I think these various ecclesiastical aspects of regionalism need to be brought together, and also applied to popular religion. This is what I would like to say a few words about, in the light of the evidence from Norwich. It has been done for some regions in other countries[46]; it needs to be done for England.

There are two aspects of this question: first, the regional church and its capital; secondly, the differences between the regional churches of England. For East Anglia there were all the normal institutional aspects of a regional church, some of them dating back to the early Anglo-Saxon period when England was indeed a heptarchy and the English Church followed these divisions. Thus the region of East Anglia, which had originally been one of the kingdoms in the heptarchy, was almost exactly co-terminous with the diocese of Norwich, with its bishop, cathedral and other aspects of episcopal organisation. The diocese had held its own ecclesiastical synods at least into the thirteenth century.[47] There were the distinctively East Anglian parish churches; a school in stained-glass;[48] and the Norwich cycle of mystery plays.[49] The city of Norwich acted as the capital of this regional church in various ways, in addition to being the seat of the bishopric and containing the cathedral. It contained a range of religious institutions unparalleled in any other town in the diocese and especially in the countryside: the cathedral priory, 4 friaries, 3 colleges of secular priests, a nunnery, some 50 parish churches, hermits and anchorites, communities resembling beguinages, craft guilds and pious confraternities.[50] This must have made the city a religious magnet for East Anglia in all sorts of ways. Some of these ways we know about, for others we can only conjecture. Thus, no doubt a fair proportion of the city's large clerical population were from the countryside;[51] many monks of the cathedral priory, for example, appear to have come from the priory's estates around the diocese.[52] We know that Margery Kempe came from Lynn to Norwich to seek advice from both the anchoress Julian, author of *Revelations of Divine Love*, and Richard Caistor, the saintly vicar of St Stephen's parish.[53] No doubt many others came to Norwich from other parts of the diocese for counsel from various holy men and women in the city or to receive the sacraments or hear sermons or attend services at various churches in the city. We know that Margery Kempe also came to Norwich to 'offer' at the cathedral before and after her pilgrimage to the Holy Land, and the sacrist's account rolls make it clear that many others came to their cathedral church to 'offer' there.[54] Indeed, a feature of East Anglian wills were bequests to Norwich cathedral, which many testators described as their 'mother' church.[55] Also, the annual performance of mystery plays, as well as other pageants and processions put on by the city's craft guilds and pious confraternities, must have been a tourist attraction.[56] This was explicitly stated by St Luke's guild, which said in 1527 that the 'many disguisings and pageants of the lives and martyrdoms of many holy saints', performed each year by the guild on Pentecost Monday, had attracted large crowds from the countryside to watch.[57] The only aspect in which Norwich does not appear to have been the religious capital of the region was Lollardy. This appears, as I said, to have made little impact on the city and yet to have been fairly widespread in some other parts of the diocese. In a sense, however, this absence of Lollardy may have increased Norwich's importance as a capital of orthodox religion.

The second aspect is that of differences between the regional churches of late medieval England. What light does Norwich shed on this topic? The basic difficulty is, as I said, that we haven't any regional studies of religion in late medieval England.[58] We are restricted to comparisons between individual towns or localities. These are of some help, however, especially for the major towns, which are likely to have been of more than local significance and representative, at least to some extent, of religion in the region. Norwich certainly highlights many of the variations. Its large number of parish churches reminds us of the great variety in this respect within late medieval England: between forty and fifty in York, Lincoln and Norwich, but far fewer in other cities of comparable importance –

Coventry, Bristol, Yarmouth and others. These differences must have had considerable effects upon the practice of religion in the cities. Like most regional capitals in England, Norwich was well endowed with religious houses for men; but its friaries were large and probably more than usually active.[59] Norwich had an exceptional number of hermits and anchorites, and the only communities resembling beguinages known to have existed in medieval England.[60] Religious bequests in Norwich wills indicate an unusually high level of support for the local church. This is in comparison with the few other cities for which comparable studies have so far been made.[61] Hull, recently examined by Dr Heath, provides perhaps the strongest contrast. He found that the religion of Hull testators was 'remarkably insular, inert and shallow, untouched by the new devotions, perfunctory almost in the old ones, uninterested in, and showing no deep acquaintance with, doctrine. . . [Thus] Protestantism came to Hull . . .as rain to a dry land.'[62] Regarding craft guilds, on the other hand, those of Norwich, although numerous and with a fair range of religious activities, did not compare with the liveried companies and craft guilds of late medieval London, nor do they appear as impressive, or as having as many charitable or ceremonial activities, as the craft guilds of Coventry or York, provincial capitals of similar importance to Norwich. None of the craft guilds in Norwich, for example, had its own guild-hall or managed a hospital or an alms-house.[63] There was the relative absence of Lollardy and anti-clericalism in Norwich, as I mentioned. Norwich was never a centre of Lollardy in the way that London, Bristol, Coventry and some other cities were.[64] There also appears to have been a relatively low level of lay initiative in running Norwich's parishes; the clergy seem to have been allowed to retain control.[65] These are further indications of a certain conformism, perhaps even of a lack of personal commitment, in the city's religion. So, in short, in many ways a remarkably vigorous and exuberant religion – almost Baroque and High Church – yet combined with elements of conformism: such would appear to have been the city's religion. Certainly Norwich seems to have had its own religious character and to have been significantly different from other English cities. That is really the point I want to make. And this suggests differences between the regional churches of late medieval England, if the regional capitals were in any way representative of their regions.

These are a few scattered and not fully digested thoughts about regionalism in the late medieval English Church. Obviously they need to be filled out with much more research. Also, I do not want to push the point too far. Clearly there were other loyalties and points of reference in the English Church: for example, western Christendom, the national church, the town, the parish. Nevertheless I think the regional church was one important point of reference, and I do not think it has yet been considered sufficiently. I hope that I have at least prompted a few thoughts about it.

Notes

1. N. Tanner, *The Church in Late Medieval Norwich, 1370–1532* (Pontifical Institute of Mediaeval Studies, Studies and Texts 66, Toronto, 1984) – subsequently referred to as: Tanner, *Norwich*.
2. P. Collinson, *The Elizabethan Puritan Movement* (London, 1967), pp. 127, 141, 186–187 and 213; J.T. Evans, *Seventeenth Century Norwich* (Oxford, 1979), pp. 84–104.
3. See especially: J. Delumeau, *Naissance et affirmation de la Réforme*, Nouvelle Clio 30 (2nd edn., Paris, 1968); id., *Le Catholicisme entre Luther et Voltaire*, Nouvelle Clio 30 bis (Paris, 1971), translated by J. Moiser as, *Catholicism between Luther and Voltaire* (London, 1977); F. Rapp, *L'Église et la vie religieuse en Occident à la fin du Moyen Age*, Nouvelle Clio 25 (2nd edn., Paris, 1980); J. Bossy, *Christianity in the West 1400–1700* (Oxford, 1985).
4. J. Scarisbrick, *The Reformation and the English People* (Oxford, 1984), *passim*, especially pp. 61–8.
5. Whiting, 'Abominable Idols: Images and Image-Breaking under Henry VIII', *Journal of Ecclesiastical History*, xxxiii (1982), pp. 46–7.
6. Around 12,000 in 1300, dipping with the Black Death and rising to around 10,000 by the 1520s, very approximately. J. Campbell, *Norwich*, Historic Towns, ed. M. Lobel (London, 1975), pp. 16–18; Tanner, *Norwich*, pp. xvi and 21.
7. Tanner, *Norwich*, pp. 2–5 and 173–8.
8. *Ibid.*, pp. 18–23.
9. *Ibid.*, p.23.
10. *Ibid.*, pp. 58 and 198–202.
11. *Ibid.*, pp. 64–66 and 202–203.
12. *Ibid.*, pp. 67–82 and 204–210.
13. *Ibid.*, pp.114–7 and 224–5.
14. *Ibid.*, pp.126–129.
15. *Ibid.*, pp. 91–104 and 220–1; E. Phelps Brown and S. Hopkin, 'Seven Centuries of Building Wages', in *Essays in Economic History*, ed. E. Carus-Wilson (London,1954–62), ii. p. 177.
16. Tanner, *Norwich*, pp. 119–120
17. *Ibid.*, pp. 118 and 222.
18. *Ibid.*, pp. 141–54.
19. *Ibid.*, pp.152–6.
20. *Ibid.*, pp. 5–7 and 158.
21. *Ibid.*, pp.23–4.
22. *Ibid.*, pp.25–6.
23. *Ibid.*, p.25.
24. *Ibid.*, pp. 162–6; *Heresy Trials in the Diocese of Norwich, 1428–1431*, ed. N. Tanner, Royal Historical Society, Camden 4th series, 20 (London, 1977), pp. 35–38, 43–50, 60 and 195.
25. Tanner, *Norwich*, pp. 101 and 220–1.
26. *Ibid.*, pp. 23 and 170.
27. *Ibid.*, pp. 163–4; R. Houlbrooke, 'Persecution of Heresy and Protestantism in the

Diocese of Norwich under Henry VIII', *Norfolk Archaeology*, xxxv (1970–1973), pp. 312–25.

28. Tanner, *Norwich*, pp. 9–10 and 51–3.

29. See above, p.134.

30. Tanner, *Norwich* pp. 138–40 and 222–3.

31. *Ibid.*, pp. 167–9.

32. *Ibid.*, pp. 29–30. The figures are largely based on the numbers who were styled 'magistri' in the records of their appointments to benefices in the episcopal registers. References to university degrees in the registers themselves, as well as other evidence, suggest that the title was indeed generally used consistently to signify a university graduate. Twenty-two of the parishes had rectors or vicars for all or part of the period 1370 to 1532; (unbeneficed) parish chaplains were in charge of the others. *Ibid.*, p.29, note 204.

33. *Ibid.*,pp. 31–5 and 191–2; John Bale, *Scriptorum illustrium maioris Brytannie catalogus* (Basel, 1557), i, pp. 473–4, 478, 495, 516–7, 527–8, 532, 534–5, 539–40, 555, 563, 579,585–6, 592–3, 597, 612–3, 629–30, and ii, pp. 53, 59, 61–2, 80, 87–8, 91, 155–6.

34. Tanner, *Norwich*, pp. 31 and 190.

35. *Ibid.*, pp. 31 and 33, quoting from: Norfolk Record Office (in Norwich), Probate Records, Registered copies of wills proved in the Norwich Consistory Court (subsequently referred to as NCC), Register Ryxe (1504-7), fol. 386[r], for Cursons's will; Lambeth Palace Library (in London), Register of Archbishop Morton 2 (1486–1500), fol.23[v], for Elys's will. The spelling of the quotations has been modernized.

36. Tanner, *Norwich*, pp. 35–42, 110–2 and 193–7.

37. *Ibid.*, p.112, quoting NCC, Register A. Caston (1479–1488), fols. 163[v] – 164[r].

38. W. Pantin, *The English Church in the Fourteenth Century* (Cambridge, 1955), pp.253–61; id., 'Instructions for a Devout and Literate Layman', in *Medieval Learning and Literature: Essays presented to Richard William Hunt*, ed.J.G. Alexander and M. Gibson (Oxford, 1976), pp. 398–422.

39. *A Book of Showings to the Anchoress Julian of Norwich*, ed. E. Colledge and J. Walsh (Pontifical Institute of Mediaeval Studies, Studies and Texts 35, Toronto, 1978), pp. 41–51.

40. Tanner, *Norwich*, chs. 1 and 2 and Conclusion (pp.1–112 and 167–71).

41. See above, p.136.

42. V. Morgan, 'Cambridge University and "The Country" 1560–1640', in *The University in Society*, ed. L. Stone (London, 1975), i, pp. 196–7, 205, 208, 218–9, 221 and 241.

43. Tanner, *Norwich*, pp. 29–33, 39, 44, 46–7, 55, 124 and 235.

44. See J. Gray, 'Canon Law in England: some reflections on the Stubbs-Maitland Controversy', in *Studies in Church History*, iii (ed. G.J. Cuming, Leiden, 1968), pp. 48–68.

45. J.A.F. Thomson, *The Later Lollards 1414–1520* (Oxford,1965), p.2 and *passim*.

46. Perhaps the best study remains: J. Toussaert, *Le sentiment religieux en Flandre à la fin du Moyen Age* (Paris, 1960).

47. *Councils and Synods,1205–1313*, ed. F.M. Powicke and C.R. Cheney (Oxford, 1964), pp. 342–64, 498–501 and 802. D. Wilkins, *Concilia Magnae Britanniae et Hiberniae* (London, 1737), i, p. 708, and ii, p. 25.

48. C. Woodforde, *The Norwich School of Glass-Painting in the Fifteenth Century* (Oxford, 1950).

49. *Non-Cycle Plays and Fragments*, ed. N. Davis, EETS Supplementary Text 1 (Oxford, 1970), pp. xxvi-xxxi.

50. See above, p.132.

51. Tanner, *Norwich*, pp. 24–5.

52. This is suggested by the monks' surnames, many of which were the names of places on

or near the priory's estates (*ibid.*, p. 25).

53. Margery Kempe, *The Book of Margery Kempe*, book 1, chs. 17–18 and 43, ed. S. Meech and H. Allen (EETS, 212, London, 1940), pp. 38–40, 42–3 and 102.
54. *Ibid.*, book 1, chs. 26 and 43, ed. Meech, pp. 60 and 102; Tanner, *Norwich*, pp. 88–90.
55. See especially the will registers of the Norwich Consistory Court and of the Archdeacon of Norwich's Court (Norfolk Record Office, Norwich).
56. Tanner, *Norwich*, pp. 70–80.
57. *Ibid.*, p. 71.
58. Wider studies do exist, for example: M. Vale, *Piety, Charity and Literacy among the Yorkshire Gentry 1370–1480*, Borthwick Papers 50 (York, 1976); P.W. Fleming, 'Charity, Faith and the Gentry of Kent 1422–1529', in *Property and Politics: Essays in Later Medieval English history*, ed. A.J. Pollard (Gloucester, 1984), pp. 36–58. But these are studies of particular groups within a region. There is, so far as I am aware, no general study of religion in a region of medieval England.
59. Tanner, *Norwich*, pp. 19–35.
60. *Ibid.*, pp. 57–66.
61. For some comparisons, see *ibid.*, pp. 113–140. The best analysis for another city is, J.A.F. Thomson, 'Piety and Charity in Late Medieval London'. *Journal of Ecclesiastical History.* xvi (1965), pp. 178–195.
62. P. Heath, 'Urban Piety in the Later Middle Ages: the Evidence of Hull Wills', in *The Church, Politics and Patronage in the Fifteenth Century*, ed. R.B. Dobson (Gloucester, 1984), p. 229.
63. Tanner, *Norwich*, pp. 68–73; G. Unwin, *The Gilds and Companies of London* (4th edn., London, 1963), pp. 155–217; *The Victoria History of the County of York: The City of York*, (Oxford, 1961), pp. 95–7 and 481–3; D. Palliser, 'The Trade Guilds of Tudor York', in *Crisis and Order in English Towns 1500–1700*, ed. P. Clark and P. Slack (London, 1972), pp. 96 and 110; C. Phythian-Adams, 'Ceremony and the Citizens: The Communal Year in Coventry', in *ibid.*, pp. 57–85.
64. J.A.F. Thomson, *The Later Lollards 1414–1520* (Oxford, 1965), pp. 20–47, 110–16 and 139–71.
65. Tanner, *Norwich*, p. 16.

8

Towns at War: Relations between the Towns of Normandy and their English Rulers, 1417–1450

Anne E. Curry
University of Reading

The development of towns in Normandy was inextricably linked with the military policies of their rulers. Some had their origins in the ducal wars as strategic and governmental centres. Others, as communes, had been elevated in the Plantagenet-Capetian struggles to the direct feudal vassalage of duke or king, and were thus committed to specific defensive and offensive obligations.[1] The war-time policies of Charles V as regent and subsequently as king formalised the defensive responsibilities of the towns. Special local purchase taxes were authorised to be levied, often in lieu of a town's contribution towards general royal taxation. These were directed towards the construction and repair of urban fortifications; although they were often initiated at royal order, it was the town's own responsibility to administer their collection and disbursement as well as to organise labour and materials, and, following earlier precedent, to man the resulting defences.[2]

These policies had several important results. In towns with already existing self-government, military organisation became one of the major aspects of urban business, creating a host of officials and consuming a great deal of municipal time and money but simultaneously generating much communal pride. To those towns without much independence, the obligation of defence gave the first taste of self-regulation. Indeed in certain Norman towns, the only urban institution discernible before the late fifteenth or sixteenth centuries concerned the financing and administration of defences.[3]

The measures taken by Charles V remained the norm into the fifteenth century when the duchy was beset by the Armagnac-Burgundian civil war and by English attack. As rulers of Normandy, the Lancastrians did little to change existing obligations within the towns but sought to exploit them as their Valois predecessors had done. Any intending conqueror had to gain possession of the towns, particularly as they formed the economic and administrative centres of the duchy. Moreover, the policies of the preceeding half-century had ensured that towns possessed the most up-to-date defences and artillery. Campaigns were thus dominated by urban sieges: when towns fell, the neighbouring villages and castles tended to surrender automatically. Once occupied, considerable attention had to be given by the ruler to the maintenance of good relations with the townspeople. The full and willing performance of urban military obligations was crucial to overall defence strategy, although urban treason, and with it the possibility of premature loss of these vital strongholds, had to be avoided at all costs.

The towns thus had to be allowed a considerable say in military policies and would inevitably bring much self-interest to bear. Their opinion could prove decisive, particularly if faced with the choice of resistance or surrender. Indeed it can easily be argued that this second stage of the Hundred Years War was won and lost not on the battlefields of Normandy but in the *maisons de la ville* and on the street corners of the duchy's towns. This paper proposes to investigate this hypothesis by examining first the role of the towns in the conquests of Henry V and of Charles VII, and by considering secondly the interplay of urban and royal policies during the whole of the English occupation. But first, for the sake of effective and concrete ilustration of the 'town at war', let us transport ourselves to Mantes at the very end of the English ocupation.

I

On Tuesday 26 August 1449, the town of Mantes, the last English-held bastion in the *Pays de Conquête*, was under threat as the French army continued its apparently inexorable advance. A large assembly of 'bourgeois, manans et habitans' gathered in the *maison de la ville* to discuss what should be done.[4] The gravity of the situation is clearly demonstrated by the large number present on this occasion – between 270 and 300 – when the regular three-weekly meetings of the town council were usually attended by not more than ten to twenty. Its singular nature is further revealed by the absence of royal officials and representatives of the English garrison, although the native-born *maréchal*, Guillaume Langlois, was present.

The *maire* reported to the assembly that Charles VII, then at Chartres, intended to lay siege to Mantes.[5] For this purpose, the French king had ordered to be sent down the Seine from Paris 'certains engins et artilleries'. The town was thus at the mercy of his troops, who would surely put it to fire and the sword (*a feu et a sang*) as indeed the laws of war permittted in the case of besieged towns which offered resistance. The *Délibérations* at Mantes record a unanimous response to the *maire's* announcement:

> veu et considere la puissance dicellui prince aussi que on ne peult avoir aucun secours des anglois au cas que le Roy Charles dessusdit feroit mettre siege devant ceste dite ville ou sommerait icelle lui faire obeissance, que on trouve moien, sans souffrir battre la dite ville de canons ne autrement, davoir bonne composition, prouffitable et honourable au mieulx que on pourra.

That very same day, the town of Mantes was delivered to the representatives of King Charles, now called by the record 'notre souverain seigneur'. The *Délibérations* clearly imply that the decision to surrender was taken by the townspeople on their own initiative.

Robert Blondel's account of the surrender of Mantes differs slightly in detail but not in spirit.[6] He suggests that Mantes initially refused to surrender, much to the French king's ire, but that the *maire,* as the only sensible member of the community, took it upon himself to write to Charles at Chartres under cover of sending, with the permission of the English lieutenant, spies to report on the strength of the French army.[7] The king's reply was positive: he wished to avoid bloodshed and promised full pardon to the town if it surrendered of its own accord. The *maire* then disclosed the true nature of the secret misssion to his fellow *bourgeois* and made a stirring speech to the English garrison inducing them to agree to the surrender. There is no specific mention of 'engins et artilleries' but the tone is much as in the *Délibérations*; resistance is useless, and will only bring death and destruction to townsman and occupier alike. Thus, 'burgenses enim et barbari unanimes, mortis terrore perculsi Gallis comitibus. . . valvas Meduntae liberas patefaciunt'. The *Délibérations* confirm that by nightfall of that same Tuesday, 26 August, Thomas Saintbarbe, lieutenant of the *bailli* and captain, Thomas, Lord Hoo, put his name to the standard form of treaty of surrender and promised to withdraw his troops within eight days.[8]

Blondel goes on to stress the war-time sufferings of the town of Mantes, dating back to the treachery of Charles of Navarre, continuing through the schisms wreaked by the Burgundians, and culminating in the 'ferrocissima crudelitas' of Henry V.[9] Basin, who claims that it was he who advised Charles VII to attack Vernon and Mantes before seeing to the conquest of Lower Normandy, asserts that the inhabitants of both towns had long been afflicted by the terrors and hardships of war, adding that the English garrisons did not object to easy surrender realising their impotence in the face of the all-powerful French army.[10]

If we were to think ourselves into the position of the inhabitants of Mantes at this point, we too would have little regard for Saintbarbe and his troops. The declining confidence of the townsmen in their English rulers, and indeed of the English garrison in their central commanders, can be seen clearly in the *Délibérations* of the previous five months. On 21 April 1449, the truce of Tours still being in force, Robert Floques, French captain of Évreux, a town which had been in French hands for the last eight years, led a sortie right up to the gates of Mantes threatening to take the town by assault ('d'emblee').[11] At the town council meeting two days later, the lieutenant, John Gregory, and other royal officials advised the *maire* to send one or two of the *bourgeois* in Gregory's company to the duke of Somerset at Rouen to inform him of the enemy's enterprise and to ask him to send more troops to the town.[12] This suggestion was received in lukewarm fashion by the town council. Whilst some thought the advice of a joint mission to Somerset wise- 'afin que le prince fut plus compte de la dite ville' – the majority felt, for what reason we cannot ascertain, that at this stage only a letter should be sent to the lieutenant-general. The municipal records do not record Somerset's reply, although the account of the *trésorier-général* of Normandy records a special payment made between 24 April and 26 June 1449 to Thomas Saintbarbe for the diligent exercise of his duties in defending Mantes, noting that he had been sent specifically 'pour obvier a plusieurs entreprises puis nagueres faictes par les gens du roy (i.e. Charles VII, for the account was not audited until Normandy was in French hands) sur la ville dudit lieu de Mantes . . .'[13]

The council met again on 12 May, when a familiar complaint was voiced.[14] Despite the truce, the cost of carrying out repairs to the fortifications of the town was ever increasing, 'qui est chose impossible a la ville de supporter sans aucune aide'. Open war in over thirty of the previous forty-nine years had undoubtedly exacerbated the burden of defence in the towns. In addition, there is a strong suggestion that, whilst towns like Mantes were quite prepared to (or had little choice but to) pay for construction and upkeep of defences in time of war, their attitude changed after the truce of Tours when expectation of peacetime conditions made them more reluctant to contribute.[15] Similarly, there was greater reluctance at Mantes to pay *guet* (watch) after the truce and a dispute had already arisen between the town authorities and the English captain over the reopening of gates which had earlier been closed for strategic reasons. It is also interesting to note that the *maire* elected shortly after the truce in November 1444 had refused to take the customary oath of allegiance to the English.[16] At the meeting of 12 May 1449, therefore, the town council decided to send the *maire* and one other *bourgeois* to Somerset 'pour lui remonstrer la povrete de ceste ville de Mantes, les grans reparations quil y fault faire chacun jour et le danger en quoy elle a este de jour en jour'.

When no reply had been received a fortnight later, the town council decided to send another leading member of the *bourgeoisie* to the lieutenant-general to ask him for a subvention from the *gabelle* (salt tax) towards the cost of repairs and of the wages of three watchmen, once again alerting him to enemy threats in the vicinity.[17] Two weeks later, on Sunday 8 June, the reply arrived and was read to a specially summoned assembly. [18] Somerset, at this stage involved in the aftermath of the loss of Pont-de-l'Arche in mid-May, had little solace to offer the town save a vague promise to allow the subvention from the *gabelle* and the following flowery phrases: 'il mercie cordialement les bourgeois, manans et habitans de ceste ville de Mantes de leurs loialtez et bonnes diligences quils ont continuelement eue tant de presente que autrefois en la seurete et saufegarde de la dite ville, parquoy ils sont dignes de recommande'.

Such pious statements may not have cut much ice with the *bourgeoisie* of Mantes, nor perhaps with the garrison of the town, for the receptivity of both groups had already been undermined by the arrival of letters at the end of the previous week from Thomas, Lord Hoo, chancellor of Normandy and titular captain and *bailli* of the town.[19] He apologised that, due to his incessant involvement in royal business, he could not attend personally to matters concerning the town nor be present in person. He had, however, been approached by Laurence Rainford with a request to be appointed his lieutenant at Mantes. This seemed a reasonable proposition to Hoo, but the latter did not want to effect the appointment without the consent of the *bourgeois* and inhabitants of the town.

At the special meeting of Sunday 8 June, the town council were somewhat confused by Hoo's letter, its being hardly what they had expected at this time of mounting crisis, for there was no mention of additional trops. Indeed, the *Délibérations* record that 'au regard des lettres de mondit seigneur le chancellier, na este donne aucune opinion'. Reassembling on the next day, the townsmen had collected their thoughts enough to decide to reply to Hoo thanking him for his good wishes. But they wanted to make clear to their absentee captain that whilst they would follow his wishes on the appointment of a new lieutenant, they had been perfectly happy with the services of the present lieutenant, Hochequin Gentil, whom they felt 'sest bien et grandement porter a la defence de la dite ville'.[20]

Rainford did not take up office. Perhaps Hoo changed his mind upon receipt of the town's equivocal reply. Hochequin Gentil was still in charge of the 'garde de la dite ville' a month later when the *maire* brought to him, after deliberation at the town council, complaints about the activities of the men of the *trésorier-général* of Normandy (Osberne Mundford) who had been seizing produce in the area. In particular, they were outraged at the removal of 'vergus aux vignes' and the threats of violence to those who had been tending the vineyards.[21] Mundford's account confirms that from 4 to 18 July he had been active, along with the earl of Shrewsbury, in the Seine valley between Vernon and Mantes attempting to resist French-backed activities and to collect local revenues to pay the English army.[22] By this stage, the English were in desperate financial straits and this had undoubtedly contributed to a decay in law and order.

Charles VII declared war on 17 July. The growing sense of crisis and disruption to ordinary life is witnessed in the subsequent *Délibérations* at Mantes. By Saturday 26 July it had been decided to cancel the banquet scheduled for 15 August to celebrate the Ascension of the Virgin: 'le receveur de la ville na point dargent . . . les aquis dicelle ville ne vallent riens a present'.[23] A curfew was imposed on the town at least from the middle of August and possibly earlier.[24] By 20 August, rumours abounded that King Charles had advanced to Chartres and that siege engines were being prepared at Paris for use against Mantes. As we have seen, it was at this stage that the town council decided to send spies to both Chartres and Paris to seek out the truth of these rumours and that, according to Blondel, the *maire* sent his own emissary to Charles VII. At the same time, the *Délibérations* record the town council's consideration of whether to write once again to Somerset 'se on voit quil soit bon de ce faire'.[25] It is not known whether any letters were sent – perhaps the town council did not think it worthwhile for the English had failed to send assistance to other towns already besieged by the French – but the spies returned within six days confirming the rumours of French preparations. So gathered, as we have seen, the large number of townsmen on 26 August to discuss immediate surrender.

Like many other Norman towns, Mantes surrendered to Charles VII without a shot being fired. After thirty years in English obedience, the Mantais sought pardon from the French king for their 'disloyalty' and attempted to re-establish good relations wiith his regime. Blondel suggests that the *maire's* secret letter had already sought promise of a general pardon from the French king: the chronicler emphasises the latter's immense clemency towards the town despite its crime of English allegiance.[26] The *Délibérations* record that at the beginning of the week following the treaty of surrender, by which time the English garrison had presumably been evacuated, the town council agreed that it would be politic to go to their new lord to seek his forgiveness.[27] The representatives elected to go on this still rather unenviable mission were also instructed to use their discretion when in the king's presence to decide if it was an appropriate juncture to ask whether exemption from the *taille* and other taxes could be granted to the town 'pour la fortification de la ville et paiement des guetteurs de dessus Notre Dame (the parish church) et de la Porte au Saint (?Porte de Seine) pour certain temps'.

II

This lengthy consideration of the surrender of the town of Mantes has been undertaken because the events of the months of the summer of 1449 as recorded in the *Délibérations* bring together so many of the characteristics and qualities of Norman towns under English rule in the first half of the fifteenth century. They also show something of the relationship between the town and its garrison and the central government of the duchy, albeit under the rather special circumstances of the end of the English occupation. They stress the town's responsibility for its own future: its defensive obligations, its sending of spies (and double agents) on its own initiative, its final decision to surrender to avoid bombardment. Throughout the *Délibérations* of the last five months of English occupation, the concerns which were uppermost in the minds of the Mantais were those which impinged most closely on the well-being and self-interest of their town.

For no other town in Normandy and the Pays de Conquête does such a detailed local record of the events of the Reconquest survive which can be compared with narrative sources. However, it is possible to show that the response of other towns to French attack was similar.

The *Délibérations* of the town council of Rouen are totally silent on the surrender, with no entries between regular financial business dealt with under English control on 28 September 1449 and the taking up of office by the newly appointed French captain on 20 November.[28] All of the principal narratives, however, give detailed accounts of the events leading up to the surrender, emphasising to a greater or lesser degree the crucial role played by the city's inhabitants.[29] Berry and Blondel both suggest that the English were prevented from withdrawing troops from Rouen for the relief of other towns because of fear of facilitating treason in the capital. With Basin, they agree (although giving slightly different accounts and chronologies) that men of Rouen approached Charles VII with plans for delivering the town to him by local collusion and subterfuge. Despite the failure of the first attempt (which Basin claims the English punished most cruelly thus stimulating further revolt), the inhabitants, fearing the damage a long siege and assault would bring but well aware of English military weakness, were finally responsible for the surrender of Rouen. This was brought about by further negotiations with the French conducted by the archbishop and leading city officials, followed by widespread armed rebellion on the part of the citizens. Basin's vivid account speaks of the erection of barricades in the street, the driving of the English into the castle, palace and bridge, the citizens' seizure of the walls and gates, and the opening of the gates to French troops. With the loss of control of the city, Somerset had little choice but to negotiate total surrender. All the narratives end with a detailed account of the formal entry of Charles VII on 10 November, and with clear evidence not only of the citizens' desire to please and placate their new master but also of his merciful and benevolent attitude towards those who had proved so vital to his bloodless and easy reconquest of the capital.

Local collusion in the French Reconquest is well-evidenced in other towns.[30] Pont-de-l'Arche, the first town to be lost, was taken by the assistance of a merchant of Louviers, a town which had itself fallen twice to the French by means of local connivance. Verneuil was betrayed by a miller of the town who had been disciplined by an Englishman for falling asleep whilst paying *guet*: the miller persuaded the watch to leave the walls early and simply admitted the French himself. Alençon was apparently recovered by local collusion, as too was Argentan, where the *bourgeoisie*, annoyed at English dissimulation in discussions for surrender, indicated to the French where they could safely enter the town. At Carentan, there were attacks on the English garrison by local men. Although Caudebec was surrendered as part of the composition following Somerset's negotiations at Rouen, a series of letters reveals earlier suspicions of urban disloyalty. Messages sent to the lieutenant-general in mid-August spoke of *division* between inhabitants and royal officials; the female spy sent to seek the opinion of the town's captain, Fulk Eyton, held captive at Pont-Audemer, brought back the following unequivocal advice about the 'enemy within': 'lequel (Eyton) manda que fort se tenissent sur leur garde les gens de guerre au dit lieu de Caudebec et les plus fors contre les bourgeois et habitans de la dite ville de Caudebec sans a eulz laisser superediter (?) ainsi que par aucuns des dessusdits a est rapporte'.[31]

Surrenders of other towns in Normandy were negotiated by their councils or by a local seigneur with scant regard for the English occcupier. As at Mantes, the principal motivation was fear of bombardment and assault, which might lead to French retribution, coupled with a certain knowledge that the English could offer no real assistance in the face of French armed might. This situation is clear at Lisieux thanks to the survival not only of the chronicle of Thomas Basin, then bishop of the city, but also of accounts and other materials in the Archives Communales.[32]

The last *compte* at Lisieux for the period of English occupation reveals that efforts were made to strengthen the town's artillery and to seek Somerset's aid shortly before the French advance. It also indicates the embassy of the bishop and representatives of the town to seek terms of composition. Basin's reasoning is made clear in his chronicle. At first he thought that the inhabitants and small English garrison could offer resistance despite the poor fortifications of the place. But then, realising that Pont-Audemer had fallen notwithstanding a much larger English military presence, he began to fear for the safety of his town, as did the English therein, although the bishop claims that the townspeople were so scared of their occupier that they dared not speak of treating for surrender. Basin thus conducted the negotiations himself, soon convincing the inhabitants and even the English garrison (Blondel gives his supposed speech *in extenso*) that non-resistance was the best option. In this way, physical damage to the town was avoided (despite the French troops' hopes of booty), the garrison left with some dignity and the bishop even regained rights in the town which he had lost during the English occupation, such as the nomination of the captain.[33]

The narratives suggest that townsmen elsewhere negotiated easy surrender for similar reasons, often persuading the English garrrison that resistance was useless (such as at Coutances and Avranches) or entering into their own independent negotiations (as at Saint-Lô, Valognes and, probably, at Honfleur). Even in towns which offered resistance, such as Caen, the inhabitants hoped to negotiate advantageous terms of surrender, avoiding the risk of legitimised plundering by the victorious army and ensuring that the defeated occupier left only after all debts had been settled. In addition, townsmen soon sought to ingratiate themselves with their new master, to seek his pardon and to ensure the preservation of their rights and privileges. The *jurés* of Caen, addressing Charles at his entry to the city, sought forgiveness for their disloyalty, arguing that they had been compelled against their will into English obedience and had suffered much in the war; the king answered that he wished his *bonne ville* to enjoy all its earlier privileges.[34] Similar urban petitions (often accompanied, as at Mantes, by a further request for exemption from taxation or financial assistance towards fortifications) and royal pardons are found in abundance for Norman towns in the wake of the French Reconquest.[35]

Urban policies in 1449–50 were not conditioned by a strong sense of pro-French patriotism. By no means had the towns of Normandy, or at least the majority of them, been waiting for liberation. Indeed, as we shall see, urban loyalty to the English had been high compared with that of other sections of the Norman population. This did not prevent the *bonnes villes* attempting to disavow their previous loyalty to the English as quickly as possible once they fell under French threat or into French hands, for towns had a strong sense of what was most prudent.

Self-preservation was undoubtedly the main motivation, for fears were largely two-fold. The first was fear of damage (which would no doubt have to be repaired at urban expense) wrought by increasingly powerful siege cannon; as Chevalier wisely comments 'par une bonne part leur (the towns') puissance militaire qui était le point d'appui et le garant de leur autonomie militaire a été compromis par le progrès de l'artillerie'.[36] The second was fear of assault, which allowed the attacker licence to pillage and slaughter. Both endangered the lives and property of individuals, and the survival of a town's governmental machinery. Surrender was often the only possible course of action unless aid was definitely known to be forthcoming; garrisons were often powerless to resist the urban will. In this respect, most towns in the French Reconquest of 1449–50 (and, as we shall see, in the English conquest of 1417–20 as well as in the intervening years), changed hands at the behest of their inhabitants.

Clearly, too, the rulers of Normandy had to take the towns into account. Charles VII actively encouraged the inhabitants of Norman towns to surrrender, assuring the preservation of their privileges and their special role within the body politic.He prevented pillage by his soldiers wherever possible, and aimed throughout at emphasising his clemency. Two principal motives for this policy can be detected. The first was a clear realisation of the strategic and political importance of the Norman towns. The second, as the principal narratives show, concerned royal propaganda. As Berry pointed out, the king's reputation in the Reconquest came not only from the strength of his army and artillery but also from his clemency.[37] Blondel offered a more specific interpretation by comparing the cruelty and rapacity of Henry V in his conquest with the mercy and 'humanitas' of Charles VII in his.[38]

III

We are often warned that history does not repeat itself. It will come as no surprise to the student of this period, however, that the policies of Henry V and his successors towards the towns of Normandy were remarkably similar to those of Charles VII, and that towns responded to English conquest in much the same way as to French.[39]

Despite Henry's stress on the legitimacy of his territorial and dynastic claims, his relations with the Norman towns were born in war. The citizens of Harfleur were harshly treated in 1415 with the taking of hostages and mass expulsions. Furthermore, Henry effectively destroyed the town's civic government, ordering its registers and charters to be burned publicly as a symbol of his authority.[40] His treatment of Caen, the first major centre to be taken in the second campaign, was equally rigorous; entering the town after severe bombardment, Henry destroyed the urban archives, allowed his soldiers to pillage at will, and began to encourage English settlement and martial rule.[41] This policy was undertaken partly to keep up the enthusiasm of the English army, and partly to impress upon other towns and strongholds that resistance was both futile and foolish.

Both objectives were fulfilled. Most of the urban centres subsequently threatened offered no resistance, although as in the 1449–50 Reconquest some intra-urban castles held out longer. The entire duchy of Alençon, for instance, fell within fifteen days. Despite Perceval de Cagny's avowal that the people of Alençon would suffer no lord but their own duke, the town and garrison had in fact begun to treat for surrender even before Henry approached the town.[42] Indeed, towns with magnate or episcopal over-lords proved no more resolute in their loyalty than did those centres directly linked to the crown.

Throughout 1418, urban self-interest predominated both in Normandy, where the fall of Falaise in February led to the easy capitulation to the English of other centres in the south and south west, and also in northern France where the Burgundians were eagerly admitted to most of the towns, including Paris,by their inhabitants.[43] In the following year, the fall of Rouen despite tenacious resistance persuaded the remaining urban centres of the duchy to surrender to the English. Caudebec, for instance, had already decided to capitulate if the Norman capital fell. The case of Mantes is once again of interest. The leading townsmen approached the duke of Clarence in early February 1419 to hand over the keys even before he had issued a summons to surrender.[44]

As in 1449–50, the towns realised that their interests were better served by surrender than resistance. They had most certainly been alarmed by English military might and by the experiences of towns which had held out against Henry. But this was not just negative fear of bombardment and assault. The English king had increasingly shown himself to be a merciful lord; his rule offered the prospect of better, or at least no worse, treatment than under Burgundian or Armagnac rule.

As early as 19 September 1417, Henry confirmed the privileges of Bayeux which had offered him no resistance.[45] The rights of Rouen had been restored in their entirety immediately after capitulation despite the lengthy siege, and there subsequently followed confirmations of privileges at Gisors, Dieppe, Caen and Pontoise.[46] The document concerning Dieppe specifically noted the loyalty of the townsmen, their readiness to surrender after the fall of Rouen and their resistance to a French plot to seize the town. The charter for Caen even cited the traditional loyalty and role of this ancient city in the Anglo-Norman heritage. Less than a month after the fall of Falaise, Henry had granted that town the customary right to levy purchase taxes to be spent on urban fortifications, and these by now traditional grants were much in evidence in the next years and throughout the English occupation.[47]

These grants and confirmations, and in particular the reasons given for their issue, only make sense when we realise that they originated in urban petitions to the English king. The towns lost no time in approaching their new royal master, as they might at any new accession, and of assuring him of their devotion in return for preservation and extension of their own interests. We know, for instance, that the Mantais sent embassies to the king in 1421 and 1422 to seek an *aide* on wine to finance fortifications along the bank of the Seine.[48] Town actions in this period parallel exactly the approaches made to Charles VII at the expulsion of the English. Henry was no less anxious to meet local requests, for he not only wished to appear a legitimate and benevolent ruler but also he, like his Valois predecessors and successors, relied to a considerable extent on the military and political support of the towns.

Henry therefore encouraged the Norman towns to see him as a just ruler, not only reducing taxation and limiting the excesses of his troops, but also making various promises to protect local interests. In January 1418, for instance, he had accorded to his uncle, the duke of Exeter, power to confirm in the king's name the rights and privileges of the towns of the duchy. Henry himself vouched in January 1420, four months before the formal signing of the Treaty of Troyes, that when he obtained the crown of France he would maintain all the rights and privileges of the peoples of his kingdom.[49] The Treaty considerably enhanced his position by making him heir and, perhaps more importantly for present policies, Regent of France. Representatives from each town were required to take oaths to the Treaty, and thenceforward incoming officials also had to take this oath to the English *bailli*. The spate of urban petitions and confirmations of privileges increased after the sealing of the Treaty as did those of other secular and religious institutions. In addition, the terms of the Treaty, by maintaining Norman separatism at least for the time being, appealed to local opinion.

Henry was well received in the Norman towns in his various progresses (much as Charles VII was feted in his Reconquest) and much lamented at his death in 1422. By then, he had already enjoyed some success in his attempts to rebuild the duchy which had been considerably damaged by decades of war. Certain aspects of his policies are worthy of note, reflecting the end of 'martial law' and the re-establishment of civil government. In January 1421, the Estates of Normandy were first summoned to Rouen thus initiating a policy of local consultation which, as we shall see, was of vital importance to the towns. Their vote of taxation ended the need for English finances and henceforward the duchy was intended to pay for, and thus have some say in, its own defence and administration.

The meeting also offered the opportunity for local complaint against the behaviour of soldiers and royal officials. The resulting royal proclamations of 24 January reveal the dominance of urban interests in the Estates. Henry banned his officers from taking exactions from the people, noting particularly the invidious practices of collecting illegal tolls on markets and merchandising, on entries and exits to towns and passage across bridges, of captains charging for 'passeports', and of the prise of victuals. The captains and officials at Pontoise, Mantes, Meulan and Beaumont-sur-Oise were specifically mentioned as the worst offenders but the proclamation was to be read in town halls and urban churches throughout the duchy (except in the *bailliage* of Alençon) 'ainsi que notre peuple puisse vivre et marchandiser en bon pais sans etre aucunement abusez ne destourbez par noz gentz ne autres'.[50]

On 25 April followed orders for the better governance of garrisons to captains of thirty-six Norman towns about whom complaints had been received, again mentioning illegal exactions, disorderly behaviour and the need (and desire of the inhabitants) for the provision of diligent defence.[51] In addition this month also saw new disciplinary measures against deserters who had been oppressing the native population.[52] Whilst these measures, along with the appointment of a seneschal and other commissions of enquiry, could not ensure the total protection of urban interest against the military, they represented Henry's sincere attempt to remedy abuses, and, even more significantly, to take account of civilian opinion.

Henry ended his reign in a spirit of conciliation although this did not preclude an element of control, for the towns still housed sizable garrisons and in some cases (particularly Harfleur and Caen) English settlers. All captains and *baillis* were English and exercised considerable control over the civilian populations, albeit often following Valois practice. At Rouen, the traditional responsibility of the city council for the defence of the walls and gates had not yet been restored. The confirmation of Pontoise's charter in January 1421 was made conditional upon good behaviour.[53] There was still considerable fear of urban treason elsewhere: at Mantes the captain was alarmed by a riotous assembly shortly before Christmas 1421 and briefly broke off relations with the town council, although the townsmen were not dilatory in seeking royal pardon.[54] Thus although the militaristic nature of the early occupation had been eroded, Henry continued to steer a middle course between conciliation and control, and the urban populations responded accordingly with some degree of caution.

IV

The English continued to rule the duchy for a further twenty-eight years. Given the length of the period, the large number of towns in the duchy each with their own characteristics and history, and the various political and military fluctuations, it is obviously impossible to consider in detail the relationship between English rulers and Norman towns. Seen at it simplest, the aims of the former remained as determined by Henry V – a balanced policy of conciliation and control. Likewise the towns continued to look to their own interests. The precise nature of the relationship depended as always upon the overall strength of the ruler's military and political position. It is important to emphasise, however, certain key features, first from the English and, secondly, from the towns' standpoint. The attitude of English rulers continued to be determined principally by the military significance of the towns. Theoretically, the English could impose control through a massive military presence, although this raised serious financial implications and could act as a potential cause of alienation of the native population. Despite constant concern for adequate protection by their rulers, towns had long disliked the presence of garrisons. The maintenance of military discipline was thus of paramount importance, and the English gave considerable attention to avoiding conflict by imposing controls on captains and their men. Indeed, the history of the relationship between Norman towns and their English rulers is inextricably linked with the system of military organisation and administration in the duchy as it developed between 1417 and 1450.

Towns zealously advanced their acknowledged ancient rights to have some say in the defence of their walls. Because the English could afford neither to provide very large garrisons nor to alienate local opinion, they had to allow town councils their traditional role in defensive provision, whilst at the same time ensuring that the burdens did not become too onerous and that adequate surveillance was maintained. At Mantes, for instance, a compromise was soon reached over control of the keys, dividing it between *bourgeois* and garrison.[55] The responsibility for defence of gates and walls was restored to Rouen in 1425, although when increased security was required, such as during the visit of Henry VI, additional English troops were introduced.[56]

In most towns, there was a division of military jurisdiction. The crown defended the castle, the townsmen their walls. This was effected by means of the obligation incumbent on all householders (usually of both the town and its environs) to pay *guet et garde*. Although there was some surveillance by English captains, the essential organisation was carried out by an elected urban official known as the *clerc du guet*.[57] Sometimes towns chose to substitute or supplement the communal watch by paying professional watchmen and *cannoniers*. The town councils of the largest towns had their own stock of armaments which could be distributed to those paying watch, and additionally saw to the construction of *guerites* and other facilities in walls and gates.[58] These military responsibilites formed a vital contribution to defence. It was in English interests to ensure that they were well and willingly performed by the townsmen, for where the local population was loyal, fewer English troops were required. The enumeration of garrisons in 1433–34 explained the small size of garrisons in Bayeux, Caudebec, Coutances, Caen, Carentan, Verneuil and Pont-de-l'Arche by commenting that these places were well-populated and peaceful: indeed many towns housed only token English garrisons except at times of crisis.[59]

The English realised, however, that urban loyalty was tenuous; if threatened such centres would always put their own interests first. All rulers needed to invest constant and considerable effort into the relationship with the towns. There is extensive evidence of English attempts to create an atmosphere of trust and community of interest. In addition to duchy-wide policies concerning economic well-being and military discipline, the English tried not only to listen to and take account of local opinion but also to shape it by dissemination of information and by regular consultation with urban interests both individually and collectively.

In many respects, the English were simply following Valois precedent, echoed, as we have seen, by the policies of Charles VII in the wake of his Reconquest. Petitions were thus received favourably and assistance granted whenever possible. Permission continued to be accorded at urban request for the levying of local purchase taxes to be spent on fortifications. Towns were given additional financial assistance from duchy revenues and even from the private purses of English captains.[60] Garrisons might be increased in size at local pressure, with towns often being prepared to meet the cost of additional protection.[61]

Attention continued to be given to local grievances against soldiers and officers of the crown, and formal channels for complaints were established in the 1420s. Governmental enquiries were launched both duchywide and locally, again commonly at urban request; the most important were the investigations and subsequent reforms ordered by the duke of Bedford in 1423, where captains were accused of billeting troops on *bourgeois* without their consent, charging tolls on entries to towns, demanding excessive *guet*, levying money and victuals illegally and imprisoning any who objected to their behaviour.[62] In like manner, the lieutenants-general and the *conseil* undertook progresses throughout the duchy, visiting the major centres, sounding out the opinion of the inhabitants, and listening to complaints and petitions. These might result in specific attempts, for instance, to improve military discipline, or to strengthen defences where both the central and urban authorities saw them as vulnerable.[63] Further governmental activity developed from practical needs, such as the rewarding of informers who had betrayed plots to deliver towns to the enemy.[64]

As in England, towns, or more precisely urban obligarchies, formed an important part of political society. Conventions of honour were thus accorded to the leading *bourgeois*. They had a special role to play in royal entries and were frequently entertained at official banquets. In recording the hospitality meted out by the earl of Warwick at Rouen in 1431, his Household Book indicates that merchants and *bourgeois* of the town were regularly guests at dinner, sometimes acompanied by their wives.[65] Local royal officials might also act to defend specific urban interests. In October 1447 it was the *gens du conseil* at Rouen who informed the town council of a petition addressed to the king by the towns of Lower Normandy which threatened to undermine the capital's privileges.[66]

The towns were undoubtedly the centres of political opinion in the duchy. Letters were frequently sent to the towns by the governments in England and in Normandy, telling them of intended policies, or sometimes answering the towns' own requests for information and assistance. There was, of course, much routine correspondence, urging towns to be on their guard against rumoured threats of attack or merely notifying them of appointments and consideration of their requests.[67] Secret missives also were sent, however, to captains warning them of rumours of urban treason and urging them to arrest the plotters.[68]

At times of crisis, greater attention was paid to keeping the towns informed and, hopefully, content. This is particularly noticeable in the crisis of 1435–36. The leading Norman towns had been invited by the English to send observers to the Congress of Arras. After the Burgundian defection, the *conseil* in Normandy was anxious to ensure that the duchy's towns were made cognisant of the duke's treachery and of the willingness of the English to negotiate a peace 'for the relief of the poor people'; it thus sent copies of the report of the English embassy to towns in the *bailliage* of Caux, an act which derives further significance from the remembrance that many of these towns had earlier been in Burgundian hands.[69] At the end of the year, and in the spring of 1436, the English council, partly in reply to a petition by the Norman Estates, sent a spate of letters to the leading towns assuring them that the sovereignty of the duchy would not be compromised and that large-scale military aid, possibly led by the young king himself, would soon be forthcoming.[70]

Town-dwellers already had considerable say in the administration of their own defences for they were largely responsible for financing them. This was, of course, a fundamental stage in the development of representative government, that those paying the taxes should share in the policy-making process. The English extended this concept in a most important way by enhancing the role accorded to the Estates General of the duchy. The Estates had been in existence before the English conquest but there is no earlier (nor later) parallel for the regularity of summons nor the extent of consultation. Prentout and de Beaurepaire together discovered sixty-four meetings of the full Estates and of local assemblies during the English occupation.[71]

Ostensibly the Estates represented all groups of the population but in practice the Third Estate was represented exclusively by delegates from the major towns. In 1443, the only year for which we know the complete composition of the Estates, twenty-one towns received summons, and dispatched in total thirty representatives, all of native origin. The clergy sent eighteen members, the nobility nine, although both groups were supplemented by royal councillors and officials.[72] The townsmen thus constituted 53 per cent of the elected representatives and must therefore have had a prominent voice in discussion of taxation (although the countryside bore the brunt of the subsidies voted) and of military policy. Their numerical dominance also explains the nature of investigations and reforms undertaken at the pressure of the Estates, most notably the general enquiry of 1423 and that of 1427 on the payment of *guet*, both of which led to important restrictions on military control of the civilian population.[73] The townsmen were also prominent in decisions to send petitions to England in 1435 and 1449, and in the growing reluctance of the Estates to vote war taxation.

There can be no doubt, therefore, that the English made considerable effort to consult urban opinion and to listen to urban demands. In many ways war helped to generate a community of interest between town and ruler. There can be no doubt, however, that a division of interest developed after the Truce of Tours, when the towns wanted an end to war-time exigencies and the English sought to preserve their military control.[74]

V

We must not forget that it needs two parties to make a relationship. We must therefore conclude by looking more closely at the urban response to English occupation, considering in particular the towns' policies towards their rulers and the incidence of urban treason.

It has been suggested that towns always placed their own interests above any feelings of loyalty. Their political allegiance can thus be seen to depend on the relative military strength of the protagonists in the war. The attitude to the English should be more accurately interpreted, perhaps, as one of resignation (as French chroniclers tended to suggest at the time of the Treaty of Troyes) or of fear (as the writers of the narratives of the French Reconquest liked to believe), although it must not be forgotten that there is enough in French chronicle and official sources to substantiate a quite widespread appreciaton of the benefits of English rule in the interim.

Towns had to maintain a delicate balancing act between protecting and advancing their own interests and, at the same time, not alienating their political masters. They wanted adequate military protection so had to agree to garrisons, high taxation and defensive obligations whilst at the same time reserving the right to object to these burdens. They desired the maintenance of privileges which gave them superiority in judicial and economic matters and were thus willing to challenge any potential encroachments on their authority by their rulers or by other towns.[75] In general, however, towns (like the central government) needed to cajole and persuade rather than threaten; only if the weakness of the ruler was thoroughly apparent would they be prepared to withdraw their allegiance.

Urban behaviour under English rule was not noticeably different from that of earlier or later decades. The towns sought constantly to 'recommend' themselves to their king and his agents. This might take the form of a general address, to remind him of their existence and their continuing loyalty to his cause. Or it could constitute a search for more practical gains, reduction from taxation, or from the *guet*,[76] the provision of additional troops, the removal or disciplining of a grasping royal official, or the remedying of a threat to their own interests.[77] Towns sought patrons much as their counterparts did in fifteenth-century England, often approaching more than one potential 'good lord'.[78] The most obvious preliminary choice was the captain, particularly if resident in the town. Towns might also approach local civilian officials, English lords with lands in the area, or important commanders, councillors and officials of the duchy's central administration, including the Regent and lieutenants-general. Finally they might address their petition to the King and Council in England.[79]

The methods by which these policies were implemented can be seen clearly in all the surviving municipal records, but of particular interest is the special account established at Lisieux in 1438. This was intended specifically 'pour employer aux dons et presents aux seigneurs passant par la ville, officiers du roi et autres come poursuivants et messagers portant lettres ou nouvelles adresses aux habitants de la ville pour le bien, prouffit et honneur dicelle'.[80] Gifts of wine, grain and *objets d'art* (including specially commissioned plate) were showered upon the English according to rank. In addition, banquets and masques were laid on for their entertainment; the Lisieux account shows the decision of the *bourgeois* in August 1439 that henceforward when 'aucuns seigneurs de guerre' or the *bailli* of Rouen came to the town, they would be ceremonially met by the town's officials and three further townsmen. Letters and gifts were sent to more distant destinations (including England), sometimes accompanied by a group of *bourgeois*.

In some cases immediate and specific return was hoped for: the captain of Mantes for instance was entertained to dinner when a dispute had arisen between him and the town council over an 'effroi' in the town at Christmas 1421.[81] In other cases, the desire was merely to recommend the town to the individual concerned in the hope that he would keep its interests in mind and perhaps help in their preservation and extension: newly-appointed officials, including the lieutenants-general, were often thus approached.[82] Finally, letters and embassies were sent in order to gain information, and perhaps, as we saw in the case of Mantes in 1449, to find out whether assistance would be forthcoming.

Generally speaking, the towns tended to act independently of each other, sometimes even in competition (as in the case of the long-running dispute between Rouen and the towns of Lower Normandy), although they made efforts to know what other towns were doing. Even in the Estates, towns sought to promote their own interests in much the same way as English towns did in Parliament; the delegates from Cherbourg, for instance, used the meeting of 1432 to complain about the 'petit gouvernement' of their captain, Robert Hungerford.[83] The Estates (and other local assemblies) did offer, however, the possibility of joint deliberation and action, of establishing enquiries which would benefit all the duchy's towns, and of petitioning the king collectively. They were thus of vital importance in enhancing the political muscle of the Norman towns.

Finally, it must be admitted that, in general, towns were loyal to the English until the final denouement. The incidence of urban treason is low compared with that of the countryside. Jouet's study showed that, of 165 executed for treason in Lower Normandy, only seven were townsmen. Despite known plots at Rouen, Gourlay admits that the capital was more a place of punishment than rebellion.[84] Indeed, most urban treason is known to us precisely because it was detected by the English or, more frequently, betrayed by other town-dwellers. This is not to deny that there were plots to deliver towns to the enemy, nor that some, such as at Louviers in 1429 and 1432, and Harfleur in 1435, were successful. Urban treason was essentially opportunistic and reflective of fluctuations in English and French military strength. Several plots were launched in 1424, for instance, when it was rumoured that the English had been defeated at Verneuil.[85] As the English position weakened from the late 1420s, so the number of plots increased, but most were still detected. The success of urban treason was largely determined by two factors; the proximity to other forms of political authority – the frontier towns were the most likely to fall – and the viability of these alternative forms of authority compared with those of the existing ruler. For most of the Norman towns, these preconditions for revolt did not occur until 1449.

Relations between Norman towns and their rulers were remarkably consistent irrespective of dynastic change. Rulers had to conciliate local interests in times of war, although they could not afford to forgo their potential to control and threaten these centres of vital political and military significance. Towns looked to their own interests, and their 'patriotism' was largely determined by the ability of the ruler to meet their desires. Towns disliked war, although it could serve to advance their interests. For the most part, however, it threatened to damage urban interests. It is not surprising, therefore, that towns tended to support whichever ruler seemed to offer the greatest possibility of peace. In such a climate of opinion, the Norman towns were prepared, even pleased, to accept Charles VII as their saviour and protector when the dynasty to which they had remained basically loyal for the previous thirty years could no longer fulfil such a role. The earlier appeal of Henry V, perhaps even of the Burgundians, had been little different.

Notes

1 C. Petit-Dutaillis, *Les Communes françaises: caractères et évolution des origines au xviiie siècle* (Paris, 1947), chapter 3, part 3.

2 C.L.H. Coulson, 'Seignorial Fortresses in France in Relation to Public Policy, c.864–1483', unpub. PhD thesis, University of London, 1972, pp. 509–21. P. Contamine, 'Les Fortifications urbaines en France à la fin du Moyen Age: aspects financiers et économiques', *Révue Historique,* cclx (1978), pp. 23–47.

3 This point is well-elucidated in the survey of urban government given in S. Deck, 'Les Municipalités en Haute-Normandie', *Annales de Normandie,* 11e année no. 4, pp. 279–300, 12e année no. 2, pp. 77–92, no.3, pp. 151–68, no.4, pp. 213–34.

4 Mantes-la-Jolie, Bibliothèque Municipale, A(rchives) C(ommunales de) M(antes), Serie BB (Délibérations de la ville), 5 ff. 27v-28v. On the archives of Mantes see S. Vitte and H. Le Moine, *Ville de Mantes: Répertoire numerique des archives communales antérieures à 1790* (Corbeil, 1931), pp. 9, 13–14, 19, and V.E. Grave, *Archives Municipales de Mantes. Analyse des registres des comptes de 1381 à 1450* (Paris, 1896).

5 King Charles had arrived at Mantes on 22 August *(Chronique du roi Charles VII par Gilles le Bouvier, dit le Heraut Berry,* ed. H. Courteault, L. Celier and M-H. Jullien de Pommerol (Société de l'Histoire de France, Paris, 1979), p. 289; Robert Blondel, 'De Reductione Normanniae' in *Narratives of the Expulsion of the English from Normandy MCCCCXLIX-MCCCCL,* ed. J. Stevenson (Rolls Series, London, 1863), p. 77).

6 Blondel, pp.78–81.

7 The *Délibérations* of 20 August record the decision to send spies to Chartres and Paris (ACM BB 5 f. 27). Blondel (p.79) reports that the letter of the *maire* and the king's reply were carried by a Franciscan friar.

8 ACM BB 5 ff. 33v-34v.

9 Blondel. p. 81.

10 Thomas Basin, *Histoire de Charles VII,* ed. and trans. C. Samaran (first edition, 2 vols, Paris, 1933–44), ii, pp. 112–13.

11 ACM BB 5 f. 19v. This event is mentioned by Blondel (p.41) and in documents emanating from the Anglo-French negotiations of June 1449 (*Narratives of the Expulsion,* p. 421). Charles VII's embassy argued that Floques had acted without royal orders but that his action was not surprising given the general French outrage at the assault on Fougères (*Ibid,*p. 460). Furthermore, Berry claimed that Mantes was one of the bases from which English troops frequently broke the truce by ambushing men en

route to Orleans and Paris (*Chroniques du roi Charles VII*, p. 294). That the English feared a raid on Mantes in the spring of 1449 is revealed by messages sent from Rouen to the captain recorded in the account of the *trésorier-général* of Normandy for 1448–49 (BL Add. Ms. 11509 f. 135v).

12 Unfortunately we cannot know for certain the size of the garrison at this time. Totalling 270 men before the Truce of Tours, it was subsequently reduced to 120. The loss of the first part of the *trésorier-général*'s account prevents us from verifying whether more troops were sent to the town in 1449 but the narratives of the Reconquest speak of 140–160 men there at the surrender (Blondel, p. 80; Berry, 'Le Recouvrement de Normandie', *Narratives of the Expulsion*, p. 267; A.E. Curry, 'Military Organization in Lancastrian Normandy, 1422-50', unpub. PhD thesis, CNAA/Teesside Polytechnic, 1985, vol. ii, Appendix II).

13 BL Add. Ms. 11509 f. 24.

14 ACM BB 5 f. 20v.

15 In May 1445, the Mantais had received an annual remission of 300 *livres tournois* for seven years on the understanding that they would employ this sum on urban fortifications. In the following year, construction continued on the Tour Saint-Martin near the parish church, despite local reluctance (ACM BB 4 f. 106v; A. Durand and V.E. Grave, *La Chronique de Mantes, ou histoire de Mantes depuis le ixe siècle jusqu'à la Revolution* (Mantes, 1883) pp. 241–42, 285. Expenditure on building works during the English occupation is recorded in the surviving *Comptes de la Commune* (ACM CC 18–20, 23–26, 28).

16 ACM BB 4 ff. 75–75v, BB 5 f. 17; Grave, *Archives Municipales de Mantes*, p. 328. For a similar situation concerning the *guet* at Lisieux see Lisieux, Bibliothèque de la Ville, A(rchives) C(omunales de) L(isieux) CC 17 f. 144. The English officials at Rouen were similarly reluctant to reopen the Porte Saint-Hillaire (Rouen, Bibliothèque de la Ville, A(rchives) M(unicipales de) R(ouen), AA 7 ff. 20v, 22, 65).

17 ACM BB 5 f. 21. The relevant account (CC 32 – compte des recettes d'un impôt extraordinaire sur le sel, juin-juillet 1449) could not be produced in 1982, but Vitte and Le Moine (*Répertoire Numerique*, p. 14) note that a payment of 182.8.0. *livres tournois* was made.

18 ACM BB f. 22.

19 *Ibid*. He served from 13 January 1438 to February 1441 and again from Michaelmas 1442 until the end of the occupation, Sir Ralph Grey being captain in 1441–42 (Curry, 'Military Organization,' vol. ii, pp. xcviii-iv). It is unlikely that Hoo visited the town after August 1448 (ACM BB 5 f. 4v).

20 ACM BB 5 f. 22v.

21 ACM BB 5 f. 24v (7 July 1449). Thomas Saintbarbe, who was presumably principal lieutenant, was absent in the English embassy at Bonport in early July 1449 (*Narratives of the Expulsion*, p. 495).

22 BL Add. Ms. 11509 f. 76v. The *Délibérations* note that the Mantais had already decided to bring their complaints to the notice of Shrewsbury then at Vernon (ACM BB 5 f. 24v).

23 ACM BB 5 f. 26v.

24 This is implied on f. 27. At the opening the civil war, the gates of Rouen had been ordered to be closed between 6 pm and 6 am (AMR A 6, 14 September 1411).

25 ACM BB 5 f. 27.

26 Blondel, pp. 79, 81.

27 ACM BB 5 f. 29 (Monday, 1 September 1449).

28 AMR A 7 ff. 55–57, 60. The accounts for 1448–49 and 1449–50 (XX 1) barely mention 'la reduction de la ville'.

29 Blondel, pp. 120–48; Berry, 'Le Recouvrement', pp. 291–320, with variation in *Chroniques du roi Charles VII*, pp. 313–28; Basin, ii, pp. 114–131.

30   The following is derived from a study of the various chronicle accounts of the Reconquest. For the earlier treason at Louviers see A. Le Prévost, *Mémoires et notes pour servir à l'histoire du Département de l'Eure*, ed. L. Delisle and L. Passy (3 vols., Évreux, 1862–69), ii, p. 336.

31   Paris, A(rchives) N(ationales) Collection Lenoir 16 ff. 319-25.

32   Blondel, p. 71; Basin, ii, pp. 95–105; ACL CC 25 pp. 181–87; ACL AA 3 (treaty of surrender 16 Aug. 1449). Berry, *Chroniques du roi Charles VII*, p. 299 gives a greater prominence to the role of the *bourgeois*.

33   J.Lesquier, 'La Reddition de 1449', *Études Lexoviennes*, i (1915), pp. 19–50. On p. 27 Lesquier suggests that some of the townspeople, realising that their own powers had been enhanced by the English occupation, may have objected to the bishop's desire to surrender.

34   Berry, 'Le Recouvrement', pp. 354–55; P. Carel, *Étude sur la commune de Caen* (Caen, 1888), pp. 137–42.

35   These petitions are listed and discussed further in my paper 'The Impact of War and Occupation on Urban Life in Normandy, 1417–50', *French History* vol 1, no. 2, pp. 157–81.

36   B. Chevalier, *Les Bonnes villes de France du xive au xvie siècle* (Paris 1982), p. 124.

37   Berry, 'Le Recouvrement', pp. 373–74.

38   Blondel, p. 220.

39   Parallels can also be drawn with the policies of John the Fearless; many Norman towns, including Rouen, welcomed his troops as liberators in 1410–11 and 1417–18 (A. Chéruel, *Histoire de Rouen sous la domination anglaise au quinzième siècle* (2 vols. in one, Rouen, 1840), ii, pp. 23–34; R.A. Newhall, *The English Conquest of Normandy, 1416-1424* (Newhaven, 1924) pp. 50, 90; R. Vaughan, *John the Fearless. The Growth of Burgundian Power* (London, 1966), pp. 85, 181.

40   This is dealt with more fully in my paper, 'The Impact of War', pp. 159, 162.

41   Carel, *Étude,*, p. 152. Unless otherwise indicated, the following resumé of Henry's campaigns is derived from Newhall, *English Conquest*, and J.H. Wylie and W.T. Waugh, *The Reign of Henry the Fifth*, (vol. 3, Cambridge, 1929).

42   *Chroniques du Perceval de Cagny*, ed. H. de Moranville (Société de l'Histoire de France, Paris, 1902), p. 111. This places a different complexion, perhaps, on the claims of Blondel (p.114) and Berry ('Le Recouvrement,' pp. 279–80) that the town of Alençon eagerly awaited liberation by its duke in 1449.

43   Duke John subsequently weakened the towns of Upper Normandy by withdrawing troops for the defence of Paris (Newhall, *English Conquest*, p. 65).

44   Mantes had surrendered in similarly eager fashion to the duke of Burgundy in September 1417(*Ibid.*, pp. 67, 127–28). Henry subsequently used the town as a base for the assault on Pontoise in July 1419 and for negotiations with the French between September and November. There are no entries in the *Délibérations* between 3 February, when town armaments were distributed, and 3 November (ACM BB3 ff. 49–50).

45   T. Rymer, *Foedera, Conventiones, Literae et Cuiusque Generis Acta Publica* (10 vols., third edition, The Hague, 1745), IV, iii, p. 16.

46   *Ibid.*, pp. 137, 146, 199; IV, iv, p. 4.

47   *Foedera*, IV, iii, p. 44; Newhall, *English Conquest*, p. 171, n. 135. J. Lesquier, 'L'Administration et les finances de Lisieux de 1423 à 1448', *Études Lexoviennes*, ii (1919), pp. 40–48, 93-100, 127–64.

48   ACM CC 20 ff. 7v, 11; PRO C64/16 m 5d. There had been a complaint to Henry in March 1420 against Englishmen setting up taverns in the town and a further petition on the wine trade was addressed to the royal council shortly after the king's death (ACM BB 3 ff. 61, 121).

49   'Rôles normands et français et autres pièces tirées des archives de Londres par Bréquigny en 1764, 1765 et 1766', *Mémoires de la Société des antiquaires de Normandie*, 3e série, 23

(1858), no. lxix; *Foedera*, IV, iii, p. 155.
50 *Ibid.*, IV, iv, p. 4.
51 *Ibid.*, p. 24. The orders were repeated in December (PRO C64/16 m. 15d). On 5 May, Sir John Radcliffe was commissioned to visit towns and castles and examine the conduct of their captains and garrisons (*Foedera*, IV, iv, p. 26).
52 Richard Woodville had been appointed seneschal on 8 January whilst the Estates were in session ('Rôles normands', no. cmxxiv, and no. cmlxxxii for disciplinary ordinances).
53 *Foedera*, IV, iv, p. 4. See n. 56.
54 ACM CC 20 f. 7v.
55 ACM BB 3 f. 124.
56 Chéruel, *Histoire de Rouen*, ii, pp. 131–32. Curry, 'Military Organization', pp. 243, 254.
57 On his role at Lisieux see ACL CC 14 f. 13v, CC8 f. 22, CC 12 f. 34.
58 In August 1422, for instance, the council at Mantes levied a tax of 2 *deniers tournois* on every animal entering and leaving the town in order to finance eight watchmen at the town gates (ACM BB 3 ff. 120, 125). On the *cannoniers* of Lisieux see ACL CC 6 f. 20. A list made in July 1448 of recently purchased armaments at Mantes is given in ACM BB 5 f. 1. The accounts of Lisieux give full details of building activities in the town.
59 J. Stevenson (ed.), *Letters and Papers Illustrative of the Wars of the English in France during the Reign of Henry the Sixth, King of England* (3 vols. in 2, Rolls Series, London 1861–64), II, ii, pp. 540-46. A study of the size of garrisons is given in Curry, 'Military Organization', chapter 2.
60 Examples of subventions to Alençon, Rouen and Harfleur are found in the *trésorier-géneral's* account for 1448–49 (BL Add Ms 11509 ff. 33v, 34v, 52v and 62v). Lord Hoo made a loan to the town of Mantes in 1441 so that it could pay its arrears to the royal receiver (ACM BB 4 f. 4).
61 The towns of the *bailliage* of Cotentin agreed to finance 120 troops in the spring of 1429 (Paris, B(ibliothèque) N(ationale), m(anu)s(crit) fr(ançais) 26051/1014, 1055, 1056).
62 Chéruel, *Histoire de Rouen*, ii, pp. 85–91; B.J.H. Rowe, 'Discipline in the Norman Garrisons under Bedford, 1422–35', *EHR*, 46 (1931), pp. 194–208.
63 For the progress undertaken by the duke of York in 1445 in Lower Normandy in order to solve the problem of military indiscipline see Curry, 'Military Organization', pp. 321–23. Edmund Beaufort attempted a full *Réformation-Général* in the same area in the summer of 1448 (*Ibid.*, pp. 332–33).
64 Colin Louvel, a *bourgeois* of Louviers, who betrayed a plot to deliver the town to the enemy was given a reward from the property of those indicted of the treasonable act (AN Collection Lenoir 22 f. 131). There are several other examples in P. Le Cacheux (ed.), *Actes de la Chancellerie d'Henri VI concernant la Normandie sous la domination anglaise (1422–35)* (2 vols., Société de l'Histoire de Normandie, Rouen and Paris, 1907–8).
65 Warwickshire County Record Office CR/1618/W, 19/5 (also Bodleian Library Film 428), ff. 18v, 30, 127v. Merchants of Paris (f.130) and Saint-Lô (f. 116v) were occasionally present. Four *bourgeois* of Rouen accompanied the countess of Warwick to Paris for the coronation of Henry VI (f.135).
66 AMR A 7 ff. 10v, 15. Note also the advice given by the French *bailli* and captain to the Rouennais in May 1450 on how they might please their new royal master by sending troops to the siege of Caen (f.77).
67 Letters sent in 1436–37 to the *bourgeois* and royal lieutenant at Saint-Lô warning of enemy activity in the Basses-Marches are detailed in AN K 64/10/3, BN ms fr 26060/2802 and ms fr 26075/3295. Of particular interest are the letters sent from England to the Mantais (ACM BB 4 f. 107) and to other towns (BN ms fr 26075/5486) by the duke of York in April 1446 informing them that he had been reappointed to the governorship of France and Normandy. In September 1445 York had written to Lisieux (by then part of his personal *appanage*) notifying his imminent departure for England

and the appointment of certain men of the *grand conseil* 'devers lesquels len poroit avoir recours en cas de necessite' (ACL CC 16 f. 14).

68 For such letters sent to Argentan in October 1428 see Stevenson, *Letters and Papers*, II, i, pp. 85–87.

69 J.G. Dickinson, *The Congress of Arras 1435: A Study in Medieval Diplomacy* (Oxford, 1955), p. 17; BL Add(itional) Ch(arter) 124.

70 'Rôles normands', nos. mccclxxxii, mccclxxxvi–vii; PRO E28/56.

71 C. de R. de Beaurepaire, *Les États de Normandie sous la domination anglaise* (Évreux, 1859); H. Prentout, *Les États provinciaux de Normandie* (3 vols., Caen, 1925–27). See also C.T. Allmand, *Lancastrian Normandy 1415–1450. The History of a Medieval Occupation* (Oxford, 1983), pp. 172–74.

72 Beaurepaire, *États*, pp. 145–49.

73 B.J.H. Rowe, 'Discipline in the Norman Garrisons under Bedford, 1422–35', EHR, 46 (1931), 201–206, transcribed from BL Birch 4101 f. 65; R.A. Newhall, 'Bedford's Ordinance on the Watch of September 1428', EHR, 50 (1935), pp. 50–54, transcribed from AN KK 325B. On complaints at the Estates of 1447 and the subsequent reissue of the 1423 ordinances see Prentout, *États provinciaux*, iii, pp. 86–89, BN ms fr 26076/5740 and Archives Départementales de l'Orne A 416.

74 See above n. 16 and Curry, 'Military Organization', pp.466, 471.

75 In 1427, for instance, the *maire et échevins* of Mantes questioned in the Paris *parlement* the duke of Bedford's claims to 'hault jurisdiction' in the town (AN Xia 4795 ff. 120–120v). Twenty years later the long-running dispute between the towns of Lower Normandy and the duchy's capital came to a head with both sides petitioning the king in England (AMR A 7 ff. 10v. 15).

76 In September 1424, for example, Rouen successfully petitioned for a reduction from 240 to eighty of those required to pay *guet* each night and an end to the levying of fines from 'defaillans' (AMR Tiroir 245). The Archives Municipales of Évreux (consultable in the Bibliothèque de la Ville) contain petitions to several English leaders, including Cardinal Beaufort and Matthew Gough, for assistance in gaining the release of a *bourgeois*, Vincent Desquetot, hostage of the French at Louviers (CC 10 pièces 1 and 3, 1431).

77 For the petition of Harfleur against its captain, William Minors, which was heard at the *Echiquier de Normandie* in 1425, see BN ms fr 26048/420. In February 1445, the townsmen of Lisieux bribed Matthew Gough with food and money to keep his indisciplined soldiers out of the town (ACL CC 17 p. 144).

78 R. Horrox, 'Urban Patronage and Patrons in the Fifteenth Century', in R.A. Griffiths (ed.), *Patronage, the Crown and the Provinces in Late Medieval England* (Gloucester, 1981), p. 148.

79 The Norman capital often approached the king directly, as, for instance, in 1444 when petitioning for collective exemption from the *arrière-ban* (AMR Tiroir 6) and in 1447–48 when responding to a threat to its privileges from the towns of Lower Normandy (AMR A 7 ff. 10v, 15).

80 ACL CC 17. Unfortunately the original manuscript does not survive but the Bibliothèque de la Ville de Lisieux holds an abstract prepared by M. Bénet in 1912.

81 ACM CC 20 f. 7v.

82 See, for instance, the missions sent by the Mantais with the very best quality wine to the duke of York in July 1441 (ACM BB 4 ff. 14v) and to Edmund Beaufort, duke of Somerset, in August 1448 (BB 5 f. 4v).

83 M. Masson d'Autume, *Cherbourg pendant la Guerre de Cent Ans de 1354 à 1450* (Cherbourg, 1948), p. 45.

84 R. Jouet, 'La Résistance à l'occupation anglaise en Basse Normandie (1418–50)' *Cahiers des Annales de Normandie*, p. 5 (Caen, 1959), 82; D. Gourlay, 'La Résistance à l'occupant anglais en Haute-Normandie (1435–44), *Annales de Normandie*, 36e année, no. 1, pp. 37–55 (esp.43–44), no. 2, pp. 91–104; P. Le Cacheux (ed,), *Rouen au temps*

de Jeanne d'Arc et pendant l'occupation anglaise, 1419–49 (Société de l'Histoire de Normandie, Rouen and Paris, 1931), pp. xcix-cxiii; Allmand, *Lancastrian Normandy,* p. 235.

85 Bernay (*Actes de la Chancellerie,* ii, CCCXXXVI), Pontaudemer (*Ibid.*, CCCLV) and Évreux (AN Collection Lenoir 22 f. 99).

9

Towns and Townspeople in Fifteenth-Century Scotland

Michael Lynch
University of Edinburgh

Of the many significant differences which distinguish the history of Scottish medieval towns from those of England the most striking is the nature of the sources. With the exception of the fragment of a single year for one town, there are for Scotland no specifically urban records as such which predate 1398. Even in the fifteenth century there is only one significant burgh archive, that of Aberdeen, which runs more or less continuously from 1398 on. There are records of some merchant guilds, principally Perth and Dunfermline, and fragments for Ayr. The Edinburgh records, both of its guild and burgh court, exist only in the form of a partial transcript made about 1580.[1] There is no evidence as to rents of fifteenth-century urban property; no testaments on which to speculate about incomes or wealth; no petitions of burghs for financial relief before the records of the Convention of Royal Burghs begin as a regular series in the 1550s. With the exception of the archive for Aberdeen, which recent work on the sixteenth century has shown to have an idiosyncratic urban oligarchy,[2] there is no basis even to consider the possibility of a general flight from civic office in the later medieval period. There are no sources akin to the English fourteenth-century poll tax records or lay subsidy returns, making it difficult to speculate about, still less establish, the extent of urban decay in later medieval Scotland.

Yet other records do exist, relating to overseas trade, coinage and exchange rates, which provide a reasonably firm context for an analysis of fifteenth-century towns. Urban decay is unquantifiable, yet it is difficult to believe that it did not exist in serious form in a society which was hit by eight separate outbreaks of plague between 1349 and 1455; or in an economy suffering reductions of some 65 per cent in the silver content of the coinage in the course of the fourteenth century, worsening exchange rates, especially in the three quarters of a century before 1450, falling customs returns on exports and the growing stranglehold of Edinburgh in most sectors of overseas trade.[3] It is likely that there was deep-seated decay, sharpened by periodic crisis, in many towns, especially those of middle-ranking status, throughout the fifteenth century and beyond. The burgh tax rolls, which begin as a series in 1535, reveal a continuing pattern of short-term crisis in more than half the fifty-odd towns which paid national taxation.[4] Overseas trade began to improve only in the 1570s and there was no decisive upswing until the 1590s. It is difficult, however, to see a general urban recovery even then, for Edinburgh accounted for 72 per cent of all customs paid on exports and the small ports of south-east Fife, which had prospered dramatically after 1540, a further 5 per cent.[5] Recovery, when it came, was spread very unevenly.

This thesis of the chronic instability of Scottish later medieval towns is based on the *Exchequer Rolls*, a difficult source which has only recently been studied in any systematic way. A rather more convenient record, the *Acts of the Parliaments of Scotland*, has tended to acclimatize the thinking of most historians of fifteenth-century Scottish towns.[6] They have in them a new wave of legislation, especially from the reigns of James I and James III, about towns – relating to their government, elections, prices, standards of workmanship, and even dove-cots and the siting of brothels. Yet this source and successive historians' preoccupation with it has probably produced an oversimplified view, which tends to view all Scottish towns in the same light and subject to the same pressures. The legislation of James III's parliaments has, in particular, contributed to the idea that the third quarter of the fifteenth century saw the beginnings of a struggle between merchants and craftsmen, which came to dominate all towns. There is a danger that historians, here and elsewhere, may risk constructing a general problem, which did not exist as such, out of legislation usually passed to resolve a specific or local difficulty, with the initiative often coming from only one town. It has, for example, been suggested that the act of 1458 prohibiting bonds of manrent between towns and landed men probably resulted from the lobbying of the burgh of Aberdeen.[7] Similarly, a much-cited act of 1487, which confined elections to 'the best and worthiest' inhabitants and insisted they be conducted 'not by partiality nor mastership which is the undoing of the burghs [from] where. . . the request comes', almost certainly also stemmed from Aberdeen, where there had been a disputed election in 1486 which had subsequently involved both the king and his council. And the well-known acts of 1467 and 1487, which sought to separate merchants from craftsmen, retailers from manufacturers, were almost certainly at least in part the product of a struggle for control of the leather trade in Edinburgh.[8] They do not necessarily prove widespread tension between the two groups in all or even many towns, for the leather trade was increasingly the preserve of only a handful of entrepreneurs. Much of this legislation was, of course, repealed or ignored, in common with other legislation of the reign of James I.[9] It had at best a marginal effect on the lives of fifteenth-century towns and townspeople. Lack of specifically urban sources has encouraged a tendency to exaggerate the importance of other sources – of central government. Those sources have in turn prompted many historians to impose a curiously centralist view of towns for a kingdom which is otherwise acknowledged to have been held by a very loose set of feudal reins. The burghs may have been subject to fairly close royal oversight in the period immediately after their legal foundation in the twelfth or thirteenth centuries, but that was no longer the case by the fourteenth century. These were local communities which, until the beginning of the long personal reign of James VI in the 1580s, had at best occasional contact with the crown and its organs of administration.[10]

The most important source for the study of fifteenth-century Scottish towns is the most awkward, the records of the Exchequer. The customs returns reflect a very limited range of staple exports – a range which was widened in the 1390s and again in the 1420s to include fish, salt and skins in addition to cloth and wool. Scotland's overseas trade had been in deficit since the 1290s.[11] The boom which had lasted from the 1250s to the 1290s was effectively shattered by the Wars of Independence and did not return for fully three centuries, although there was a brief recovery in the 1370s. The combination of the loss of Berwick to the English and the settling, by the mid-fourteenth century, of a staple port at Bruges drastically altered the league table of Scottish towns and forced many to reshape their internal economies, which had hitherto been heavily dependent on the wool and cloth trade. By the middle of the fourteenth century the burghs of Edinburgh, Aberdeen, Perth and Dundee were recognized by Bruges as 'the four great towns of Scotland'[12] and the customs returns for the 1370s confirm their pre-eminence: 58 per cent of customs revenue was paid by them. The vast bulk of that revenue came from the wool trade, in the form of the export, for the most part, of raw wool and woolfells. Edinburgh had 24 per cent, Aberdeen 15 per cent, Dundee 10 per cent and Perth 9 per cent. The next four towns – Linlithgow, Haddington, Lanark and Montrose – totalled between them 20 per cent, with Linlithgow coming close to Perth.[13] Yet by 1500 the combined share of the four great towns had risen to 81 per cent, a figure by then derived from a much wider range of commodities. The share of the second four had dropped to 9 per cent and only Haddington had maintained its position: Montrose had dropped to ninth of the exporting burghs and Linlithgow to tenth, their places being taken by the modest west-coast ports of Ayr and Dumbarton.[14]

The fifteenth century saw the bulk of the export trade coming increasingly to be funnelled through a small number of larger centres, all strategically placed on the east coast, on the main trade route to Flanders. This basic pattern varied in its extent and timing from one staple commodity to another.[15] It was in the wool trade that Edinburgh first gained its striking ascendancy: it had a 21 per cent share of the export trade in wool in the late 1320s, 41 per cent by 1410–15, 57 per cent by the late 1440s, and 71 per cent by the late 1450s. Its next significant gain came in the 1530s, by which time it claimed over 87 per cent. By contrast, Edinburgh's share of the market in hides was then 68 per cent, although by the 1590s it would stand at 83 per cent. The inroads made by Edinburgh into the market in hides were more gradual and less overwhelming: in the late 1440s it paid 28 per cent of customs, only half of its share of wool customs. By the late 1450s it had nearly 37 per cent but its share slipped in the 1460s. Its decisive gains were made in the last thirty years of the century, when it doubled its stake in the trade. Yet there was an important difference between the trade in these two basic commodities. With the wool trade Edinburgh was in the course of the fifteenth century fast gaining a near-monopoly of a trade which was in steepening decline after 1400; by the end of the fifteenth century Scotland exported less than a quarter of the amount of wool it had done in the 1370s. There had also been a drop in the number of hides exported over the same period but only of a third, and there were signs of some expansion in the last quarter of the fifteenth century, even if it was fluctuating and uneven.[16]

The trade battleground amongst the Scottish burghs had been in wool in the fifty years after the loss of Berwick, Scotland's premier wool town, in 1334. By the second half of the fifteenth century the battleground had shifted to the trade in hides and skins. In the late 1440s the four great towns together held just 52 per cent of the trade: but five other medium-sized towns held 40 per cent.

TABLE 1: PERCENTAGE SHARE OF CUSTOMS PAID ON EXPORTED HIDES, 1445–99

	1445–9	1455–9	1465–9	1475–9	1485–9	1495–9
Edinburgh	28.2	36.6	26.6	48.0	55.7	66.0
Inverness	13.9	11.0	6.1	0.8	–	1.0
Ayr	9.6	2.3	7.0	6.0	4.9	6.8
Perth	9.3	4.2	5.0	4.3	4.6	2.5
Aberdeen	8.8	9.1	5.9	5.3	8.4	3.3
Linlithgow	8.6	6.4	10.6	3.4	2.7	0.7
Stirling	8.0	4.6	5.5	2.7	3.4	5.5
Dundee	5.6	7.4	9.1	8.4	8.8	6.7
Kirkcudbright	–	5.6	9.4	6.5	2.4	1.0

By the 1470s the league table of exporting burghs specialising in hides and skins had been transformed. The share of the middle-ranking towns had dropped by fully a half, whereas Edinburgh's had increased by over 40 per cent. It is an illustration of the general context of the continuing slump and uncertainty in Scotland's markets overseas, with both France and the Hanse towns; trade with Flanders was even more unsettled, with a series of shifts of the staple port betwen Bruges and Middleburg.[17] This in turn was reflected in a chronic instability in the economy of most Scottish towns, especially those of middling rank, as they came under pressure from larger rivals in their traditional specialised markets. Certain towns, like Stirling, had diversified their economies in the fourteenth century to accommodate Edinburgh's increasing stake in the wool trade,[18] but found themselves under renewed pressure in the fifteenth century in the very areas into which they had moved.

The scale of dislocation in individual towns is better revealed if actual figures of exports and custom are considered rather than percentage shares. Some of the middling towns, like Ayr and Stirling, were able to weather the slump in their leather trade over the course of the second half of the fifteenth century but in others, like Inverness, Kirkcudbright and Linlithgow, it collapsed.

TABLE 2:   AVERAGE ANNUAL CUSTOM PAID (IN £ SCOTS) ON EXPORTED HIDES, 1445–99.

	1445–9	1455–9	1465–9	1475–9	1485–9	1495–9
Edinburgh	91	113	55	180	95	235
Inverness	45	34	13	3	–	3
Ayr	31	7	15	23	8	24
Perth	30	13	10	16	8	9
Aberdeen	28	28	12	20	14	12
Linlithgow	28	20	22	13	5	3
Stirling	26	14	11	10	6	20
Dundee	16	23	19	32	15	14
Kirkcudbright	–	17	20	25	4	3

The two great towns which suffered a real drop in their exports of hides – Aberdeen and Perth – were large enough to find room to diversify again.[19] There are indications that their share of inland trade was increasing, at the expense of smaller inland towns.

The fifteenth century saw a very different economic climate from the twelfth and thirteenth, when the *Burgh Laws* and *Statutes* of the Berwick guild had been drawn up during a boom in the wool and cloth trades. These regulations, so frequently cited as shaping burgh life in the fifteenth century and beyond, had only marginal importance in what in effect was a trade war between the larger and medium-sized towns for a greater share of declining and fluctuating markets. The basic context for the study of fifteenth-century Scottish towns is, as revealed by customs records, one of a lingering long-term economic decline which was exaggerated by periodic short-term crises. Few towns outside the four great burghs escaped the cycle of urban decay or outright decline.

If the available sources for the study of the Scottish medieval town are decidedly sparser than for its English counterpart, there are also a number of points of real difference in their shape and development. These form the substance of this chapter. The easiest to illustrate is the fact that Scottish towns and townspeople were, by English standards, very lightly taxed throughout the medieval period. Aberdeen, the second or third largest town in fifteenth-century Scotland, had 445 taxpayers in 1448. This would place it seemingly well below such small English towns as Wells or Barking, which had tax-paying populations of about 900 and were ranked fortieth or below in the league table of towns paying the lay subsidy of 1377. Even Edinburgh had only 1,245 taxpayers in 1583, when its actual population, measurable by other means, was about 13,500.[20] Comparisons of the tax-paying populations of English and Scottish towns are consequently meaningless.

Another contrast which is simple to outline is the single-parish urban community which in Scotland persisted throughout the whole of the medieval period. The new parishes carved out to complement the legal foundation of the king's burghs in the twelfth and thirteenth centuries, with fashionable biblical and continental saints of that period, such as St John, St Mary and St Nicholas, remained untouched until at least the end of the sixteenth century. By that time Edinburgh had 8,000 adult communicants in the one parish.[21] It is not possible therefore to measure urban decay by the counting of derelict medieval parish churches, as in some English towns. The most striking development of the second half of the fifteenth century was rather the recasting of the urban parish in new foundations of collegiate churches designed to accommodate the whole of the population. The spread of the burgh collegiate church, such as St Giles' in Edinburgh, with its array of new altars, all with their own saints, in the century before the Reformation of 1560 was the complement of the formal incorporation of craft guilds which belonged to the same period. Each new craft, when incorporated, was granted its own altar, saint and chaplain, under its own close supervision. This also coincided with the development, which was strikingly late in Scotland, of a civic cult, imported for the most part from Flanders: merchant guilds adopted the cult of the Holy Blood from Bruges.[22] The notion of the organic unity of medieval urban society thus reached its mature expression distinctly late in Scottish towns. The identity of burgh community and *corpus christianum* remained, but it was by 1500 being stretched to new lengths, as populations of the larger towns began to increase for the first time for centuries.

The fact that Scottish burghs did not subdivide their original parish and few significantly overspilled their medieval town plans,[23] added to the compelling sense of a burgh community. The Scottish burghs were more uniform in burgh law and custom than were English boroughs and from a certain point in fifteenth century, perhaps from 1405, had a much more unified voice in national politics than was the case in England.[24] The twelfth-century *Burgh Laws* were copied out in the book of the Dunfermline guildry three centuries later and by a burgess of Inverness sometime in the 1580s.[25] They and much else provide a common thread which in a genuine sense linked burghs and burgesses in 1200 and 1500 or even 1600.[26] Yet the characteristic uniformity of Scottish burgh institutions, law and custom needs to be set against the demonstrable diversity of Scottish towns – as marketplaces, finishing centres, ports or regional centres. The *Burgh Laws* have been described as 'a jumble' even when they were first drawn up;[27] they provided, at best, a common core of customs and regulations which was subsequently embellished, qualified or ignored by different towns as they saw fit, as was the case with parliamentary legislation. The *Burgh Laws* were by the fifteenth century probably most cherished in smaller towns, like Dunfermline; there may be an analogy, as time went on, of the smaller the town the greater were the economic pressures on it and the greater its attachment to early medieval burgh custom and law. By the late fifteenth century it is possible to demonstrate widespread evasion of the *Burgh Laws* in the larger towns, like Edinburgh and Perth.[28] In this respect, as in others, a sharper distinction needs to be made than has conventionally been done between the history of Scottish towns before and after 1300. The contrast with English boroughs may here have been less marked in practice than it might appear at first sight.

Although Scottish towns had a single parish church, in other respects the ecclesiastical presence was rather larger than in their English counterparts. In twelfth- and thirteenth-century Berwick, for example, there was a considerable stake held by monastic houses in urban property; fifteen monasteries and priories ranging from the abbey of Kinloss in Moray to nearby Coldstream held land in Berwick.[29] Large grants of urban property to religious houses became much less common after 1300 but the ecclesiastical position was still in the mid-fifteenth century probably consolidating rather than weakening, with the founding of a number of friaries at the urban periphery; in Aberdeen 29 per cent of all recorded property transactions then involved the church. The Edinburgh Dominicans (founded in 1230) had still over a hundred small property rents at the Reformation.[30] Most towns, whether diocesan centres like Glasgow or St Andrews, or not (and it is as well to remember that none of the largest four towns was) continued to have a sizeable ecclesiastical presence into the fifteenth century and beyond.

The fifth of the contrasts follows on. Most Scottish towns had a larger ecclesiastical presence than a noble one. It is possible to point to towns, like Aberdeen, where the great market place of Castlegate was flanked by the town houses of landed men, both local, like Lord Forbes and the Earl Marischal, and not so local, like the earls of Buchan and Erroll. But this was somewhat unusual. Noble interest in towns certainly existed but, like the nobles themselves, it tended to be peripatetic: a number of important fifteenth-century nobles seem, like the king himself, to have regularly been on the move, visiting and issuing writs in various towns,[31] but the precise degree of their influence was usually intangible because it was rarely pushed to the issue. Certain towns did pay pensions to nobles; more than half of Aberdeen's regular income flowed out in the form of pensions – to no less than four magnates and one bishop in 1494. Yet not included in that list was the earl of Huntly, with whom the burgh had its closest relationship. The fifth earl of Crawford had pensions from no less than six burghs, as far apart as Banff and Crail and ranging in size from Aberdeen to Forfar. It is difficult to believe that Crawford had the muscle to collect protection money from all six. Sometimes money flowed the other way, from noble to town, as when the earl of Huntly lent the burgh of Aberdeen £220 in 1441; he was still owed £100 of it ten years later.[32] The relationship between towns and landed men is a subject which has yet to be extensively examined in or before the fifteenth century. The issue of town and country was, however, the most important issue in urban politics in the sixteenth century, centring on the gentrification of urban government. In Perth and Stirling the process began in the 1520s and 1530s and was being put into reverse by the closing years of the sixteenth century, by when the gentry were retiring to their estates and leaving a void in urban government which, in some cases, provoked a jostling for power as new groups sought to fill their places. Yet in Aberdeen the process had begun earlier, in the 1490s, if not before.[33]

There was otherwise seemingly little sign in Scotland of serious disputes between towns and noble overlords or between towns and local gentry throughout the medieval period. One reason for this may have been, as shall be seen, the relatively low percentage of private seigneurial burghs, at least when compared with England. Yet the transformation of the higher nobility, which was near-complete by the end of the 1450s,[34] often had the the effect of recasting in a more clear-cut way local and regional spheres of magnate interest. This, in turn, must seriously have affected the thinking of many burghs, both large and small, about their standing in the community of the realm. Legislation of James IV's reign tried to regulate the new relationships which seem to have been emerging between some burghs and landed men: an act of 1491, which was probably again directed at Aberdeen, forbade the purchase of rural lordships by burgesses and another of 1503 prohibited rural landowners holding burgh office or entering into bonds with burghs.[35] This legislation, which demonstrably failed to halt this two-way traffic, suggests a drift together of town and country towards the close of the fifteenth century.

The boundaries between town and country were being revised in their economic aspect as well as the political. The most striking difference between the make-up of urban life in Scotland and England in the medieval period lies in the marked contrast in the general mix of different kinds of towns. The simplest of the contrasts to demonstrate is the fact that in 1400 two-thirds of all English towns were seigneurial boroughs, whereas in Scotland the proportions were appreciably different – in 1400 half of all Scottish burghs were royal. There had been no headlong rush of Scottish lords to gain charters for village markets in the thirteenth century. There was no rush in the century after 1450, but there was a steady trickle, with over ninety private burghs being erected or confirmed.[36] Significantly, almost a quarter of the new erections had ecclesiastical superiors; the ecclesiastical presence was almost as significant in the urban hinterland as in the town itself.

There were in Scotland few inland regional centres of any size, both inland and overseas trade being dominated by and funnelled through towns which stood on tidal water. Although very little is known about inland trade in this period, there are indications that far from trade draining away from larger centres, like Perth and Aberdeen, either to smaller regional centres or to new private burghs, the largest towns were consolidating and gaining ground – in both inland and overseas trade.[37] Edinburgh had no less than fifteen separate markets in 1477 and habitually complained of the daily influx of 'miserable creatures' from its hinterland.[38] The evidence of an isolated tax roll of 1485 listing burghs north of the Forth, when compared with the next available roll of 1535, shows that Aberdeen paid more in national taxation than all the burghs within its sheriffdom. Indeed Aberdeen paid more than all the burghs combined between it and Inverness; their total amounted to 86 per cent of Aberdeen's. In 1535, by the same measure, they paid only 50 per cent.[39] So if inland trade was increasing, and there are some indications that it was, the share of the cake was going not to inland regional centres but to the new private local market centres and, pre-eminently, to the larger towns, which also already dominated overseas trade.

There were in Scotland few if any one-industry towns, like Worcester. The simplest and most important of the reasons for this lies in the slightness of the cloth trade for Scotland. The explanation for this lies in two distinctive aspects of Scotland's overseas trade, most of which had since 1350 been funnelled through the staple port of Bruges. The arrangements with Bruges included the banning of all exports of finished cloth, except of the very cheapest and coarsest varieties. Scottish cloth was banned from Flanders by a treaty of 1427, unless it was shipped there for dyeing and finishing and then shipped back to Scotland.[40] So the cloth trade, which is often taken as the measure of economic growth of towns, simply does not apply in the same way to Scotland, at least between the fourteenth and sixteenth centuries. Dyers had been prominent in the Perth guild in the thirteenth century and would rise again as a craft aristocracy in the seventeenth century. In Perth and most other Scottish towns the various sectors of the textile industry were not conspicuous thorughout the later medieval period, either in numbers or in wealth or influence. The second phenomenon lies in the near-monopoly increasingly taken by Edinburgh of what there was of a cloth industry. Details of exports of woollen cloth become available only in the 1430s, when Edinburgh paid over 59 per cent of all custom on exported cloth; Aberdeen paid a mere 2.7 per cent and Dundee a little less. By the 1450s Edinburgh had accumulated no less than 87 per cent.[41]

Here the customs returns are, however, partly misleading since they did not take account of poorer quality cloth. These figures conflict with what is known of Dundee's occupational structure in the later sixteenth century when its dyers paid almost 7 per cent of total taxation – a phenomenal assessment which was proportionately more even than Edinburgh's tailors, then the boom craft in the capital.[42] Much of Dundee's cloth products probably went to the Baltic: 17 per cent of Danzig's imports from Scotland were in poor quality cloth and it probably also made up a large component of the mixed packages of *Krämerwaren* which made up a further 52 per cent of imports.[43] In the fifteenth century, as in the twentieth, 'Scots prices' were renowned through the Baltic and there was a stream of legislation in North German towns against Scots pedlars hawking their wares. But elsewhere – outside Dundee – textile trades were often located in the suburbs or hinterlands of the larger towns. Even Edinburgh, which controlled so much of the cloth trade, had only thirteen weavers in the town itself in 1558 and numbers in the capital's textile trades were actually falling in the later sixteenth century, despite its continuing grip over the export of customed cloth. It is likely that most of the stages of carding, spinning and weaving were put out to the suburbs or rural hinterland of the larger towns, which acted usually only as reception centres.[44]

The final contrast between English and Scottish towns lay in the marked differences in parts of their occupational structure and the make-up of craft guilds. Both also stemmed from the distinctly unusual patterns of Scottish overseas trade and its unbalanced distribution amongst the royal burghs which still enjoyed a protected monopoly over both the import and export trade. Scottish towns were not 'specialised', at least in the terms of the debate over English towns, but many did have unevenly diversified economies as a result. Crafts were late to be given incorporated status as self-governing guilds in Scottish towns. In Edinburgh the process began in 1474, coinciding with the town's sharp increase in the share of the export trade in leather, when the skinners were incorporated. It was not completed until 1523, by which time fourteen guilds had been formed. Yet Norwich, a town of roughly comparable size, had seventy-nine different trades in 1525.[45] The latitude given to Bruges craftsmen to flood the Scottish market with a wide range of quality manufactured goods had a telling and long-term effect, lasting well beyond its demise in the late fifteenth century as the staple port, on urban craft skills in Scotland. As late as the 1580s English observers commented on the narrowness of the range of handicrafts in Scottish towns.[46]

These new craft incorporations were often amalgamated: the Edinburgh hammermen, the second to be granted a 'seal of cause' and certainly by 1550 the largest guild in the capital, combined all metal workers and also fringe trades like saddlers and beltmakers as well as workers in pewter, gold and tin. So Edinburgh had only fourteen craft guilds, Perth and Dundee nine, and Aberdeen and Stirling seven.[47]

The composite structure of Scottish craft guilds, which allowed a craft aristocracy to emerge relatively quickly within each guild, is important, for it points to a revision of the accepted nature of the urban hierarchy in fifteenth-century Scottish towns. The conventional view is that the fifteenth century saw the emergence of an aristocracy of overseas merchants, 'the best and worthiest' as legislation habitually termed them; their growing monopoly of burgh government and the merchant guild had the effect, it is held, of inducing serious conflict between merchants and craftsmen, which indelibly marked the history of most Scottish towns well into the next century. Yet much of this analysis seems overdrawn. An elite of overseas merchants was emerging, but much the same process was taking place in other key parts of the urban economy, especially in the leather and metal trades.

With the contraction of overseas trade both burgh establishments and the crown took steps to try to restrict access to wealthier, established traders: in 1425 parliament limited exporters to those with at least three sacks of wool or their equivalent in value; in 1467 it decreed that only the 'famous and worshipful' could trade abroad.[48] Yet this applied largely to the trade in wool and woollen cloth. Much the same narrowing of influence was also happening within the leather trade, but there the entrepreneurs were craftsmen – usually skinners, who gained increasing control of its long and diverse manufacturing processes, some also, as with the textile trade, put out to the suburbs and rural hinterland. Leading craftsmen were also granted the right by town councils and parliaments, especially in the 1420s, 1460s and 1470s, to fix prices and wages and to prescribe standards of work. The formal incorporation of craft guilds, which began in the 1470s, completed the trend. The skinners and the metal workers, both amalgamated crafts, were usually amongst the first to gain confirmation of their status. Power and control over the economic monopolies which were the mainspring of urban life were passing to the 'best and worthiest' in urban society and this was true of both the retailing and the manufacturing sectors of the town economy. The larger merchants tended to deal in a variety of commodities; the more prosperous craftsmen tended to supervise a number of stages in long manufacturing processes.[49] A new aristocracy, of both overseas merchants and certain kinds of craftsmen, was emerging in the larger towns by the last quarter of the fifteenth century.

All of this was part of the quiet and often camouflaged transformation of the society of Scottish late medieval towns which accompanied the diversification of their economies following the catastrophic and prolonged slump in the wool trade in the fourteenth century. It is a mistake to try to trace the outlines of this change using only the increasingly outmoded *Burgh Laws* or the measuring stick of the merchant guild. When individual cocket books become available, in the sixteenth century, they reveal that in Edinburgh the export trade in skins and hides was inhabited by craftsmen as well as merchants, and by traders who were both in and out of the merchant guild.[50] The constitution of the merchant guild was apparently similar in various towns but its composition varied quite strikingly: there were sixty-three in the Aberdeen merchant guild in 1445, only a few more than in the very much smaller town of Dunfermline, which averaged fifty – some one-third of all male inhabitants. In Perth, which was probably a little smaller than Aberdeen, there were over one hundred in the guild in the 1450s. In Perth, craftsmen made up over 40 per cent of entrants to the merchant guild; in early sixteenth-century Edinburgh the proportion was 15 per cent; and in Aberdeen it was 13.5 per cent over the course of fifteenth century. In each of these three large towns the kind of craftsmen most commonly entering the guild also varied: in Edinburgh the craft hierarchy was headed by the leather and metal workers in 1500; in Perth by the metal workers and the bakers; in Aberdeen, where the craft presence was slighter and the hierarchy less clear-cut, by the fleshers, bakers, tailors and cordwainers.[51] Again the distinction between the early and late medieval periods needs to be made. The statutes of the Berwick guild had been drawn up for a town in which the guild merchant was filled with provision merchants and entrepreneurs who controlled the key stages in cloth manufacture.[52] There were by the fourteenth century some nineteen Scottish burghs with a merchant guild but by then most were operating in the wool and leather trades rather than in cloth. Much of the history of the Scottish burgh has been told in terms of its institutions and the growing exclusiveness of the guild merchant as a club for overseas merchants. Much of the history of the Scottish town from 1370 onwards needs to be told in terms of its markets, especially in wool and leather and the fluctuating boundaries within these trades between middlemen and manufacturers.[53] This was the basis for the emergence of a new urban aristocracy in the larger towns.

The later fifteenth century, it has been argued, saw an economic revolution, occasioned by the combined effects of trade slump and fluctuations in the exchange rate, which produced a shift of climate in favour of urban craftsmen, at the expense of overseas merchants.[54] The general thesis is plausible, but two further questions remain to be settled. Which towns and which craftsmen benefited most? It has been seen that larger towns were claiming a greater share of most parts of the export trade as it fluctuated or declined. The losers were towns such as Linlithgow, which provides a typical case study of the middle-ranking town in decline in the fifteenth century. It was ranked fifth of the exporting burghs in the 1370s but had sunk to ninth by 1550. Its share of the wool trade fluctuated between 9 per cent and 12 per cent from the 1350s until the 1430s; in the late 1440s it dropped to 6 per cent and it collapsed in the next decade. Its share of the market in hides was slipping at the same time and, despite a recovery in the 1460s, had been eclipsed by the 1490s (see Table 2). Its share of cloth exports was modest and held steadier at between 3 per cent and 5 per cent until 1450, before crashing to less than 1 per cent in the 1470s. The economic decline of Linlithgow, which oddly coincided with its re-emergence as a royal centre, was part of the price to be paid for the rise of Edinburgh. Other towns of a similar size, such as Haddington or Ayr, weathered the shifts in overseas trade better: Ayr almost recovered its trade in hides after a disastrous slump in the 1450s and Haddington which had held 9 per cent of the trade in wool in the 1360s, recovered from a drop to 2 per cent in the 1410s to 8 per cent in the 1420s. Some historians might see this as restructuring rather than decay, but if so the restructuring lasted for a long period indeed: sixteenth-century evidence, from both customs returns and tax assessments, shows no let up in the distinctive cycle of localised, short-term crises and lingering decay which afflicted most small and medium-sized Scottish towns.[55]

As overseas trade came increasingly to be concentrated in some of the larger towns, certain crafts, particularly in leather and textiles which were most closely tied to export markets, must have been affected. The growing hold of Edinburgh on the export of hides and skins – it handled 24,340 of the 36,430 hides exported in 1499 and 28,740 of the 32,526 skins – had inevitable consequences on the occupational structure of the capital. Nineteen master skinners were listed in the craft's 'seal of cause' of 1474; there were forty-two by 1558. The numbers of fleshers and cordwainers were also appreciably increasing, as were those of tailors.[56] Yet what was happening to a town like Perth, whose share of overseas trade was slipping, especially in leather (see Table I), but which was, according to the tax rolls, holding its position, particularly in relation to the smaller inland towns around it? In 1485 it paid almost 28 per cent of the tax levied on the Tay towns and in 1535 it paid 25.5 per cent. Perth was variously described by its inhabitants as a 'craft town', different from other 'merchant towns' of Scotland, and, located on the silting River Tay, as 'a dry town far from the sea'. It had its own craft aristocracy, of bakers and hammermen, who imported iron from the Baltic. Both must have prospered modestly in the later fifteenth century by an increase in inland rather than overseas trade: bakers once admitted to the merchant guild could buy grain direct and in bulk; its metal workers, whose customers extended far beyond the boundaries of the sheriffdom, supplied the specialist needs of rural agriculture.[57]

These were the crafts – skinners, metal workers, tailors and bakers in the four great towns – which were the clearest beneficiaries of the changing economic circumstances of the late fifteenth century. They were usually the first to be given incorporated status as guilds and were granted the most prestigious positions in the new Corpus Christi processions. Closest to the Holy Blood, which belonged to the merchant guild, were the banners of St. Eloi of the hammermen, St. Crispin of the skinners and St. Obert of the bakers.[58]

Much of this would change in the course of the sixteenth century. Both craft saints and civic ritual disappeared with the Reformation. More fundamental was the change in the economic climate: falling wage rates, increasing pressure by burgh authorities on food trades to hold down their prices in a period of steep price inflation, and a slump in demand for domestic handicrafts.[59] This contrasted sharply with the economic circumstances of the period when the craft aristocracy was given its formal recognition. The sudden removal of the Corpus Christi procession, in which the urban hierarchy had reassuringly been depicted, combined with straitened economic circumstances to induce a crisis of identity for the old craft aristocracy of the fifteenth century. By the 1580s various crafts, the privileged and the not so privileged, were beginning in many towns to demand a new kind of recognition of their status, in the form of seats on town councils. And a new craft aristocracy was also beginning to emerge – of previously unincorporated maltsters, dyers and glovers – who were shaking off the control of their overseeing guild.[60] Many of the troubles which beset Scottish urban society in the century after 1550 were the result of the various urban aristocracies established in the later fifteenth century clinging to their accustomed places in the burgh community. In this respect, as in many others, the pivot on which the history of the Scottish medieval town moves was the fifteenth century.

Notes

The abbreviations conform to the 'List of abbreviated titles of the printed sources of Scottish history', *Scottish Historical Review*, xlii (1963), supplement.

1   I.Flett and J. Cripps, 'Documentary sources', in M. Lynch, M. Spearman and G. Stell (eds.), *The Scottish Medieval Town* (Edinburgh, forthcoming), ch. 2.

2   A. White, 'Religion, politics and society in Aberdeen, 1543–1593' (Edinburgh Univ. Ph.D., 1985), pp. 8–20

3   A. Grant, *Independence and Nationhood: Scotland 1306–1469* (London, 1984), pp. 72–3, 80–81.

4   M. Lynch, 'Continuity and change in urban society, 1500–1700', in R. Houston and I. Whyte (eds.), *Scottish Society, 1500–1800* (Cambridge, forthcoming).

5   I. Guy, 'The Scottish export trade 1460–1599, from the Exchequer Rolls', (St. Andrews Univ. M. Phil., 1982), pp. 166–74.

6   See e.g. *Scottish Historical Documents*, ed. G. Donaldson (Edinburgh, 1970), pp. 84–5.

7   J. Wormald, *Lords and Men in Scotland: Bonds of Manrent, 1442–1603*, (Edinburgh, 1985), p. 138.

8   Aberdeen City Archives, MS Council Reg., vii, p.27; *Acts Parl. Scot.*, ii, 178 c. 14 (1487). In 1500, after the Court of the Four Burghs, sitting in Edinburgh, reiterated the acts of 1467 and 1487 (ibid., 86, cc.2, 3; 178, cc. 12, 13), Edinburgh's council ordered skinners to 'occupy no merchandise'. Four days later it admitted ninety-one 'mercatores burgenses' and a further twenty a month later. Identification is seldom possible, because of lack of other records, but they included some fleshers, cordiners and skinners as well as merchandisers, such as a fruitseller and chapman. (*Edin. Burgh Recs.*, i, 86–9; Edinburgh City Archives, MS Register of Burgesses, i, fos. 8v-10v). The numbers suddenly entered reflects the scale of illicit trading within the town as well as the uncertain boundaries between merchandise and manufacturing.

9   A. A. M. Duncan, *James I, King of Scots 1424–1437* (Univ. of Glasgow, 2nd ed., 1984), pp. 9–10.

10   M. Lynch, 'The crown and the burghs, 1500–1625', in M. Lynch (ed.), *The Early Modern Town in Scotland* (London, 1987), pp. 58–67.

11   See A.W.K. Stevenson, 'Trade between Scotland and the Low Countries in the later middle ages' (Aberdeen Univ. Ph.D., 1982), esp. ch. 1; also his 'Trade with the south, 1070–1513', in Lynch *et al.*, *Scottish Medieval Town*, ch. 11.

12   K. Hohlbaum (ed.), *Hansisches Urkundenbuch* (Halle, 1882–6), iii, no. 131.

13   Stevenson, 'Trade between Scotland and the Low Countires,' 228n.

14   Lynch, 'Continuity and change'.

15   The detailed statistics drawn from *Exchequer Rolls of Scotland*, vols. ii-vi, covering the period 1359–1460, depend on the work of Dr. A. Grant, who generously lent them to me. Those for the period after 1460, based on vols. vii-xxiii, depend on the research of Isabel Guy, whose data was kindly supplied to me by Professor T.C. Smout.

16   Stevenson, 'Trade between Scotland and the Low Countries,' p. 290.

17   Ibid., pp. 43–116.

18   E. Ewan, 'The burgesses of fourteenth century Scotland: a social history' (Edinburgh Univ. Ph.D., 1984), 216n.

19   M. Lynch, 'The social and economic structure of the larger towns, 1450–1600', in

Lynch et al., Scottish Medieval Town, ch. 15.

20 Aberdeen City Archive, MS Co. Reg., iv, pp. 512–18; W.G. Hoskins, Local History in England (London, 2nd ed., 1972), p. 176; M. Lynch, Edinburgh and the Reformation (Edinburgh, 1981), p. 378, prints a 1583 tax roll and his 'Whatever happened to the medieval burgh? Some guide lines for sixteenth and seventeenth century historians', Scottish Economic and Social History, iv (1984), p. 7, details an ecclesiastical census of 1592, which revealed 8,000 adult communicants.

21 G.W.S. Barrow, Kingship and Unity: Scotland 1000–1306 (London, 1981), p. 90; Lynch, Early Modern Town, p. 28.

22 D. McRoberts, The Fetternear Banner (Glasgow, n.d), pp. 16–17.

23 Perth was a significant exception, with some fifteenth-century suburbs; see the maps in M. Spearman, 'The medieval townscape of Perth', in Lynch et al., Scottish Medieval Town, ch. 3.

24 R. Nicholson, Scotland: The Later Middle Ages (Edinburgh, 1974), p. 265.

25 The Gild Court Book of Dunfermline, 1433–1597, ed. E.P.D. Torrie (Scot. Record Soc., 1986); the Inverness transcript forms part of Scottish Catholic Archives, Fort Augustus MS Al.

26 Barrow, Kingship, p. 84.

27 A.A.M. Duncan, Scotland: The Making of the Kingdom (Edinburgh, 1975), p. 482.

29 W. Stevenson, The monastic presence in Scottish burghs in the twelfth and thirteenth centuries', SHR, lx (1981), pp. 97–118.

30 Edinburgh City Archives, MS Accounts of Collector of Kirk Rents, vol. i.,

31 C.A. Kelham, 'Bases of magnatial power in later fifteenth century Scotland' (Edinburgh Univ. Ph.D., 1986), p. 52.

32 Ibid., pp. 337–8; H. Booton, 'Economic and social change in later medieval Aberdeen', in J.S. Smith (ed), New light on Medieval Aberdeen (Aberdeen, 1985), pp. 51–2.

33 Lynch, Early Modern Town, pp. 12–14; White, 'Religion, Politics and Society', pp. 12–17.

34 Grant, Independence, pp. 123–4.

35 Acts of Parl. Scot., ii, pp. 226–7 c. 17 (1491); 245 c.43 (1503) which was repeated in 1504 (ii, pp. 252 c. 33). See also Balfour, Practicks, p. 58.

36 R. Hilton, 'Towns and societies in medieval England', Urban History Yearbook (1982), pp. 9–11; G.S. Pryde, The Burghs of Scotland: A Critical List (Oxford, 1965), nos. 1–45, 82–132.

37 Lynch, 'Continuity and change'.

38 Edinburgh Burgh Recs., i, pp. 34–5; ii, 104.

39 Burghs Convention Recs., i, pp. 514–15; 543. The 1485 tax is wrongly dated as 1483 in the printed edition; I am grateful to Dr. N. Macdougall for his advice on this point. It was granted by a parliament opening on 21 March, which must be that of 1485.

40 Stevenson, 'Trade between Scotland and the Low Countries', p. 223

41 Stevenson, 'Trade with the south'.

42 Lynch, 'Social and economic structure'.

43 D. Ditchburn, 'Trade with northern Europe, 1297–1540', in Lynch et al., Scottish Medieval Town, ch. 10.

44 Lynch, 'Social and economic structure'.

45 J.D. Marwick, Edinburgh Guilds and Crafts (Edinburgh, 1909), pp. 47–73; Lynch, 'Social and economic structure'; J.F. Pound, 'The social and trade structure of Norwich, 1525–1575', Past and Present, xxxiv (1966), p. 55.

46 Cal. State Papers Scot., xii, no. 906.

47 Edinburgh Burgh Recs., i, p. 47; E. Bain, Merchant and Craft Guilds: a History of the Aberdeen Incorporated Trades (Aberdeen, 1887), p. 308; D. Murray, Early Burgh Organisation in Scotland (Glasgow, 1924), i, p. 359; Lynch, 'Social and economic structure'.

48 Stevenson, 'Trade with the south'; *Acts Parl. Scot.*, ii, pp. 8 c.16 (1425); 86 c.3 (1467).
49 Lynch, 'Social and economic structure'.
50 E.g. Scottish Record Office, E71/30/12 shows one-third of Edinurgh's skinners involved in the export of hides and skins 1562–3; only 31 per cent of the exporters were members of the merchant guild.
51 E.P.D. Torrie, 'The guild in fifteenth century Dunfermline', in Lynch *et al.*, *Scottish Medieval Town*, ch. 14; Lynch, 'Social and economic structure'. The information on Perth was kindly supplied by Marion Stavert, who is preparing an edition of the Perth Guild Book, which begins in 1452, for Scot. Record Soc.
52 Duncan, *Scotland*, pp. 490, 499.
53 Lynch, 'Social and economic structure'.
54 Grant, *Independence*, pp. 85–6; Stevenson, 'Trade between Scotland and the Low Countries', pp. iv, 262–3.
55 Lynch, 'Continuity and change'.
56 Lynch, 'Social and economic structure'; *Edinburgh Burgh Recs.*, i, p. 28; *Exch. Rolls.*, xi, pp. 218–35.
57 Lynch, 'Social and economic structure'; *Burghs Conv.Recs.*, i, pp. 514–15, 543; M.B. Verschuur, 'Perth and the Reformation: society and reform 1540–1560' (Glasgow Univ. Ph.D., 1985), 611, 616.
58 Bain, *Merchant and Craft Guilds*, pp. 49–61.
59 S.G.E. Lythe, *The Economy of Scotland in its European Setting, 1550–1625* (Edinburgh, 1960), pp. 30, 113–14, 248, 251–2; Guy, 'The Scottish Export Trade', p. 173.
60 Lynch, 'Social and economic structure'.

Index

GENTRY & LESSER NOBILITY
IN LATER MEDIEVAL ENGLAND

Edited by Michael Jones

Discussion of 'the rise of the gentry' generated one of the liveliest historical debates in England since the Second World War and one which is still not entirely resolved. But in recent years specialists of the later Middle Ages have also increasingly concerned themselves with 'the middling ranks of society who used their abilities as stewards, councillors, lawyers, and soldiers, or their positions as substantial landowners serving as knights of the shire, justices and commissioners, to rise in wealth and status' and the consequent shifts in economic and political power this entailed. Nor is the phenomenon limited to England. The adaptation or transformation of traditional aristocratic society on the Continent in the wake of analogous movements has been the focus for much recent work. This book provides a synthesis of much of this and, by adopting a comparative approach, highlights parallels and contrasts in social evolution over the larger part of north-western Europe.

232pp   216mm × 138mm
Illustrated
ISBN 0 86299 280 X (case) £18.00

PEOPLE, POLITICS AND COMMUNITY IN THE LATER MIDDLE AGES

Edited by *Joel Rosenthal and Colin Richmond*

This book contains a collection of papers focusing on fifteenth-century England, presented at the International Congress on Medieval Studies at Western Michigan University in May 1985, and at a symposium at the University of Keele in July 1986.

Rosemary Hayes: 'The Pre-episcopal Career of William Alnwick Bishop of Norwich and Lincoln'

Virginia Davis: 'William Wainfleet and the Educational Revolution of the Fifteenth Century'

Kate Mertes: 'The English Noble Household as a Religious Community'

Simon Payling: 'Arbitration and the Law in Nottinghamshire 1399–1461'

Ian Arthurson: 'The Rising of 1497: a Revolt of the Peasantry'

Marjorie Drexler: 'Fluid Prejudice: Scottish Origin Myths in the Later Middle Ages'

James Gillespie: 'Cheshiremen at Blore Heath'

Michael Bennett: 'Careerism in Late Medieval England'

Ben McRee: 'Religious Guilds and Regulation in Late Medieval Towns'

216pp   216mm × 138mm
ISBN 0 86299 359 8 (case) £17.50